No Neutral Ground?

Dilemmas in American Politics

Series Editor **L. Sandy Maisel,** *Colby College*

Dilemmas in American Politics offers teachers and students a series of quality books on timely topics and key institutions in American government. Each text will examine a "real world" dilemma and will be structured to cover the historical, theoretical, policy relevant, and future dimensions of its subject.

BOOKS IN THIS SERIES

No Neutral Ground? Abortion Politics in an Age of Absolutes, Karen O' Connor

Onward Christian Soldiers? The Religious Right in American Politics, Clyde Wilcox

Payment Due: A Nation in Debt, A Generation in Trouble, Timothy J. Penny and Steven E. Schier

Bucking the Deficit: Economic Policymaking in the United States, G. Calvin Mackenzie and Saranna Thornton

"Can We All Get Along?" Racial and Ethnic Minorities in American Politics, Paula D. McClain and Joseph Stewart Jr.

Remote and Controlled: Media Politics in a Cynical Age, Matthew Robert Kerbel

FORTHCOMING TITLES

Welfare Policy in American Politics, Anne Marie Cammisa

The Dilemma of Congressional Reform, David T. Canon and Kenneth R. Mayer

Immigration and Immigrants in the Contemporary United States, Rodolfo O. de la Garza and Louis DeSipio

Participation, Democracy, and the New Citizenship in Contemporary American Politics, Craig A. Rimmerman

The Angry American: How Voter Rage Is Changing the Nation, Susan J. Tolchin

No Neutral Ground?

Abortion Politics in an Age of Absolutes

Karen O'Connor
American University

To my mother,
Norma Wilton O'Connor,

who has always been there to encourage me

Dilemmas in American Politics

Published in 1996 in the United States of America by Westview Press, 5500 Central Avenue, Boulder, Colorado 80301-2877, and in the United Kingdom by Westview Press, 12 Hid's Copse Road, Cumnor Hill, Oxford OX2 9JJ

A CIP catalog record for this book is available from the Library of Congress.
ISBN 0-8133-1945-5 (hc.) — ISBN 0-8133-1946-3 (pbk.)

The paper used in this publication meets the requirements of the American National Standard for Permanence of Paper for Printed Library Materials Z39.48-1984.

10 9 8 7 6 5 4 3 2 1

Contents

Illustrations

Tables

Figures

Photos

Cartoons

Boxes

Preface

This book has been a long time in coming together—even longer than Jennifer Knerr at Westview and series editor Sandy Maisel know. In fact, I've been interested in women's rights since I wrote my first term paper on Susan B. Anthony in the seventh grade. One of the first issues I remember avidly following was the New York State legislature's legalization of abortion when I was in high school. I had grown up at a time when young girls who got pregnant had little alternative than to go to a "home" for unwed mothers or seek an illegal abortion. I still remember how happy we were in my all-female (Catholic) high school to have been the first class not to have someone leave school to have a baby (although one of my classmates was visibly pregnant and we did our best to make certain that someone always walked in front of her so the nuns wouldn't catch her and expel her).

Given my long-standing interest in women's issues, I knew I wanted my Ph.D. dissertation to be about women's rights. When I first began to write the dissertation about twenty years ago, I hoped to explore the role of women's rights groups in bringing about change in the status of women through litigation. My interest in litigation was a natural one, for I was taking classes in the joint J.D./Ph.D. program at SUNY Buffalo at a time when most members of the faculty seemed to be involved in litigating or studying litigation for social change. But because abortion is such a complex issue—one that cuts across so many legal, moral, and social contexts, to name just three areas of analysis—I quickly decided to limit the scope of my dissertation to nonabortion-related matters of importance to women. Still, even while I was writing my dissertation, the overarching impact of legalized abortion on women's status in society continued to haunt me.

Although I wasn't planning on using any of the early abortion cases in my dissertation, I conducted extensive interviews with Margie Pitts Hames, who argued *Doe v. Bolton* (1973) before the U.S. Supreme Court; with Ruth Bader Ginsburg, about her early role in trying to convince the Supreme Court that abortion restrictions were violations of the Fourteenth Amendment's equal protection clause; with Rhonda Copelon of the Center for Constitutional Rights, who had filed an amicus curiae brief in *Roe v. Wade* (1973); and with Sylvia Law of New York University Law School, who had filed amicus curiae briefs in several cases subsequent to *Roe*.

I used little of that information in my dissertation but did strike up a friendship with Margie Pitts Hames. After I had moved to Atlanta to take a teaching position at Emory University and had passed the Georgia bar, Margie, by then on the national board of the National Abortion Rights Action League (NARAL), asked me to come work with her on a federal challenge to the Hyde Amendment. I did so gladly because I believed then, and continue to believe, that constitutional rights should be available to all, not just to those who can afford to exercise them. The years during which I worked and finally litigated in federal court with Margie, as well as Elizabeth Appley, were memorable in many ways. After all, how many lawyers who are themselves seven months pregnant get to appear in federal court on behalf of pregnant plaintiffs unable to afford an abortion that their physicians deem medically necessary? During that time, the three of us also were part of a larger group that founded the Georgia Abortion Rights Action League, an affiliate of NARAL that continues today. During that period I also met several courageous women. Among them was Lynn Randall (now the president of the National Abortion Federation), who had recently established the Feminist Women's Health Center—one of the prime targets of Randall Terry's Operation Rescue during the 1988 Democratic National Convention.

Once I gave birth to my daughter, the pressures of motherhood, teaching, and publishing pushed my interest in abortion to the back burner. But in the late 1980s, like many other women, I was struck by the specter of losing rights already won. I began to think and write about abortion and was invited to serve on the board of the Feminist Women's Health Center. This close-up experience with the day-to-day operation of a clinic amid picketing, threats, and regulatory harassment (whether in the form of daily clinic inspections or annual IRS audits) drove home the point as to how precarious reproductive rights had become, even though they were still technically guaranteed by the Constitution. Meanwhile, my interest in abortion and reproductive rights, coupled with my supervision of Tim Haas's dissertation on surrogate parenthood, led me to develop a course on the "Politics of Reproductive Rights" at Emory that I've continued to teach at the American University.

It was around this time in my life that Sandy and Jennifer asked if I would like to write a book on abortion for the Dilemmas in American Politics series. I jumped at the opportunity—but quickly became overwhelmed by the task in front of me. Unlike other policy areas such as women's rights and civil rights, which I had studied or written about before, this issue could not be approached without evoking awe over the deep tensions that divided those on both sides of the debate. Bluntly put, I believe that the decision to have an abortion should always be the woman's under any circumstances. Yet I also understand that, to those who believe that abortion is the taking of a life, laws or judicial rulings that allow abortion are abhorrent. The problem is that I'm not going to change my position and others are not likely to change theirs. Therein lies the dilemma for policymakers: How to develop policy in an issue area where both sides are intensely polarized and where, even at "the middle," there is little agreement on specific kinds of restrictions that might be acceptable.

In this book, I have tried my best to be objective and to respect the full range of opinions held by individuals and the public regarding the abortion issue in particular and reproductive rights more generally. The challenge has been tricky, though. I've always prided myself on the way that I've taught these issues; yet the first draft of this manuscript—I can see now—was woefully unequal in its coverage of the right-to-life movement. My hope is that, by discussing this dilemma within a policy framework, I have begun to show readers just how difficult it is, and will always be, to develop a policy on abortion rights that can make everyone happy.

I owe considerable debts to several people—first and foremost to Jennifer and Sandy, who kept after me to finish this book. I hope their efforts and all of their time, helpful comments, and news clippings were worth it. I'd also like to thank several of my Ph.D. students at Emory for their ideas, assistance, and encouragement—especially Tim Haas and Maria Bevacqua in Women's Studies and John R. Hermann (now at Trinity University) and Bernadette Nye (now at Union College) in Political Science. In addition, Bernadette, Sue Davis at Emory, and Jessica Brodey at New York University Law School read the entire manuscript and gave me numerous suggestions and comments to help me make the book a better one. And in the final stages of this book, Sue and Jessica Waters at American University helped me track down all sorts of last-minute odds and ends.

I have also incurred a huge, quantity-time debt to my family over the last few years, during which I was trying to complete this and several other projects. My husband, Richard Cupitt, has made my life an easier place in which to write, and my daughter, Meghan, has put up with hearing me talk about abortion rights since the moment she was born. On the day that *Webster* was decided, just before the local TV reporters arrived to interview me about it, Meghan rolled out of bed and (at the age of nine) asked: "Was it 4 to 4, with O'Connor the swing?" Such is the world that children of academics grow up in.

If the abortion dilemma is ever to be solved by the political process, it won't likely happen soon. Emotions on both sides are running too high. More to the point is the question, Will there come a time when the need for most abortions is eliminated by education, safe and reliable forms of birth control, and, for that matter, common sense? But birth control, too, is a controversial issue, often fraught with moral and even racial overtones. Thus, although I hope this volume will provide readers with food for thought, I realize that abortion is intertwined with a whole other set of policy issues that I have not even begun to tackle here.

Karen O'Connor

Acronyms

ABCL	American Birth Control League
ACLU	American Civil Liberties Union
AFLA	Adolescent Family Life Act
ALI	American Law Institute
AMA	American Medical Association
CBN	Christian Broadcast Network
CC	Christian Coalition
CDC	Centers for Disease Control; later Centers for Disease Prevention and Control
EEOC	Equal Employment Opportunity Commission
ERA	Equal Rights Amendment
FACE	Freedom of Access to Clinic Entrances Act
FDA	Food and Drug Administration
FOCA	Freedom of Choice Act
HHS	U.S. Department of Health and Human Services
IUDs	intrauterine devices
KKK	Ku Klux Klan
MM	Moral Majority
NAACP	National Association for the Advancement of Colored People
NARAL	National Association to Repeal Abortion Laws; became National Abortion Rights Action League; became National Abortion and Reproductive Rights Action League
NBCL	National Birth Control League
NCCB	National Conference of Catholic Bishops
NOW	National Organization for Women
NRLC	National Right-to-Life Committee
NWP	National Woman's Party
NWPC	National Women's Political Caucus
OR	Operation Rescue
PAC	Political Action Committee
PETA	People for the Ethical Treatment of Animals
PLAL	Pro-Life Action League
PP	Planned Parenthood Federation of America
RFP	Reproductive Freedom Project
RICO	Racketeer Influenced and Corrupt Organizations Act
YWCA	Young Women's Christian Association

1

Abortion: The Search for a Neutral Ground

Whenever these forces struggled to prevail—in the courts, the Congress, the executive regulatory process, the state legislatures and city councils—there were HEW and its Medicaid program. And there was no neutral ground on which HEW and its Secretary could comfortably stand, for any decision—to fund all, or none, or some abortions—would disappoint and enrage millions of Americans who were convinced that theirs was the only humane position.

—Joseph A. Califano, Jr., former secretary of the Department of Health, Education, and Welfare, in *Governing America* (1981), p. 50

WHEN JUSTICE HARRY A. BLACKMUN retired from the U.S. Supreme Court on April 7, 1994, he gently reminded reporters that ***Roe v. Wade*** (1973) was a 7-to-2 decision and not his opinion alone. Blackmun was still clearly proud of the fact that he wrote the opinion for the majority, which made a woman's decision to have an abortion a constitutionally protected right. When asked to comment on *Roe*, he told reporters: "I think it was right in 1973, and I think it is right today. I think it's a step that had to be taken as we go down the road toward the full emancipation of women" (Goodman 1994, p. 15).

The publicity that surrounded Blackmun's retirement announcement and the speculation about possible successors to him highlight the prominent role that the U.S. Supreme Court—an unelected body—has played in the abortion debate. Through its interpretation of the U.S. Constitution in 1973, state laws concerning abortion were invalidated throughout the country, and the stage was set for twenty-plus years of debate about the morality, legality, and rationality of its decision.

The abortion controversy that was triggered by *Roe v. Wade* provides an excellent opportunity to illustrate how a divisive issue can affect American politics at all levels of government. More specifically, it highlights a major dilemma: How does the polity come to agreement on issues for which compromise is unlikely or very difficult to achieve? The abortion issue has put policymakers and citizens in myriad political and personal dilemmas because many people view the abortion issue in moral or religious terms; others view it as a matter of personal liberty. Thus, to compromise concerning abortion goes against many individuals' firmly held religious, moral, or ideological beliefs.

Moreover, the abortion issue is a particularly interesting one because it was not until *after* the Supreme Court decided *Roe v. Wade* that abortion prompted extensive, long-lasting national debate. It also presents an interesting case study of a policy issue in which much of the action has been designed in response to or as a way of persuading the U.S. Supreme Court—supposedly immune from political pressure—to change its interpretation to include *or* not include a woman's right to terminate a pregnancy. In addition, the abortion controversy underscores the tendency of Americans to frame all such issues in terms of rights while relying on undemocratic institutions, especially the courts, to allocate those rights.

As government has tried to grapple with this controversy, the courts have played a major role. And flowing from the Supreme Court's abortion decisions have been a host of other ancillary questions. The federal system, for example, produces a systemic dilemma concerning which level of government, if any, has the responsibility to regulate abortions, the testing and distribution of drugs like **RU-486** (what some call the abortion pill), abortion funding, and even access to contraceptives. Another dilemma is what may be termed a civil liberties question: What are the limits of free speech and assembly protections contained in the First Amendment with regard to federal laws designed to punish clinic violence?

The abortion controversy highlights how the use of symbols and rhetoric can affect the way governmental policymakers at all levels—local law enforcement officers, elected national, state, and local governmental officials, judges, and even jurors—think about an issue. Abortion is also a matter in which responsibility for policy has shifted from the local level to the state level to the national level and then, in the 1990s, like many other policy issues, back to the state level—albeit with some guidance from the U.S. Supreme Court.

In that respect, the abortion issue calls to mind many other policies that present the age-old question of which level of government, if any, is best suited to the effort to settle a particular societal problem. Most of these other policy issues, however, have failed to stir the heated emotions that have been the hallmark of the abortion discussion. For example, welfare reform and health care, while important to many, are not frequently viewed as life-or-death issues. In many ways, the abortion controversy is much more like the dilemma posed by racial relations in the United States than are other policy issues. At first, at least especially in the South, racial equality and desegregation appeared to be matters about which people refused to compromise. Though not universally considered a matter of life or death, civil rights, like abortion, has produced exceptionally strong reactions from people on both sides.

Since the founding period, when the Framers opted not to deal head on with slavery, that issue and its legacy have produced major dilemmas for American society. While moral reformers viewed slavery as wrong, Southern plantation owners deemed it necessary to their way of life. Ultimately, it took a Civil War that tore the nation in two, as well as the passage of the Thirteenth, Fourteenth, and Fifteenth Amendments, to resolve the slavery issue. Still, its legacy soon surfaced in the Southern states' passage of the Black Codes and Jim Crow laws, which were designed to institutionalize a strictly segregated society in terms of education, employment, housing, and even voting. It was not until the Supreme Court ruled that *state* maintenance of segregated schools was unconstitutional in *Brown v. Board of Education of Topeka* (1954), and the U.S. Congress passed the Civil Rights Act of 1964 and the Voting Rights Act of 1965, that black Americans began to receive even an approximation of the full citizenship rights long enjoyed by white Americans. Furthermore, although the most visible forms of race discrimination have since been erased, the public's divided reactions to and views on O. J. Simpson's acquittal in 1995 underscore the fact that blacks and whites still view the political system and its treatment of them very differently.

Even though abortion has not been an issue on the public agenda for nearly as long as race, the emotionalism that has attended its rise to prominence, its initial treatment as a local or state issue, and the eventual role of the U.S. Supreme Court in enunciating a national constitutional policy allows for some comparisons to racial issues as well as to other pressing policy concerns. Indeed, just as there were numerous demonstrations against court-ordered busing to desegregate public schools, many violent demonstrations have occurred in protest against the federal court decisions seeking to legalize abortion, limit governmental restriction on abortion, and maintain women's access to abortion clinics.

The purpose of this book is not to resolve the question of whether one should have an abortion or even to state definitively whether abortion is right or wrong; rather, it is to clarify how the polity struggles to make major policy decisions in areas about which people express little agreement but very strong feelings. In short, abortion policy and the issues that emanate from it are treated in the following pages as vehicles by which to understand the policymaking process more clearly.

The Policymaking Process

No matter what the policy issue involved, be it the environment, civil rights, health care, or abortion, some variation or permutation of what political scientists term the **policymaking process** occurs. At each stage of the process, a variety of political actors and institutions are involved, as revealed in Figure 1.1. Often, as in the case of the abortion issue, a policy may make several laps around the policy cycle as it is defined and redefined.

The Stages of the Process

The policymaking process generally has seven identifiable stages, although it is often difficult to delineate where one stage ends and the next begins (Anderson

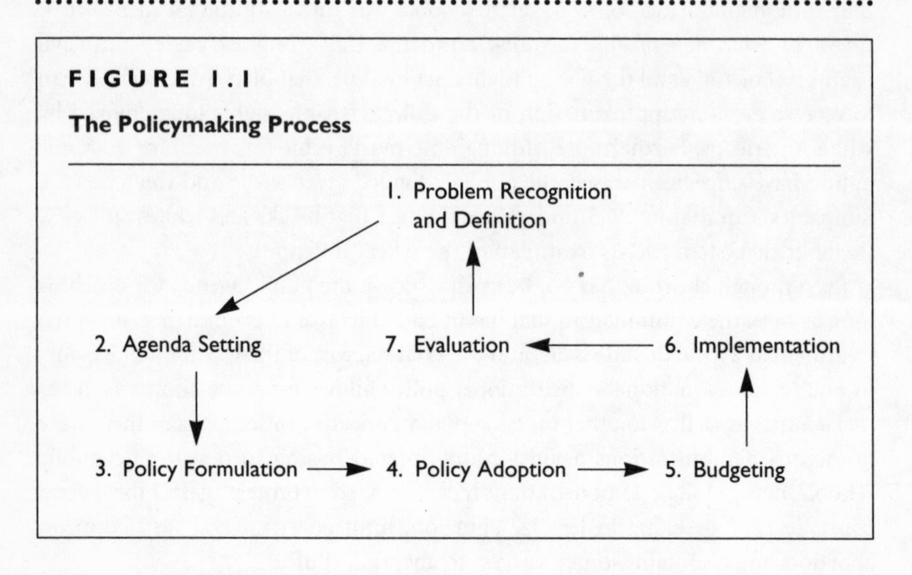

FIGURE 1.1
The Policymaking Process

1994). Stage 1 involves **problem recognition** and **problem definition.** It is during this stage that individuals, interest groups, or lawmakers determine that a problem exists. Historically, in the case of abortion (see Chapter 2), the process began when some isolated individuals and then a physicians' group, the American College of Gynecologists and Obstetricians, as well as a lawyers' group, the American Law Institute, called for decriminalization, that is, for changing state laws that made abortions illegal. In Stage 2, the **agenda-setting stage,** the media as well as a variety of new women's rights and abortion rights groups focused on the problems faced by women who were forced to seek illegal abortions. Wire coat hangers, often used by desperate women to abort their own pregnancies, became the groups' symbol; and the right of a woman to control her own body, their call to arms. In Stage 3, that of **policy formulation,** some groups continued to seek changes in state law, whereas others (much like those in the civil rights arena) sought to bring challenges in the federal courts, believing that a decision from the U.S. Supreme Court that invalidated restrictive abortion laws would be a much faster way of achieving their goal.

Although many public policies are initially formulated by either state or national legislatures, abortion policy, at least since 1973 through the early 1990s, has been the bailiwick of the federal courts. Accordingly, when the Supreme Court decided *Roe v. Wade* (1973), it not only formulated policy but also required that all states comply with its ruling—thereby also requiring **policy adoption,** which occurs in Stage 4. In the case of abortion, the outcome was that no state could restrict a woman's right to an abortion through the point of fetal viability, the point after which, as determined by the Court, the fetus had a chance of surviving outside the mother's womb.

A key component of many public policies is **budgeting,** Stage 5 of most policy processes. How the Head Start program or the Social Security retirement fund is to be financed, for example, is a key question with which members of Congress and the president must grapple every year. In the case of federal civil rights laws, federal courts required local school districts to pay for busing to integrate previously segregated schools. But budgeting was not envisioned as a major factor by those who originally recognized and defined abortion as a women's rights issue. Once abortions were legal, you could get one if you could afford it. Soon after *Roe v. Wade*, however, members of Congress opposed to abortion targeted federal funding of abortions for indigent women, who relied on federal funding for their other medical needs, as one way to counter the reach of the Court's decision. In fact, budgeting, often called Congress's power of the purse, has been a major tool by which Congress has been able to assert itself in an issue area where the courts have been such prominent actors.

The **implementation** stage of the policy process, Stage 6, is one in which considerable variation occurs. For example, despite current implementation of civil rights laws, African Americans in many walks of life continue to be denied true equality and the debate about affirmative action rages on. Many public schools are still almost exclusively black, and, despite laws that prohibit on-the-job discrimination, many African Americans continue to report discrimination in the hiring and promotion processes. By contrast, initial implementation of the Supreme Court's edict concerning abortion—which prohibited states from interfering with a woman's right to secure an abortion—was easier. The Court's decision was clear-cut: Abortion could *not* be criminalized. Thus, clinics were opened around the country to provide abortion services so long as a woman could afford to pay. Yet anti-abortion groups quickly mobilized to try to pass national and state abortion restrictions as well as a constitutional amendment to overrule *Roe*, in actions reminiscent of many Southern states' reactions to *Brown v. Board of Education of Topeka* (1954). Although the Supreme Court ordered the desegregation of public schools in *Brown,* the scope of its decision prompted recalcitrant school boards to seek ways to evade or prolong efforts to desegregate their schools.

The last stage of the policymaking process, Stage 7, is that of **evaluation.** In the context of abortion policy, evaluation is perhaps more difficult than for other policies. This difficulty is exactly what sets abortion policymaking apart. Where there is little or no consensus in the polity regarding the desirability of outcome, the effectiveness of a policy is very difficult to measure. If, for example, policymakers want to determine whether a childhood immunization program is working, they can count the number of children inoculated or the number of reported cases of a particular disease. Almost all Americans agree that the reduction of cases of measles is a measure of success and that the eradication of *any* disease is good public policy. Similarly, most Americans—today, at least—agree that discrimination based on race is wrong and look to the increasing numbers of African Americans in college or in high-paying positions as indications of program success. But they are divided regarding the proper remedies for the problem of discrimination, as evidenced by the continuing debate over affirmative action.

When considering how to evaluate the success of abortion policy, not only the public but lawmakers, too, are often at odds about what constitutes success. To those opposed to abortion, any abortion is a failure. To those committed to full implementation of *Roe v. Wade*, parental notification or consent requirements, an absence of Medicaid funding for abortions for indigent women, blocked access to clinics, and the declining number of physicians willing to perform abortions are all measures of failed policy implementation. As with most public policies, these different perceptions of policy effectiveness have led both opponents and supporters of abortion rights to continue to make varied demands on the political system, thus bringing the policy cycle full circle back to Stage 1.

The Fluidity of the Process

The stages of the policymaking process are often fluid; that is, once the process begins, the stages may occur simultaneously, one stage may trigger either another stage or a new policy definition or redefinition, new events may occur that bring the issue to the forefront in a different manner, or the courts may intervene and reformulate the debate. For example, as the abortion controversy has evolved in the United States, how it is defined has changed. At one time, some individuals sought only the decriminalization or *reform* of abortion laws; they did not challenge the right of the state to limit abortions in certain circumstances. Later, others recast the debate in terms of the right of a woman to control her body free from governmental interference as opposed to the right of a fetus to life, as the *repeal* of all abortion laws was sought. By focusing on the humanity of the fetus, the debate as it was shaped by abortion opponents in the wake on the *Roe* decision became one of right-to-life versus a woman's right to choose—or murder versus bodily integrity. By 1977, the abortion debate had become a matter of right-to-life versus pro-choice. Right-to-lifers were quick to recognize that it was morally preferable to be *for* the right of a fetus to life instead of *against* a woman's right to control her body. Similarly, as medical technology has advanced, even questions about fetal viability have prompted legislators and the courts to reexamine basic policy assumptions. Clearly, then, the way in which the debate (as well as the issue) is defined can have important consequences for the other stages of the policymaking process.

Throughout this book, how governments and lawmakers—at the national, state, and even local levels—have reacted to the abortion issue as it has been defined and redefined within the policy cycle will be analyzed as a way of highlighting some key facets of the American political system. Sometimes, as we shall see, the system has appeared to work well; at other times it has not. Given the complex nature of the issue, and the tendency of Americans to frame all such matters in terms of rights while relying on undemocratic institutions, especially the courts, to allocate those rights, the political system's inability to forge and maintain coherent and consistent policy in the face of widely divergent, and possibly irreconcilable, views on diverse abortion issues is not surprising. Should the government be in the business of regulating abortion or banning it altogether? Some argue that the right of privacy should preclude *any* government regulation of abortion. At the opposite end of the spectrum, probably as many Americans believe that abortion under any circumstances is murder, and that drastic measures to prevent it are justified. Compounding the problem—at least for some—are improvements in medical technologies that have moved forward the point of fetal viability to a time not anticipated by the majority's decision in *Roe* in 1973.

Most politicians—both elected and appointed—have attempted to walk a tightrope across the abortion issue, and their positions have often vacillated depending on where the political winds happen to be blowing and whether abortion is an important issue in that election year. As governor of California, Ronald Reagan signed into law in 1967 the most liberal abortion statute to date. Later, in 1980, while running for president of the United States, he disavowed this stance and allied himself instead with a Republican Party platform that called for "a constitutional amendment to restore protection of the right to life for unborn children." His vice-presidential running mate, George Bush, also exhibited an apparent reversal of his position on abortion. For example, as a member of Congress in the late 1960s, Bush appeared to support abortion rights when he co-sponsored legislation to fund family planning clinics; but when he first ran for the Republican presidential nomination in 1980, Bush modified his stand to oppose abortion except in cases of rape or incest, or when the life of the mother was in danger. In the same year, once selected as Ronald Reagan's running mate, he quickly adopted Reagan's new anti-abortion position. In 1988, as Bush sought the nod of the Republican Party to be its presidential candidate, he directed his supporters to reject efforts to amend the GOP platform to permit the Medicaid funding of abortions when pregnancies were the result of rape or incest (Kenworthy 1988). And in 1992, during his ultimately unsuccessful bid for reelection to the presidency, Bush again narrowed his support for abortion. This time, he was advocating "adoption, not abortion," inasmuch as he argued that abortion should be legal only when the life of the mother was at stake. Said Bush about his first abortion conversion, "I'm a practical man. I like what works" (Kenworthy 1988).

Switching sides doesn't always work, however—especially on an issue sparking very strong opinions. As one close Bush adviser put it: "People say, 'Doesn't this guy believe in anything, doesn't he have any principles of his own that he thinks are more important than expedient politics?'" Thus, Bush's stand on abortion in 1992 may have backfired. During the 1992 elections, when abortion emerged as a key issue for many voters, the two major-party presidential candidates held diametrically opposed views on the issue. Many citizens appeared to be more interested in supporting pro-choice rather than pro-life candidates as George Bush and many Republicans were defeated and replaced by pro-choice Democrats, particularly in the House.

By the 1994 midterm congressional elections, the controversy over abortion politics had subsided somewhat and most candidates' stand on abortion and abortion-related issues—at the national level, at least—did not appear to be important factors in their races. As a result of President Bill Clinton's appointment of two pro-choice justices to the Supreme Court, Ruth Bader Ginsburg and Stephen Breyer, abortion rights were less likely to be negated by the Court. In fact, the Planned Parenthood Federation of America (PP) hired a new director with managed health care experience, in the belief that the continued legality of abortion would no longer be an issue.

But the abortion issue has not gone away. It continues to be in the news and on the public agenda. The role of abortion in the 1996 national and state elections, the prominence of the Christian Right's "Contract with the American Family" (which calls for a ban on abortion funds for the poor and on late abortions), and the U.S. Senate's refusal to confirm Dr. Henry Foster as surgeon general because he performed thirty-nine abortions during his lengthy medical career underscore the continued turmoil produced in the polity by the abortion issue—as did congressional attempts to criminalize certain late-term abortion techniques.

An Eye for an Eye, a Tooth for a Tooth?

Although the abortion issue has appeared to ebb and flow, the war over abortion continues. The Clinton administration authorized testing of RU-486 in selected clinics in 1994. And clinic violence has limited the availability of surgical abortions as fewer and fewer doctors are trained in the procedures or are willing to perform them in the face of ongoing threats to themselves and their families.

Clinic violence began in 1977 but increased dramatically in the 1990s. Physicians who perform abortions have been threatened, injured, and even killed. In the wake of attacks on doctors, fewer physicians are willing to perform abortions, making a guaranteed "right" often inaccessible to many. On March 10, 1993, for example, Dr. David Gunn began another routine day at the abortion clinic where he worked in Pensacola, Florida. As he stepped out of his car near the clinic back door, the shouts of anti-abortion protesters rang out. His name had appeared on posters urging pro-life activists to make his life, and those of his loved ones, miserable. As he approached the clinic, Dr. Gunn was shot three times in the back at point-blank range by a clinic protester. Pro-choice activists argue that his death was yet another casualty of the war over abortion that has been waged in the United States for several years; in stark contrast, pro-lifers see aborted fetuses as the casualties of that war. Yet, given the constitutional nature of our federal system, much of the legislation concerning clinic violence has been defined as a free speech/assembly issue. Thus far, the U.S. Supreme Court has come out on the side of allowing some free speech/assembly restrictions to protect the safety and personal liberty of abortion providers and seekers.

Abortion no longer presents a simple issue for lawmakers. What started out as an effort to reform restrictive abortion laws that banned physicians from performing a now relatively safe procedure has escalated and expanded into many other, more complex areas. Which level or levels of government—state, local, or national—should be responsible for making abortion policy? Should some level of government fund abortions for poor women? If the right to an abortion is a constitutional right, can a state be required to provide free surgical services for indigent women? For any reason, or only for situations of rape or incest? Does the constitutional right to an abortion include the right of a minor female to secure an abortion without her parents' permission or notification? Should the question of how or why a woman got pregnant (e.g., birth control failure, rape, or incest) or why she wants to terminate a pregnancy (e.g., sex selection, convenience, economic difficulty, or fetal abnormality) be considerations that affect a woman's ability to secure a safe *and* legal abortion? Will distribution of RU-486 encourage abortion, or will it deter the need for late-term abortions? These are all questions with which various state legislators as well as the U.S. Congress and often the Supreme Court have grappled in the last two decades since abortion was first legalized nationally by the Court in *Roe v. Wade* (1973).

Is There a Common Ground?

The politics of abortion present a difficult situation for most political decision-makers as they attempt to wrestle with questions of women's rights and whether a fetus has rights in the context of moral, scientific, religious, constitutional, and more overtly political debates. As we will see throughout this book, the fact that deep divisions concerning abortion exist within the public mind makes it an area in which political compromise has been virtually impossible. Since *Roe* was decided in 1973, one public opinion poll after another has revealed fairly constant positions on abortion—although fewer people today believe that it should "always" be illegal. As shown in Table 1.1, about 15 to 20 percent of the U.S. population has consistently reported believing that abortion should always be illegal. In stark contrast, an even larger number—usually between 20 to 30 percent of the population—has believed that abortion should always be legal. Moreover, a majority of those polled have consistently believed that abortion should be permissible in some circumstances. It may be that the large number of people who hold

TABLE 1.1

Public Opinion Polls Showing Support for Legal Abortion, 1975–1995

Date	*Always Legal*	*Legal Under Some Circumstances*	*Always Illegal*
1995	32	50	15
1994	33	51	13
1993	32	51	13
1992	31	53	14
1991	32	50	17
1990	31	53	12
1989	29	51	17
1988	24	57	17
1980	25	53	18
1977	22	55	19
1975	21	54	22

Gallup poll question: Should abortion be legal under all circumstances, legal only under some circumstances, or illegal in all circumstances?

Source: Gallup Poll Monthly, January 1992, p. 6; "Religion and Abortion," *The Gallup Poll*, April 22, 1993, p. 76; "Religion and Abortion," *The Gallup Poll*, March 1995, p. 29.

what may be termed a middle-ground position on abortion is consistent with and reflective of the dilemma faced by the polity.

Not only are there "firm" positions on both sides but, as the table illustrates, there also appears to be little room for easily articulated compromise between the two extremes. More precisely, support for abortion rights decreases (or, conversely, opposition to legalized abortion increases) dramatically when pollsters interject a variety of reasons as "conditions" to temper a woman's right to terminate a pregnancy. Many Americans, for example, oppose legal abortion for unmarried women or for women who do not believe that they have adequate resources to support a new child. Others, as discussed later in the book, believe that abortion should remain legal but approve of, or are not willing to object strongly to, myriad restrictions—including, but not limited to, parental consent, spousal consent, informed consent, and waiting periods. Yet in 1973 *Roe v. Wade* actually legalized abortion for *any* reason—through the end of the second trimester—so long as a woman makes the decision to abort in consultation with her physician. The "right of privacy," concluded seven of nine Supreme Court justices, was "broad enough to encompass a woman's decision whether or not to terminate her pregnancy." (See Box 3.1 for the text of the *Roe v. Wade* decision.)

Strong positions on both sides of the abortion debate make for little agreement even in "the middle." Cartoon used by permission.

Legalized abortion—as constitutionally guaranteed by *Roe*—quickly created a political "hot potato" for many lawmakers and became a matter that many lawmakers wished to evade whenever possible. As discussed in Chapters 5 and 6, many pro-choice lawmakers in Congress opted to avoid bringing to the floor for a vote the Freedom of Choice Act, which would codify the Supreme Court's decision in *Roe* through national legislation. Many representatives believed that a pro-choice president, coupled with new appointments to the U.S. Supreme Court, were enough to protect the continued legality of abortion in some form. Yet only three years after the presidential victory of pro-choice Bill Clinton, the Republican-controlled 104th Congress enacted several new policies that, as critics charge, have severely curtailed abortion rights for both the poor and government employees. Others, such as the Partial Birth Abortion Ban Act, were vetoed by the president.

To understand how abortion got on the public agenda and why it poses a dilemma for lawmakers and citizens alike, we must first consider both the historical context in which the issue developed and the process through which the dilemma was created. Toward this end, we turn next to Chapter 2, "Defining the Abortion Issue and Getting on the Public Agenda," which presents a short history of abortion as an issue of legislative and public debate. There we will see how the problem was initially defined as a policy issue and how it got on the public agenda. Chapter 3, "Abortion, the Constitution, and the Federal System," complements this history by presenting the constitutional context in which *Roe v. Wade* (1973) and its companion case, ***Doe v. Bolton*** (1973), arose and were decided. Also discussed in that chapter is the nature of the federal system created by the U.S. Constitution and the way in which the abortion dilemma fits within it as the polity grapples with the question of which level of government, if any, should set abortion policy. Chapter 4, "The Aftermath of *Roe* and *Doe*," then covers the immediate aftermath of the Supreme Court's enunciation of a national abortion policy and the formation of a social movement in response to the abortion decisions. Chapter 5, "The Politics of Abortion, 1980–1988," examines the interdependent roles of the courts, the president, the Congress, interest groups, political parties, the media, the states, and public opinion in the adoption and redefinition of abortion policy, as well as the ways in which each of the actors has affected and been affected by the abortion dilemma. Chapter 6, "The Politics of Abortion, 1988–1992," examines the resurgence of the abortion issue in the wake of *Webster v. Reproductive Health Services* (1989) and its effects on the states, policymakers, public opinion, and the 1992 elections. Finally, Chapter 7, "The Clinton Years and Beyond: From Abortion Politics to Abortion Policy," surveys recent abortion cases, executive directives, increasing clinic violence, state and local responses to abortion, and the potential effect of RU-486 on the abortion dilemma. It also speculates about the future of abortion politics in the United States and addresses several questions—among them, Will the dilemma ever be resolved? And does the difficulty involved in resolving it reflect simply the strengths (or weaknesses) of the American political system?

2

Defining the Abortion Issue and Getting on the Public Agenda

> The regimen I adopt shall be for the benefit of my patients according to my ability and judgement, and not for their hurt or for any wrong. I will give no deadly drug to any, though it be asked of me, and I will counsel such, and especially, I will not aid a woman to procure abortion. . . .
>
> —Hippocratic oath taken by all physicians

As NEARLY THREE HUNDRED prominent American historians noted in an **amicus curiae** ("friend of the court") brief submitted to the U.S. Supreme Court in ***Webster v. Reproductive Health Services*** (1989), abortion was legal in America in colonial times. Perhaps more important, however, is the point made by historians that, in spite of the commonality of abortion, *no government*, be it local, state, or national, attempted to regulate the practice. It was simply not an issue of public debate or considered a proper object of governmental regulation or legislation. Given the dilemma that the abortion issue now presents to the polity, the purpose of this chapter is to explore how abortion was transformed from a private dilemma to a public problem (as it came to be defined) and how it initially arrived on the public agenda.

Because the practice of abortion is as old as pregnancy itself, many women have attempted to control their fertility or to terminate their pregnancies when family planning methods, whether by natural or artificial means, fail. Even the U.S. Supreme Court has noted that abortion was practiced in ancient Greece as well as in the Roman Empire. Most Greek philosophers, moreover, saw little wrong with abortion, so long as it took place before fetal viability, the time at which a fetus is considered able to live outside its mother's womb. Even the Roman Catholic Church, now a major opponent of legalized abortion, allowed abortion before **quickening,** the time when a woman first feels movement of the **fetus** in utero—usually between the sixteenth and eighteenth weeks of pregnancy. Note, too, that under English **common law,** the basis of the colonial legal system, abortions in the early stages of pregnancy were never considered a crime and abortions were routinely performed before quickening. Thus, at the time that the U.S. Constitution was adopted, and throughout most of the nineteenth century, women enjoyed the legal right to terminate a pregnancy. An 1812 ruling by a Massachusetts state court, for example, declared that an abortion performed before quickening, with the woman's consent, was not punishable. Accordingly, it was not until 1821, when Connecticut became the first state to include abortion after quickening within its criminal law prohibitions, that a polity began to address the issue. When Connecticut legislators opted to make it a crime to give a woman any kind of poisonous substance to induce an abortion, they had no idea of the dilemma that their actions would later pose for future lawmakers. But the die was cast once a state government decided to criminalize some kinds of abortions (Rubin 1994).

Early Legal Trends

Once Connecticut—a heavily Catholic state—outlawed abortions *after quickening* in keeping with the new policy of the Roman Catholic Church, three other states followed suit. In 1828, for example, New York State enacted legislation that was to become the model for others. It barred destruction of an unquickened fetus but allowed for abortions when necessary to save the life of the mother. The distinction between before and after quickening is one that state legislators had little problem making, although it would later become a thorny problem for modern-day policymakers.

State legislators were also concerned with public safety issues. In 1830, for example, prompted by public health concerns in an era of little understanding of antiseptic procedures, New York outlawed *any* surgery unless two physicians could attest that it was essential to the life of the patient. Surgery, including abortion surgery, was simply deemed too dangerous to risk.

After the Civil War (1861–1865), efforts to make abortions illegal were renewed in the states. These efforts were instigated by an "influential anti-abortion movement" led largely by the newly formed American Medical Association (AMA). According to historians, the AMA's creation between 1850 and 1869 provided the "single most important factor in altering the legal policies toward abortion in this country" (*Brief of 281 American Historians* 1988). In 1854, interestingly enough, Pope Pius IX initiated a dramatic change in Roman Catholic policy toward abortion. By 1869 excommunication had been declared the official policy of the church for physicians who performed abortions (Blanchard 1994, p. 11). Thus, in response to the powerful lobbying efforts of the AMA, support for (or at least adherence to) new Roman Catholic Church policy, and the similar stance taken by some Protestant churches (Byrnes and Segers 1992, p. 4), most states passed laws that severely restricted abortions. Religious belief was not noted as a reason for this action. Instead, most legislators noted their interest in passing laws to protect women from the unsafe practices of untrained abortionists (Luker 1984); the Catholic Church's influence on legislation was undeniable, however.

Physicians campaigned for restrictive abortion laws for several reasons, including (1) their desire to professionalize the practice of medicine and drive midwives out of the medical business; (2) their perception of a need to boost the national population because of declining birthrates (children were no longer as "useful" to parents in the face of increasing industrialization); (3) their discriminatory ideas about the natural subordination of women, bolstered by the Victorian ethic that encouraged chastity (women who had abortions could thereby escape censure for their immoral acts) (Petchesky 1984, p. 82; *Brief of 281 American Historians* 1988); and (4) their concern for maternal health.

The New Jersey Supreme Court even publicly recognized health concerns by noting that the state's anti-abortion statute had been passed "not to prevent the procuring of abortions as much as to guard the health and life of the mother against the consequences of such attempts" (*State v. Murphy*, 1858). In fact, it was not until the late 1800s that antiseptic techniques became widely accepted, in spite of discoveries that had taken place soon after the Civil War. Thus, although many legislators opposed abortion as morally wrong, most state anti-abortion laws were passed as the result of a concerted lobbying effort by doctors—not women, the Roman Catholic Church, fundamentalists, or any other professional or interest group active in the policy arena today. Indeed, the Roman Catholic Church in the United States did not take an *active* role in the abortion debate until the 1950s, even though its stance regarding the immorality of abortion after quickening had been adopted by most states before then (Byrnes and Segers 1992, p. 4).

The anti-abortion message sent by physicians had a captive audience among the U.S. populace during the Victorian era and proved to be an effective way of defining the problem. Because Puritan notions of sin and propriety continued to prevail, holding white women to a high standard of sexual purity and making women responsible for the moral well-being of the entire community, abortion restrictions became another way to ensure that such moral standards would be upheld (Petchesky 1984, p. 72). Legalized abortion was thus a means by which unmarried women could "avoid their shame and escape punishment," as one state anti-abortion law explained (Lader 1991, p. 3). The law sent out the message that women who violated the moral code should bear all accompanying public humiliation. This prevailing ethos strongly supported abortion restrictions. It also helped redefine abortion as a moral rather than medical issue—although initially it was a woman's morals and not the morality of abortion that was stressed.

As the move toward state criminalization of abortion grew after the Civil War, many moral reformers and most women's rights advocates supported the idea of **voluntary motherhood,** a woman's right to limit her family size by natural means (Gordon 1977, p. 95). But they were nearly unanimous in their distaste for *artificial* forms of birth control, an idea that was not to gain acceptance for several more decades. Echoing moralist sentiments of the day, they believed that contraceptive devices were "a standing reproach upon, and a permanent indictment against American women" (Gordon 1977, p. 97). Connecticut, for example, outlawed artificial birth control at the same time it restricted abortion.

This is not to imply, however, that most women wished to give birth every year. Elizabeth Cady Stanton, a key mover for women's rights in the 1800s, who herself had eight children and did not become active in the women's movement until many of them were grown, believed that before women could gain full equality, they had to have control over their bodies. A staunch supporter of voluntary motherhood, Stanton frequently addressed "women-only" audiences during the **suffrage campaign** to win for women the right to vote. At those meetings, she regularly talked about the need for women to limit the size of their families so as to improve their overall status (Degler 1980, p. 204).

Because of the moral beliefs and purity standards cited earlier, late nineteenth- and early twentieth-century family planning advocates focused their discussion on birth control rather than on abortion. Though still not a socially acceptable topic of public discourse, preventing conception was widely perceived as less morally objectionable than aborting a fetus. Birth control advocates could still claim to favor strong, healthy families while objecting to abortion.

Public discussions of morals and birth control were extremely controversial and soon were basically outlawed with the passage of the **Comstock Act** in 1873, which prohibited the use of the U.S. mails for distribution of "obscene" materials. It specifically labeled as obscene "the dissemination of any pornography, abortion devices and any drug, medicine, article or thing designed, adapted, or intended for preventing conception" (Banner 1984, p. 17). It also "branded as smut" and therefore as "obscene" many essays that urged abstinence as a method of family planning (Reed 1978, p. 37). Proponents of the act, including its sponsor, Anthony Comstock, believed that this kind of information could only lead to moral decay and more abortions.

In the aftermath of passage of the Comstock Act, little new information was disseminated about birth control or abortion. Writing about those matters in public meant near-certain arrest. It wasn't until the early 1900s that women again began to speak out publicly about the need to control family size.

The Birth Control Movement

Birth control was an exceptionally controversial issue during the suffrage era. Although the Comstock Act barred dissemination of birth control information through the mails, many educated, middle-class women were clearly using artificial forms of contraception. Poorer and immigrant women, however, continued to have very large families. Soon, Margaret Sanger, a nurse with strong ties to the socialist movement, and a growing number of women active in the progressive movement began to believe that family planning was the only way out of poverty for many.

Sanger, concerned about the death and poverty suffered by immigrant women who did not know how to limit family size and influenced by nativist sentiments of the day, traveled to Europe to learn more about contraceptive devices, since their dissemination was not banned there. On her return, she began publishing her newspaper, *The Woman Rebel*, in which she explained available contraceptive

Nurse Margaret Sanger, who risked prison time by distributing information about contraceptives, viewed birth control as a social reform issue. Photo shows Edythe B. Tichell applying adhesive tape to Margaret Sanger so that she could not preach birth control while attending a banquet. Photo courtesy of UPI/Corbis—Bettmann Archives.

devices and called on women to take the responsibility of limiting the size of their families (Reed 1978, p. 87). Soon, Sanger was indicted for violating the Comstock Act. To avoid a possible forty-five-year prison sentence, she fled to Europe in 1914. In her absence, a group of women founded the National Birth Control League (NBCL), whose creation Sanger had urged in *The Woman Rebel.* It was directed by Mary Ware Dennett.

When Sanger returned from Europe, she and Dennett clashed over goals as well as over who would lead the NBCL. They also sharply disagreed on strategy. Dennett believed in total repeal of laws like the Comstock Act; Sanger abandoned her previous support of nonphysician dissemination of birth control. Now she sought only a change in anti-contraceptive laws to allow physicians to fit birth control devices. As a result of this move, her goals became more acceptable not only to physicians, a powerful political group, but also to many suffragists who distrusted Dennett for her work in the controversial peace movement.

Sanger's arguments for birth control closely paralleled those made earlier by suffragists; her tone was often racist as she lectured on the evils of increasing immigrant populations. When in 1921 Sanger founded a new organization, the American Birth Control League (ABCL), out of dissatisfaction with Dennett, she supported birth control as a social reform, not a woman's issue.

"Her Legal Status," from *Birth Control Review* (May 1919). Used by permission of the New York Public Library.

Although the ABCL was far more acceptable to both physicians and suffragists than the NBCL, Sanger still faced an uphill battle because birth control was an issue far more controversial than suffrage. Even after ratification of the Nineteenth Amendment, which enfranchised women, Sanger was unable to attract the support of many women's organizations to her largely separate movement (Gordon 1977, p. 221).

Hostility to Sanger and birth control was evidenced by the refusal of the largest women's club, the General Federation of Women's Clubs, even to discuss a birth control resolution at its national meeting. A similar action also was taken by the League of Women Voters. In fact, the only women's organization to go on record publicly in support of the ABCL's activities was the National Women's Trade Union League. Even the liberal National Woman's Party (NWP) refused to adopt a resolution favoring birth control, out of the fear that doing so would confuse public perceptions of its goal—an equal rights amendment—that had nothing to do with birth control. In fact, the NWP leaders took great pains to dissociate their goals from any ideas that could be considered to be anti-family. Talk of abortion was absolutely out of the question.

The failure of many of the major women's groups to support the birth control movement is not surprising. Many ministers, priests, and even suffragists vehemently objected to it. In declining to be a sponsor of the ABCL, Carrie Chapman Catt, president of the National American Woman Suffrage Association, wrote to Sanger, "Your reform is too narrow to appeal to me and too sordid" (Gordon 1977, p. 228). Even many socialists believed that association with the birth control movement made their economic radicalism less acceptable. Thus, declining support from conservative feminists and isolation from many radicals and socialists largely accounted for the movement's relative lack of progress during this period. And if birth control could draw no vocal supporters, neither could the cause of abortion rights.

Public discussion of birth control and abortion was finally "legalized" by a federal court decision that forced reinterpretation of the Comstock Act in light of new scientific and clinical data accumulated by Sanger's Clinical Research Bureau. The litigation was orchestrated by the Committee on Federal Legislation for Birth Control—also founded by Sanger. The court found that the Comstock Act had to be read in light of medical advancements, and that to punish physicians for importing or selling birth control devices that "might intelligently be employed . . . for the purpose of saving life or promoting the well-being of their patients" was not the design of the statute (*United States v. One Package*, 1936).

This decision was Sanger's victory over the Comstock Act, and it allowed her American Birth Control League to speak to state legislatures to urge them to amend or repeal their individual Comstock-like acts preventing discussion or distribution of birth control devices (Baer 1991, p. 185). Soon thereafter, Sanger's group merged with the National Birth Control League and changed its name to the **Planned Parenthood Federation of America** to dissociate itself from the more controversial term *birth control.* Despite continued public disfavor over this term, in the late 1930s a *Ladies Home Journal* poll revealed that 79 percent of American women approved of limiting their families through artificial means (D'Emilio and Freedman 1988, p. 248). And in 1937, North Carolina became the first state to sanction the distribution of birth control in its public health clinics. Six southern states quickly followed suit when they learned that African-American births were accounting for as many as 85 percent of all births in their respective states (D'Emilio and Freedman 1988, pp. 247–248). Although the overall birth control movement consequently made great strides, the racist motivation behind the action is obvious.

By the late 1950s, Planned Parenthood had succeeded in winning repeal of restrictive birth control statutes in all states but Connecticut and Massachusetts. In those two states, the Roman Catholic Church effectively lobbied state legislators to keep the laws. Indeed, by 1950 the church was teaching that all forms of artificial birth control were immoral. Thus, church leaders argued that repeal of restrictive laws would lead to higher incidences of sin. Planned Parenthood, then, was forced to initiate test cases in those states when efforts to repeal restrictive laws were stymied by strong Roman Catholic lobbying.

Abortion Gets on the Public Agenda

Just as Planned Parenthood was working to force repeal of restrictive state laws that prevented it from dispensing birth control information and devices in its family planning clinics, the issue of abortion was garnering some public attention and groups and individuals were beginning to take positions on opposite sides of the debate. Further, as eventually defined by the courts, both access to contraceptives and legal abortions were considered by some to be issues involving the constitutional right to **privacy,** whereas others viewed contraceptives as immoral and abortion as the taking of a human life. Thus, the issue of privacy, as defined by the courts in the birth control cases, ultimately became the basis for challenging restrictive state abortion laws.

Problem Recognition

Prior to the 1960s the topic of abortion was not widely discussed, although some, particularly the Roman Catholic Church, denounced it. Even Sanger, one of the first to call for women's access to birth control, publicly spoke out against abortion. But in the late 1950s and early 1960s, a series of events prompted many to call for changes in restrictive state abortion laws, which generally allowed abortions only to save the life of the woman. At that time, police experts called illicit abortion "the third largest criminal activity in the country, surpassed only by narcotics and gambling" (D'Emilio and Freedman 1988, p. 253). The American College of Gynecologists and Obstetricians weighed in, voicing its opinion that abortion should be decriminalized. And in 1959, the influential American Law Institute (ALI) suggested revisions in its widely copied Model Penal Code to decriminalize abortion in three circumstances:

1. When continuation of the pregnancy would gravely impair the physical or mental health of the mother.
2. When the child might be born with a grave physical or mental defect.
3. When pregnancy resulted from rape, incest, or other felonious intercourse, including illicit intercourse with a girl below the age of sixteen.

Problem Definition

Soon thereafter, events occurring almost simultaneously led to an abortion rights movement in the United States, as highlighted in Figure 2.1. Abortion first became an issue of public debate in 1962 when Sherri Finkbine, a television personality in Phoenix, Arizona, sought an abortion after realizing that she had taken thalidomide, a drug proven to cause grave fetal abnormalities. For the first time in history, abortion received prominent national attention: The issue was spotlighted when Finkbine was forced to fly to Sweden for an abortion because she was unable to secure one legally in the United States. As her plight was broadcast in minute detail, attention also turned to scientific advances that had lessened the medical risks associated with abortion.

The Finkbine incident not only helped to define the problem and put abortion on the public agenda; it also spurred pollsters, for the first time, to begin asking Americans about their views on abortion. In August 1962, for example, the Gallup poll posed the following question: "As you may have heard or read, an Arizona woman recently had a legal abortion in Sweden after having taken the drug thalidomide, which has been linked to birth defects. Do you think this woman did the right thing or the wrong thing in having this abortion operation?" Of those surveyed, 52 percent believed Finkbine was right; 32 percent responded that she was wrong; 16 percent of those polled had no opinion.

Soon after the Finkbine incident, in 1963 and 1964, a German measles epidemic swept through the United States. More and more pregnant women found

FIGURE 2.1

Cycle One of the Policymaking Process

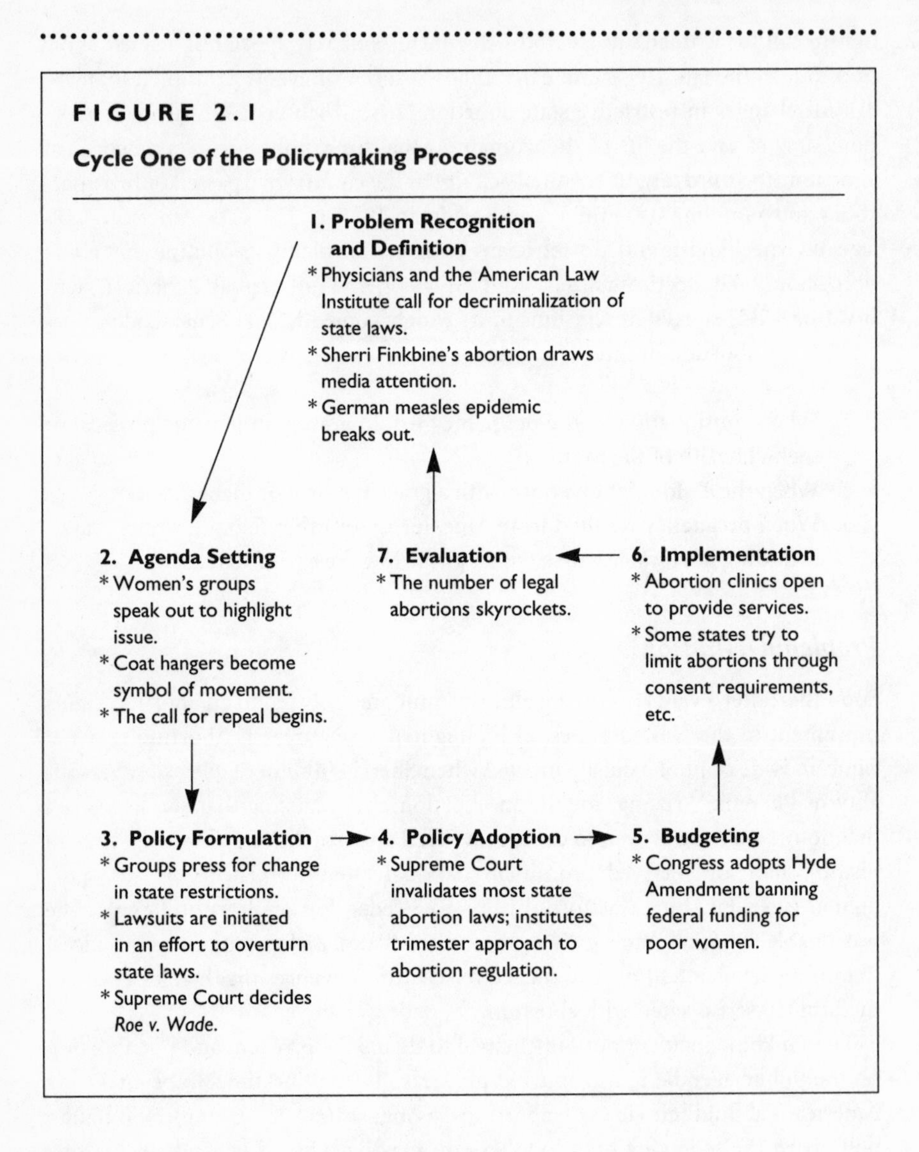

themselves exposed to the measles, which, if contracted during the first three months of pregnancy, often disrupts the development of the fetus. As they unsuccessfully sought legal abortions, public concern over abortion reform increased. However, although more than twenty thousand children were born with deformities directly traceable to measles, concern and publicity were inadequate to forge a full-scale abortion rights movement. And public opinion continued to be divided. A 1966 Gallup poll, for example, revealed that 54 percent of the public believed that "abortion operations should be legal when the child may be born deformed," while 32 percent disagreed.

In spite of mixed public opinion, these factors prompted several individuals to become increasingly concerned with abortion reform. In the mid-1960s Lawrence Lader, the author of a book about Margaret Sanger (1955), began to advocate abortion reform in public speeches and to refer women to physicians who would risk performing the illegal procedure. Around the same time, Patricia Maginnis, a California woman who had undergone three illegal abortions, began to advocate publicly the total repeal of all abortion laws—a radical proposal that went far beyond the ALI Model Penal Code.

The isolated actions of Lader and Maginnis and the founding, in 1964, of two pro-choice groups, the Association for the Study of Abortion and the Parents' Aid Society—even when coupled with news accounts of the horrors of illegal, back-alley abortions and the birth of children with fetal deformities—would not have been enough to start an abortion rights movement without the infusion of potential supporters provided by the birth control movement and the fledgling women's rights movement (McGlen and O'Connor 1995). At the same time that abortion began to be debated anew, Planned Parenthood was testing the constitutionality of restrictive state birth control laws. Supreme Court rulings, especially *Griswold v. Connecticut* (1965), laid the foundation for women to claim that the right to terminate a pregnancy was grounded in a woman's right to privacy—a principle the Court declared loudly and clearly in ruling, ultimately, that state laws banning the sale of birth control information or devices were unconstitutional. The grounding of contraceptive rights in notions of privacy was to have a profound impact on the way that abortion would be debated and evaluated.

By 1967 Lader, Maginnis, and their supporters had successfully raised the level of discourse about abortion in several states and were able to secure passage of abortion statutes in California, Colorado, and North Carolina despite localized protest from the Catholic Church. As the abortion issue was defined, however, these laws were not based on women's right to privacy or right to control their bodies; instead, these reformers chose to define the debate more narrowly by seeking modest changes in the law; each new statute followed the ALI Model Penal Code and expanded the reasons for legal abortion from "saving life" (of the mother) to "preserving health" (of the mother) (Lader 1991, p. 10). Still, few women were able to find physicians willing to approve an abortion under even these less restrictive standards.

Calls for Repeal: The Issue Defined

Although abortion rights activists were making some headway, the first *formal* call for the repeal of restrictive abortion laws can be traced to the Bill of Rights for Women adopted by the National Organization for Women (NOW) at its first annual convention in 1967. The last section demanded "[t]he right of women to control their own reproductive lives by removing from the penal codes laws limiting access to contraceptive information and devices and by repealing penal laws governing abortion" (NOW 1967).

This provision sought to alter the nature of the debate and was passed over strong opposition within the group. Some members believed that abortion was not a civil rights issue; others argued that NOW's association with abortion would bring unfavorable publicity that would make other, more attainable goals such as equality in pay or employment opportunities increasingly difficult to achieve. This resolution marked the beginning of the formal and informal link between the women's rights movement and the movement to achieve abortion rights and underscored its transition from a medical issue to a political one for many women.

NOW's public support of abortion added the members and even some of the leaders necessary for the start of a real movement for change. Significantly, soon after NOW's call for repeal, other "rights"-oriented organizations followed suit. For example, in 1968 the Citizens Advisory Council on the Status of Women, a presidential commission established by President John F. Kennedy, called for the repeal of all restrictive abortion laws, as did the American Civil Liberties Union (ACLU).

Women's rights advocates became increasingly active in campaigns to repeal restrictive state laws. Abortion was now on the public agenda. In 1968, the National Association to Repeal Abortion Laws was formed; originally known as the New York Abortion Rights Action League, it later became the **National Abortion Rights Action League (NARAL)** (after *Roe v. Wade* was decided). Lawrence Lader was instrumental in the founding of NARAL and became its first chair. By 1970, the combined activities of these groups, along with support from physicians, had allowed the abortion issue to be redefined in the eyes of many policymakers from "a moral, ethical, religious, social, legal, or economic problem" (Luker 1984, pp. 42ff) to a medical problem.

Thus, by 1971, the pressure from these women's rights groups, abortion rights groups, and professional medical and legal associations had led fourteen states to revise their abortion laws to allow abortions in some circumstances. Four additional states had repealed their restrictive abortion statutes (Rubin 1994, p. 117). But change in the states was a slow, piecemeal process. In New York State, for example, NARAL, Planned Parenthood (which endorsed abortion rights in 1970), the Young Women's Christian Association (YWCA), and other interest groups used conventional lobbying methods to pressure the state legislature for abortion reform. More radical women's groups, which generally drew a younger membership, held public "speak outs" where diverse women talked about their own illegal abortions. The goal of these groups was to raise public awareness of the abortion issue.

The Anti-Abortion Movement

The state of New York was an early battleground for abortion rights advocates and opponents. It was there that the legislature debated the most liberal abortion bill to date—a bill that removed all abortion restrictions during the first six months of pregnancy. In 1967, in the aftermath of the Supreme Court's decision in *Griswold v. Connecticut* (1965) and the reform efforts in several states, the **National Conference of Catholic Bishops (NCCB)** established the Family Life Division, whose purpose it was to educate Catholics about the evils of abortion. Because the Catholic Church teaches that life begins at conception, it considers abortion to be the taking of a life. Thus, its prominent role in this debate is not surprising.

As part of its plan to prevent further liberalization of state abortion laws, the national Family Life Division created local divisions, often called bureaus, throughout the states to monitor proposed changes to state abortion laws *and* to seek the indictments of physicians who violated existing laws. Bishop James McHugh of the Family Life Division gathered together several anti-abortion lay citizens to act as his advisers, calling them his National Right-to-Life Committee. These advisers and the Family Life Division were instrumental in leading the opposition to proposed liberalization of the New York state law (Lader 1973).

At this time, Roman Catholics made up 40 percent of the electorate in New York. In spite of the Catholic Church's strong opposition to liberalization of the New York law, the bill was passed in 1970, and New York was dubbed the "abortion capital of the United States." By 1972, pressure from the Catholic Church and other abortion opponents had led the legislature to repeal the liberalized law, but liberal Republican Governor Nelson A. Rockefeller vetoed the change. The New York victory both fueled the abortion rights movement and provided the catalyst for the formation of an **anti-abortion movement,** which arose to fend off attempts by liberal activists to repeal New York's restrictive abortion laws. Though initially successful in a handful of states, abortion law repeal advocates experienced several legislative setbacks owing to the efforts of the growing anti-abortion movement. Many of its first members were Roman Catholic professional men and women who were upset with their professional associations' positions on abortion reform. For example, in 1967 the American Medical Association endorsed abortion law reform for the first time since 1871, after a survey of physicians revealed that 86.9 percent favored liberalized laws (Paige 1983, p. 44). When combined with forces from the Catholic Church, who argued that fetuses, too, should be guaranteed the constitutional right to "life, liberty, and due process of law," this new anti-abortion movement became quite powerful. In Michigan and North Dakota, for example, proposals for abortion law *reform* were put to the voters and overwhelmingly rejected. Not only did the anti-abortion movement stymie efforts at reform or repeal, it also was instrumental in convincing local prosecutors to charge and try physicians who performed abortions in violation of existing laws.

Despite this litigation, women's rights advocates increasingly came to believe that the courts were their best chance to change restrictive abortion laws, because a single positive judicial opinion from the federal court could be much more effective than years of effort in many states. Just as blacks earlier had viewed litigation as a more effective way to garner constitutional rights, women's rights activists believed that litigation offered the potential for deciding the issue far more quickly than would be achieved through a state-by-state effort to win repeal. Instead of seeking a constitutional amendment to secure a national right to an abortion, they opted to try to convince the federal courts that state restrictions violated rights that could already be found in or traced to the U.S. Constitution. Feminists who sought abortion law repeal were simply not sufficiently well organized on the state and local levels to launch a nationwide, state-by-state assault on abortion laws. Thus, the movement to reform restrictive abortion laws in state legislatures was largely abandoned in favor of a movement to repeal abortion laws through the courts.

Consequently, between 1969 and 1973, scores of cases brought both by abortion opponents and by supporters of abortion rights were initiated. Abortion opponents brought cases to court against physicians who performed abortions; supporters of reform or repeal often defended physicians from those charges (Blanchard 1994). Later, abortion rights advocates brought cases on behalf of women who sought abortions but were unable to secure them because of restrictive state statutes. These cases are discussed in Chapter 3.

Conclusion

From colonial times through the early 1970s, abortion evolved from a practice left to the discretion of women to one severely restricted by the law. Movements geared toward reversing restrictive nineteenth-century birth control and abortion laws sprang up due to the dedicated efforts of a few individuals. In the 1960s a series of events—including calls for reform of laws that criminalized abortion, the birth of babies with congenital defects caused by drugs or German measles, and growing concern about women's rights and the right of women to control their reproductive capabilities—brought national attention to this once private issue. After abortion was put on the public agenda by abortion rights advocates, movements both for and against the repeal of restrictive abortion laws grew more powerful, as epitomized by the confrontation of pro- and anti-abortion forces in New York State.

Groups continued to mobilize on both sides of the issue as it became defined in terms of women's rights instead of the right of a fetus to life. As this debate expanded, the abortion issue was placed on the public agenda in the form of new abortion reform/repeal statutes, and several lawsuits challenged the constitutionality of existing state laws as incompatible with protections found in the U.S. Constitution. These actions were soon to have far-reaching policy implications as the polity was called on to grapple with questions regarding which level of government should have authority to legislate about abortion. How the issue was defined often determined how individuals thought the dilemma should be resolved.

3

Abortion, the Constitution, and the Federal System

Different states and political subdivisions will approach [the abortion issue] and strike their respective balances in different ways. Some will adopt laws diametrically opposed to others. But . . . the diversity that results from state and local authority to attack a common problem in different ways, even opposing ways, is part of the genius of a federal system of government.

—Solicitor General Rex E. Lee, in oral argument before the U.S. Supreme Court in *Akron v. Akron Center for Reproductive Health* (1983)

As groups on both sides of the abortion debate squared off, much of their activity was structured by the nature of the U.S. federal system. Whereas abortion rights advocates looked to the federal courts for a single sweeping decision to apply to all of the states, opponents continued to press for victories on the state level. The question of how the polity makes decisions concerning abortion—an issue on which there is little agreement or compromise due to its moral, ethical, religious, and ideological facets—is complicated by the fact that government in the United States is a **federal system.** Thus, the question of which level of government—national, state, or local—is best suited to address the range of policy issues that stem from adoption of any governmental position on the legality or illegality of abortion is one that has been revisited almost every time the abortion issue has reached the public agenda.

When the Framers met in Philadelphia during the summer of 1787 to draft a new Constitution, neither women's rights nor abortion was on their minds. Instead, two of the key questions facing the Framers were how best to design the new national government and what its relationship to the states should be. In the end, they fashioned a new, as yet untried governmental system—what we today call the federal system. In this new federal system, both the states and the national government derived their powers directly from the people. Unlike the system that had existed when the United States was governed by the Articles of Confederation (whereby the national government derived all of its power and authority from the states), the new Constitution specified that certain enumerated powers were to be exercised by the national government. All other powers were retained by the states or the people.

Most of the powers specifically granted to the new national government by the Constitution dealt with commercial matters. There was no mention of the personal rights or liberties that Americans enjoy today. In fact, because the new Constitution was silent about those rights, many of which were already protected against state infringement by individual state constitutions, some citizens, especially Anti-Federalists, were reluctant to ratify the Constitution as it was proposed. The concerns of Anti-Federalists—those opposed to the new Constitution—were sufficiently justified in the minds of many to make passage of a proposed Bill of Rights to amend the Constitution the first order of business for the new Congress in 1789.

The **Bill of Rights,** which was quickly ratified by the states, consists of the first ten amendments to the U.S. Constitution. Many of the rights contained in those amendments were very near and dear to the hearts of colonial Americans and reflected American concern with abuses by the English crown. For example, the First Amendment guaranteed freedoms of speech and association, and the Fourth Amendment protected all citizens from unreasonable searches and seizures. Just as important, the Ninth Amendment specifically noted that the "enumeration," or listing, of "certain" rights in the Constitution or Bill of Rights should "not be construed to deny or disparage others retained by the people." This phrase was later to have significant importance in the war over abortion rights.

In the 1820s, when the states first began to enact statutes criminalizing abortion, they did so under their **police powers,** the right of the states to legislate for the public health and welfare of their citizens. Several states, in fact, made specific mention of their police powers in their charters and the rights the charters allowed the states to retain in the federal system.

These police powers were underscored by the **Tenth Amendment,** which specifies that all powers not delegated to the national government, nor prohibited by it, are "reserved" to the states—that is, to the people. These reserved powers are generally thought to include a state's right to regulate criminal conduct, public health and morals, and family law. But the state police powers suggested by the Tenth Amendment have always eluded a clear definition. As Justice William O. Douglas commented with respect to the Tenth Amendment, "An attempt to define its reach or trace its outer limits is fruitless" (*Berman v. Parker*, 1954). Yet the courts have often had to make such an attempt, because many states have assumed that they had the authority to regulate access to birth control and abortion under their respective police powers.

In particular, once the U.S. Congress had enacted the Comstock Act in 1873, several states banned the sale or dissemination of birth control information. The Comstock Act—because it was a federal, or national, law—was passed under Congress's authority to regulate interstate commerce under the **commerce clause** contained in Article I, section 8, of the U.S. Constitution. Thus, Congress had the power to ban the sale or dissemination of information it considered obscene only when it *went across state lines* or somehow involved interstate commerce. And once a particular item was deemed obscene, it was no longer protected by free speech guarantees provided in the First Amendment, because obscenity is not protected by the First Amendment or by any state constitution. But just as individual states had moved to outlaw abortions beginning in the 1820s, most states by the late 1800s had banned the dissemination of birth control information or devices as obscene under the authority of their state police powers.

Birth Control and Test Cases Challenging Restrictive State Laws

By the early 1960s, Planned Parenthood had made significant progress in bringing birth control information and access to many Americans. But the path to this outcome took many turns. For one thing, a 1936 federal court ruled that the federal Comstock Act violated the U.S. Constitution, but it did not invalidate *state* "Comstock" laws. In fact, two states—Connecticut and Massachusetts—still had Comstock-like laws that banned the sale or use of birth control devices or information. The Connecticut law, for example, had been enacted in 1879, soon after passage of the Comstock Act. This law specifically made it a crime for anyone to use any drug, article, or instrument to prevent conception or to give assistance or counsel in its use.

As early as the 1940s, Planned Parenthood, assisted by lawyers from the American Civil Liberties Union, attempted to challenge the Connecticut law. Unsuccessful in its efforts to persuade enough legislators in the heavily Roman Catholic state to support a change in the law, Planned Parenthood turned to the courts instead. There, it initiated what are called **test cases,** whereby plaintiffs are chosen to challenge or test the constitutionality of a law or practice in order to advance an interest group's policy goals in court. By launching test cases, Planned Parenthood and the ACLU hoped that the federal courts would find the restrictive state laws unconstitutional and, therefore, null and void. In one such test case involving birth control, Dr. Wilder Tileston, a Planned Parenthood physician, asserted in court that the Connecticut law prevented him from giving his best professional advice to three of his patients whose health, he believed, would be endangered by childbearing. His legal complaint alleged that local law enforcement officers would be likely to arrest him if he counseled his patients appropriately—but in violation of state law. However, since Tileston had not actually been arrested or even charged with violating that state law, the U.S. Supreme Court dismissed his lawsuit. The Court ruled that Tileston had no **standing,** or legal basis to bring the case, because he had not been directly or personally injured by the law. In other words, the Court noted, the law did not place *his* life in danger. Moreover, the patients to which his complaint referred had not been a party to the lawsuit (*Tileston v. Ullman,* 1943).

Planned Parenthood did not give up. In the late 1950s, it again initiated several test cases in an attempt to invalidate the Connecticut law. And again, it used a physician as a plaintiff. This time, Dr. C. Lee Buxton, chair of the Yale University Medical School's Department of Obstetrics and Gynecology, alleged that the statute prohibited him from exercising his best professional judgment in treating a married woman whose health indicated that it was unwise for her to get pregnant. Again, the U.S. Supreme Court ruled that since the Connecticut law had rarely been enforced, and that since Buxton had not been prosecuted under the law, his case, as well as that of two married women wishing to be informed about contraceptive options by their physicians (who sued under the assumed name of Poe), did not present controversies justifying adjudication of a constitutional issue (*Poe v. Ullman,* 1961).

Undaunted, Planned Parenthood opened a clinic in New Haven, Connecticut, specifically to challenge the state law (Friendly and Elliott 1984). Its director, Estelle Griswold, and its doctor, C. Lee Buxton, were quickly arrested for their flagrant violation of the law. They were tried, convicted, and fined for this violation, and their conviction was appealed to the U.S. Supreme Court, which could no longer claim that an actual controversy did not exist.

In ***Griswold v. Connecticut*** (1965), the Supreme Court ruled that the state law was unconstitutional. The Court concluded that the U.S. Constitution contained a broad right to privacy, which was a **fundamental freedom.** According to judicial precedent, when a state restricts fundamental freedoms, the actions of the state are subject to greater scrutiny and, therefore, to added protection by the Court.

The right to privacy, the Court concluded, could be found in the "penumbras emanating" from several specific guarantees in the Bill of Rights. These **penumbras** allowed the Court to state that a right to privacy must be inferred from all of the rights that were specifically spelled out in the national Constitution, including the First Amendment's protection of association; the Third Amendment's bar on the quartering of soldiers in private homes in peacetime without consent; the Fourth Amendment's protection from unreasonable searches and seizures of homes and property; the Fifth Amendment's guarantee of freedom from self-incrimination; and the Ninth Amendment, which gave to all citizens rights not specifically enumerated in the Constitution. The right to privacy, the Court concluded, was so basic that the Framers had not seen the need to spell it out more clearly in the Constitution. Nevertheless, all of these amendments, especially the Ninth, could be taken at face value to imply a privacy right. Once this right to privacy was found within the Bill of Rights' guarantees, the Court went on to conclude that it included a married couple's right to use birth control. Seven years later, in 1972, the Court used the same privacy right to strike down as unconstitutional a Massachusetts law that allowed only married couples access to contraceptives.

State Law and Abortion Policy

Although *Griswold* was met with little attention or consternation, it was soon to provide the basis for a much more controversial ruling. Soon after the founding of the National Abortion Rights Action League (NARAL) in 1968, its leadership decided to pursue a two-pronged strategy to bring about repeal of restrictive state abortion statutes. NARAL continued to pursue change on a state-by-state basis, but it also believed that a litigation strategy to achieve change through the courts might be just as effective, and possibly quicker. Then, as now, it took a significant amount of organization and tremendous resources to lobby state legislatures effectively. Instead of lobbying one body with 535 members in one city—the District of Columbia—groups had to be mobilized in the state capitals of every state where change was sought. And even if a group was successful in a particular state, its success, given the nature of the federal system, was limited to that state. In contrast, if a particular law was attacked in the federal courts as being in violation of the U.S. Constitution in a test case, the decision of the U.S. Supreme Court, if the Court agreed that a violation had been committed, was binding *on all fifty states.*

Early Challenges in State Court

The first breakthrough on the abortion front came in a state court in California, where reformers were well on the way to putting abortion reform on the public agenda. In early 1967, one prominent physician announced that he was referring patients for abortions in violation of California law. At the urging of California anti-abortion groups, he was quickly indicted and tried in state court. Two years later, in 1969, the California supreme court ruled that the state law was unconstitutional, and soon thousands of abortions were being performed by licensed physicians in that state (Lader 1991, p. 11).

Early Challenges in Federal Court

Around the same time, Milan Vuitch, a physician in Washington, D.C.—in anticipation of his own arrest after anti-abortion groups put pressure on local authorities—followed NARAL suggestions and began keeping detailed records of the health status of the women who came to him for an abortion. The D.C. abortion statute permitted abortions only when they were necessary for the "health or life" of the mother. Vuitch was soon indicted for violating the D.C. law. But a federal court judge (the case was in federal court because Washington, D.C., is not a state) dismissed his indictment, finding the law unconstitutionally vague and therefore unenforceable because it provided no adequate guidelines for law enforcement officials to decide whether, in fact, the law had been violated. The federal court added that "a woman's liberty and right of privacy extends to family, marriage, and sex matters and *may well include the right to remove an unwanted child, at least in early stages of pregnancy*" (emphasis added) (*United States v. Vuitch*, 1969). The U.S. Supreme Court, however, sent the case back to the lower court for trial, on the grounds that the law was not unconstitutionally vague. Women's "health," it ruled, could be defined by a judge or a jury, so Vuitch could be prosecuted if adequate health reasons for the abortions he performed could not be provided (*United States v. Vuitch*, 1971).

The activities of Planned Parenthood, NARAL, and *anti*-abortion groups illustrate some of the myriad ways that interest groups have tried to affect public policy in the United States. Just as the National Association for the Advancement of Colored People (NAACP) Legal Defense and Education Fund brought a series of test cases to invalidate the "separate but equal doctrine" that had culminated in the U.S. Supreme Court's decision in *Brown v. Board of Education* (1954), the aforementioned groups resorted to litigation when their efforts to seek change in state laws and/or practices appeared to be going nowhere. Litigation in state and federal courts, however, is just one of the many tools wielded by interest groups to advance their policy interests. It is common for such groups to try to persuade state or national lawmakers to propose legislation to foster group goals. But when this more conventional form of interest-group activity appears to be futile (as was the case when the NAACP tried to lobby segregationist Southern legislators) or difficult to bring about on a state-by-state basis (because of strong opposition in some states or a lack of group organization in others), the courts have often proved to be a quicker means for groups advocating major policy change—especially when they are advocating that change based on rights guaranteed under the U.S. Constitution. Given the nature of the federal system, then, it is often quicker and cheaper for interest groups to seek policy declarations from the U.S. Supreme Court, which, under the U.S. system of law, is the supreme law of the land. Thus, any single U.S. Supreme Court decision interpreting the U.S. Constitution is binding on all fifty states.

Invalidation of State Abortion Laws by the U.S. Supreme Court

United States v. Vuitch (1971) was just one of scores of test cases that were launched around the country by liberal interest groups in an effort to invalidate restrictive abortion laws (O'Connor 1980; Rubin 1994). Against this background of increasing litigation and expanded support for change among women's rights groups, the U.S. Supreme Court agreed to hear two more cases involving abortion rights. The first of these, *Roe v. Wade* (1973), involved Jane Roe's challenge to a Texas law that prohibited abortions except when necessary to save a mother's life. (The woman is referred to as "Jane Roe" because most abortion cases involving individuals use pseudonyms instead of actual names, to spare the individuals unwanted media attention.) Because Roe's pregnancy was not life threatening (thus making her ineligible for a legal abortion in Texas), she was advised to seek one out of state. She did not have the money to do so. So, after obtaining legal counsel, she went to court to challenge the constitutionality of the Texas law. Roe's original lawsuit was filed in a federal district court. Again, given the nature of the U.S. federal system, her challenge to the state law could have been filed either in state court because it involved a state law or in federal court because her lawyers were alleging that the state law violated rights guaranteed by the national Bill of Rights. Her lawyers opted to proceed in federal court. They recognized that elected state court judges, who regularly face reelection, would be less likely to rule as unconstitutional a law made by elected state representatives than would unelected federal judges who serve for life. As with many issues involving race discrimination, most lawyers challenging restrictive laws or practices have opted (at least until recently) to try their cases in the historically more liberal federal courts.

Roe's lawsuit alleged that the Texas law deprived "women and their physicians of rights protected by the 4th, 5th, 9th, and 14th Amendments" to the U.S. Constitution, and that she was deprived of the "fundamental right . . . to choose when and where to have children." Clearly, her lawyers relied heavily on the right to privacy enunciated by the U.S. Supreme Court in *Griswold v. Connecticut* (1965).

Unlike the Texas law, the Georgia statute challenged in *Doe v. Bolton* (1973), the companion case to *Roe*, was based on the Model Penal Code of the American Law Institute (ALI). Doe's lawyers, acting on behalf of Planned Parenthood and several doctors, nurses, clergy, and social workers, alleged that the Georgia law was an undue restriction of personal and marital privacy and a denial of equal protection of the laws.

Pro- and anti-abortion forces had gone head-to-head in numerous states where abortion reform was being debated, but *Roe* and *Doe* marked the first major, direct, national confrontation between these forces. Amicus curiae briefs were submitted in support of the plaintiffs in both abortion cases by several physicians' groups and women's rights organizations, including the American Association of University Women, the Young Women's Christian Association (YWCA), the National Organization for Women (NOW), and Planned Parenthood. Though not as numerous, anti-abortion groups also filed amicus curiae briefs in large numbers. Among these latter groups were the National Right-to-Life Committee, Americans United for Life, Women for the Unborn, and Women Concerned for the Unborn Child.

Federal Responses to the Abortion Issue

Although *Roe v. Wade* and *Doe v. Bolton* presented challenges to state laws, some expected that the national government might try to intercede in the abortion debate. Interestingly, *Roe* and *Doe* were decided within days of President Richard M. Nixon's second inauguration. Although Nixon made no public comments on the cases at the time, as early as 1971 he had publicly stated that his "firm personal and religious beliefs" led him to "consider abortion an unacceptable form of population control" (*New York Times Abstracts*, April 4, 1971, p. 103). In fact, as evidenced by a letter to Secretary of Defense Melvin R. Laird from Richard Nixon, the president was sufficiently concerned about the abortion issue that he directed his secretary of defense to follow state laws regarding abortion for military personnel rather than set a uniform federal policy. This letter vividly illustrates the president's recognition of the dilemma posed by the federal system: Should federal or state law apply? On the one hand, if state law were to take precedence, thus doing away with a national standard, government employees and dependents on federal military bases would have different rights depending on where they were stationed by the federal government. On the other hand, if it were inherently the responsibility of the federal government to set national policy, abortion rights would be given to all citizens of the fifty states. Apparently, President Nixon subscribed to the former view (see Figure 3.1).

Although President Nixon indicated that state law should apply to federal military bases, he was not above entering into the fray of state politics to lobby for restrictive state abortion laws. He personally intervened in an attempt to convince fellow Republican Nelson A. Rockefeller to veto the liberal New York law (Rubin 1994, p. 146). And he rejected proposals made by his own Commission on Population Growth, which recommended that restrictive state abortion laws be liberalized and contraceptives be made available to teenagers (Dixon-Mueller 1993, p. 66).

Notwithstanding Nixon's stated policy preferences, when the abortion cases were accepted for argument before the U.S. Supreme Court, his administration took no action—even though it is not unusual for the United States to file an amicus curiae brief advocating a position on important policy matters. This inaction is even more surprising given that **Solicitor General** Erwin Griswold, the member of the U.S. Justice Department appointed by the president to represent the United States and its interests before the Supreme Court, had defended the District of

FIGURE 3.1

Nixon Memo to Laird

THE WHITE HOUSE
WASHINGTON

March 24, 1971

Dear Mel:

I've been made aware of the Department of Defense's policy on abortions.

As you know, for many years I have had strong personal convictions on this subject which I have expressed both privately and publicly. I realize that it is a difficult and touchy problem which has divided national opinion.

Nevertheless, I feel strongly that this Administration should not support a policy contrary to local state laws. Accordingly, if the Department of Defense maintains medical or hospital installations which perform abortions contrary to applicable law in the locality of the installation, I must request that you immediately modify that policy.

I do not believe that the statutory requirement of "uniformity" is any inhibition to your compliance with this request since it is my desire that this be a uniform policy of the Department wherever it maintains such installations.

Sincerely,

Honorable Melvin R. Laird
The Secretary of Defense
Washington, D. C.

Letter to Secretary of Defense Melvin Laird from President Richard Nixon (1971), directing federal military bases to follow local laws on abortion.

Columbia's abortion restrictions at issue in *United States v. Vuitch* (1971). Perhaps Nixon believed that the Court, which now included four of his own nominees, shared his views. Ironically, however, it was Harry A. Blackmun, one of Nixon's appointees, who wrote for the majority in *Roe.*

The Supreme Court Decides

Groups on both sides of the abortion issue recognized the tremendous power that the federal courts have in making and monitoring national policy. Although the Framers, when originally drafting the Constitution, anticipated that the judiciary "would be the least dangerous branch" (Hamilton, *Federalist* No. 78), over time the power and role of the courts in national policymaking has increased a thousandfold. Today, groups often start the policy cycle by bringing cases to court. In that way, they can attempt to define the issue, get it on the public agenda, and obtain a relatively quick decision (which in turn can serve the purposes of either policy formulation or policy implementation). This policy cycle is essentially what characterized *Roe v. Wade.*

Roe v. Wade. On January 22, 1973, the Supreme Court handed down its momentous decision in *Roe,* formulating a national abortion policy for the first time. In a 7-to-2 decision, although the majority did not adopt the view that abortion was a totally private matter as urged by some, seven justices clearly concluded that a woman's *constitutional right to privacy* was more important than a state's right to regulate abortion under its police powers. The Court also implicitly recognized that it was within the role of the federal courts to standardize abortion policy throughout the nation. In essence, the majority of the Court interpreted the Bill of Rights to provide protection for all women, regardless of the state in which they lived. Abortion policy was thus largely transferred to the responsibility of the federal courts, and state police powers were forced to take a role secondary to individual federal constitutional rights.

The two dissenters, Justice William H. Rehnquist (appointed by President Richard M. Nixon) and Justice Byron White (appointed by President John F. Kennedy), voiced strong opposition to the majority opinion. They criticized the Court for finding a right not specified in the Constitution to overturn the carefully considered laws of several states that had acted to criminalize abortion under their police powers.

More than simply finding the Georgia and Texas laws unconstitutional, however, the seven justices in the majority in *Roe* effectively invalidated the abortion laws of all but four states, as indicated in Table 3.1. In doing so, they rejected state arguments that the states had the authority under the U.S. Constitution to protect the public health and welfare of their citizens as they saw fit.

TABLE 3.1

State Laws and the Effect of *Roe v. Wade*

States Not Affected			
Alaska	Hawaii	New York	Washington
States with Reformed Laws in Need of Rewriting			
Alabama	Arkansas	California	Colorado
Delaware	Florida	Georgia	Kansas
Maryland	Mississippi	New Mexico	North Carolina
Oregon	South Carolina	Virginia	
States with Unreformed Laws in Need of Total Rewriting			
Arizona	Connecticut	Idaho	Illinois
Indiana	Iowa	Kentucky	Louisiana
Maine	Massachusetts	Michigan	Minnesota
Missouri	Montana	Nebraska	Nevada
New Hampshire	New Jersey	North Dakota	Ohio
Oklahoma	Pennsylvania	Rhode Island	South Dakota
Tennessee	Texas	Utah	Vermont
West Virginia	Wyoming		

Source: Congressional Record, January 23, 1973, S 1, 862.

In finding a right to privacy in the national Bill of Rights, the justices in *Roe* divided pregnancy into trimesters and defined different rights as applying to each of the three categories. The Court—including three Nixon appointees, Harry A. Blackmun, Lewis Powell, and Chief Justice Warren E. Burger—held that during the first trimester, a woman, in consultation with her physician, had an absolute right to obtain an abortion free from state interference. With respect to the second trimester, the Court found that the "State, in promoting its interest in the health of the mother, may, if it chooses, regulate the abortion procedure in ways that are reasonably related to maternal health." Thus, the question would eventually become one of delineating what kinds of restrictions states could apply to abortion rights. Finally, regarding the last trimester of pregnancy, the justices concluded that the states, to promote the interests of "potential human life," could regulate or prohibit abortions, except when they were necessary to preserve the "life or health of the mother." (See Box 3.1. for the text of the *Roe v. Wade* decision.)

BOX 3.1

Excerpts from *Roe v. Wade*

Legal citation: 410 U.S. 113
Argued: December 13, 1971
Decided: January 22, 1973
Opinion by: Justice Blackmun

. . . One's philosophy, one's experiences, one's exposure to the raw edges of human existence, one's religious training, one's attitudes toward life and family and their values, and the moral standards one establishes and seeks to observe, are all likely to influence and to color one's thinking and conclusions about abortion.

Our task, of course, is to resolve the issue by constitutional measurement, free of emotion and of predilection. We seek earnestly to do this, and, because we do, we have inquired into, and in this opinion place some emphasis upon, medical and medical-legal history and what that history reveals about man's attitudes toward the abortion procedure over the centuries. . . .

The State has a legitimate interest in seeing to it that abortion, like any other medical procedure, is performed under circumstances that insure maximum safety for the patient. This interest obviously extends at least to the performing physician and his staff, to the facilities involved, to the availability of after-care, and to adequate provision for any complication or emergency that might arise. The prevalence of high mortality rates at illegal "abortion mills" strengthens, rather than weakens, the State's interest in regulating the conditions under which abortions are performed. Moreover, the risk to the woman increases as her pregnancy continues. Thus, the State retains a definite interest in protecting the woman's own health and safety when an abortion is proposed at a late stage of pregnancy. . . .

This right of privacy, whether it be founded in the Fourteenth Amendment's concept of personal liberty and restrictions upon state action, as we feel it is, or, as the District Court determined, in the Ninth Amendment's reservation of rights to the people, is broad enough to encompass a woman's decision whether or not to terminate her pregnancy. The detriment that the State would impose upon the pregnant woman by denying this choice altogether is apparent. Specific and direct harm medically diagnosable even in early pregnancy may be involved. Maternity, or additional offspring, may force upon the woman a distressful life and future. Psychological harm may be imminent. Mental and physical health may be taxed by child care. There is also the distress, for all concerned, associated with the unwanted child, and there is the problem of bringing a child into a family already unable, psychologically and otherwise, to care for it. In other cases, as in this one, the additional difficulties and continuing stigma of unwed motherhood may be involved. All these are factors the woman and her responsible physician necessarily will consider in consultation.

On the basis of elements such as these, appellant and some amici argue that the woman's right is absolute and that she is entitled to terminate her pregnancy at whatever time, in whatever way, and for whatever reason she alone chooses. With this we do not agree. Appellant's arguments that Texas either has no valid interest at all in regulating the abortion decision, or no interest strong enough to support any limitation upon the woman's sole determination, are unpersuasive. The Court's decisions recognizing a right of privacy also acknowledge that some state regulation in areas protected by that right is appropriate. As noted above, a State may properly assert important interests in safeguarding health, in maintaining medical standards, and in protecting potential life. At some point in pregnancy, these respective interests become sufficiently compelling to sustain regulation of the factors that govern the abortion decision. The privacy right involved, therefore, cannot be said to be absolute. In fact, it is not clear to us that the claim asserted by some amici that one has an unlimited right to do with one's body as one pleases bears a close relationship to the right of privacy previously articulated in the Court's decisions. The Court has refused to recognize an unlimited right of this kind in the past. We, therefore, conclude that the right of personal privacy includes the abortion decision, but that this right is not unqualified and must be considered against important state interests in regulation.

Doe v. Bolton. In *Doe v. Bolton*, another 7-to-2 decision authored by Justice Harry A. Blackmun, the majority also struck down the Georgia Model ALI–type abortion statute as unconstitutional. At issue in *Doe* was the state statute that allowed abortion only in three cases: (1) when carrying a pregnancy to term would result in a threat to the health of the mother; (2) when the fetus was likely to be born with a grave permanent and irremediable physical or mental defect; or (3) when the pregnancy was a result of forcible or statutory rape. The statute required the attending physician to certify, by means of signatures from two additional physicians, that the abortion was to be performed for one of those specified reasons. It also required that the hospital be licensed and accredited, and that a hospital abortion committee approve the abortion. Alleged instances of rape had to be certified, and all women seeking abortions had to be state residents. Clearly, in

BOX 3.2

Where Are They Now?

In late summer 1995, the pro-choice community was caught off guard when a longtime symbol of the movement, its own poster child Norma McCorvey—aka Jane Roe of *Roe v. Wade* fame—denounced the decision that bore her name (or pseudonym, to be more exact). The strange and sad life of this poor, uneducated former carnival barker had taken yet another bizarre turn. McCorvey, whose unsuccessful attempt to secure an abortion had led to the Supreme Court's stunning ruling in *Roe*, now was not only turning her back on pro-choice activists but also announced her recent baptism by a national Operation Rescue (OR) leader. Despite the fact that McCorvey is a lesbian who has lived with her partner for twenty-six years, one leader of Operation Rescue, which is normally quick to denounce homosexuality, stated that McCorvey "doesn't have to desert Connie [her partner], just so long as everything is pure."[1]

Her sexual orientation is not the only potential cause of friction between McCorvey and the Christian right. Much to the latter's chagrin, she persists in her belief that first-trimester abortions should be legal.

McCorvey never really felt comfortable with the better-educated, more affluent leaders of the pro-choice movement—among them Sarah Weddington, her lawyer in *Roe*. Having told *ABC News* that she had been exploited by the pro-choice movement, McCorvey, whose baby was adopted by her mother, also appeared to have been stunned by revelations in Weddington's book, *A Question of Choice* (1992). It was there that Weddington disclosed, for the first time, that she herself had secured an abortion four years before *Roe*. Unlike McCorvey, however, Weddington had the money and wherewithal to find out where an illegal abortion could be performed. Weddington's failure to be "up front" with McCorvey about her past abortion may be one reason for McCorvey's abortion conversion. "She kept that from me and I still don't forgive her and I never did have an abortion," said McCorvey. "When I first met her, I asked Sarah if I could get an abortion. She said that she didn't know. That was a damn lie and she knew it, but she needed me to be pregnant, so she could have a case to fight and I was too dumb to know she wasn't telling the truth."[2]

For many years after *Roe*, McCorvey told no one other than her partner that she was Jane Roe. Then, during the Reagan years, McCorvey went public and often participated in pro-choice rallies. More recently she had found employment as a marketing director for a Texas abortion clinic—a job option no longer open to her. In 1995, moreover, she authored a book entitled *I Am Roe*. Now, having found a new appreciative audience among the ranks of the right-to-life movement, she is writing a second book about both her conversion and her experience working as a filing clerk for Operation Rescue.

"I wish I had chosen a different plaintiff," said Sarah Weddington shortly after McCorvey's surprise announcement. "Frankly, I'm not sure she really has figured out what she does believe. Because on [the] one hand, she was saying she was opposed to abortion, but on the other hand, [she said] it should be legal in the first trimester, but that women should not have more than two."[3]

Weddington's life contrasts sharply with that of McCorvey. After arguing *Roe*, Weddington was elected to the Texas legislature at the age of twenty-six. An early president of the National Abortion Rights Action League (NARAL), she subsequently served as an assistant to President Jimmy Carter in the area of women's issues. Still an outspoken advocate of abortion rights, Weddington teaches at the University of Texas and is now writing a book on political leadership.

Mary and John Doe, the named plaintiffs in *Doe v. Bolton*, went on to become lawyers and to have two children; their lawyer, Margie Pitts Hames, continued as a pro-choice activist. Like Weddington, Hames served as president of NARAL; later, she founded the Georgia chapter of that organization. In fact, Hames worked on behalf of many Atlanta abortion clinics until her death in 1994. Dorothy Beasley, who as an assistant attorney general argued *Doe* for the state of Georgia, now sits on the Georgia Court of Appeals. And Robert Flowers, who argued *Roe* for the state of Texas, is now employed by a state agency there.

Notes

1. Quoted in Daniel Jeffreys, "Her case legalized abortion in the U.S. She is the very symbol of the prochoice movement. But now 'Jane Roe' has switched sides. She tells Daniel Jeffreys why," *The Independent*, August 24, 1995, p. 4.
2. Ibid.
3. Quoted in Judy Thomas, "*Roe vs. Wade* Lawyer Regrets Picking McCorvey as Plaintiff," *Kansas City Star*, October 26, 1995, p. A-8.

enacting all of these provisions, the state of Georgia believed it was exercising its constitutional right to legislate for the public health and safety of its citizens.

The same seven-man majority opinion struck down each of these provisions as unconstitutional under the First, Fourth, Fifth, Ninth, and Fourteenth Amendments. However, *Doe*, like *Roe*, left unanswered numerous questions about what kinds of restrictions could be imposed by states on individuals seeking or performing abortions. Taken together, *Roe* and *Doe* underscored the important role that physicians had long played in the abortion debate. Although both rulings upheld a woman's right to secure an abortion and limited the kinds of restrictions that states could impose, they ultimately left the decision about whether to obtain an abortion with the woman in consultation with her physician.

In his opinion in *Roe*, Justice Blackmun noted, "I fear what the headlines may be, but it should be stressed that the Court does not today hold that the Constitution compels abortion on demand." Yet Blackmun's fears did not cause the instant uproar he predicted. *Roe* and *Doe* were decided on the day that former president Lyndon B. Johnson died, thus temporarily diverting national attention from *Roe*. Torrents of rage against the decision, however, were soon to come. (See Box 3.2 for a discussion of what has become of the major actors in *Roe* and *Doe*.)

Conclusion

The U.S. Constitution is silent on the issues of birth control and abortion. Yet that document and the federal system have played key roles in determining the way the polity has addressed the abortion issue. Although public opinion polls have shown only mixed support for abortion, several state legislatures have acted to decriminalize abortion in certain circumstances; others have repealed their restrictive abortion laws. In most states, groups mobilized on both sides of the abortion issue. Those groups that favored reform and/or repeal of restrictive abortion laws quickly recognized that the state-by-state route would be long, tedious, and fraught with possibilities for potential losses. Thus, they launched a series of test cases to build on the Supreme Court's enunciation of the privacy doctrine in an effort to invoke the right to privacy as protection of a woman's right to terminate her pregnancy. In *Roe v. Wade* (1973), the Court ruled that the right to privacy—a right derived from the penumbras or emanations of rights contained in the First, Third, Fourth, Fifth, Ninth, and Fourteenth Amendments to the Constitution—protected a woman's right to an abortion. In *Doe v. Bolton* (1973), the Court also ruled that states could not limit how or why abortions could be performed in the early stages of pregnancy. It concluded in both cases that a state's right to legislate abortion policy before fetal viability could not interfere with a woman's right to privacy. However, the Court left open the question as to what extent the state could legally regulate abortion in later stages of pregnancy. The Court's decision in these abortion cases ignited the debate as the focus shifted from the states to the national level—at least for the time being.

The Supreme Court's decisions in *Roe v. Wade* and *Doe v. Bolton* went far beyond even the most liberal state statutes. The Court ruled that a woman's constitutional right to privacy included the right to secure an abortion "free from undue state interference," a phrase that would later take on increasing importance. To the Court in *Roe*, however, such freedom initially meant that states could not limit abortion rights in any significant way during the first two trimesters of pregnancy.

In terms of the policy process, freedom from undue state interference also meant that the abortion issue, at least initially, had been clearly defined and put on the public agenda. In addition, both *Roe* and *Doe* signaled that a *national* abortion policy had been articulated by the Court to supersede any existing *state* policies. It was now up to other actors in the policymaking process—the president, Congress, interest groups, political parties, voters, state legislatures, and even the public—to become involved in that process, even though the Court would continue to be the ultimate arbiter of constitutional controversies.

4

The Aftermath of *Roe* and *Doe*

The emphasis has got to be on implementation. . . . I don't feel these fanatics on the other side will just sit back and take this. I think they'll press for whatever legislation they can get away with, and they'll be pushing for a constitutional amendment.

—Lee Gidding, executive director of NARAL, quoted in Malloy (1973)

I feel this opinion will be reversed. It may take a quarter of a century. It may take fifty years. But I think it will happen.

—Monsignor James McHugh, director of the Family Life Division of the U.S. Catholic Conference, quoted in Malloy (1973)

THE SUPREME COURT'S DECISIONS in *Roe v. Wade* and *Doe v. Bolton* functioned "as a catalyst rather than as the last word on abortion" (Devins 1995, p. ix). *Roe* read like a piece of legislation in its careful differentiation of the rights of a woman to an abortion across the three trimesters of pregnancy and its delineation of the limits of constitutional state action permitted during each trimester. *Roe* and *Doe* together, however, opened up the question as to precisely what could be restricted by the states. The abortion decisions themselves, as well as their ambiguity, not only spurred the creation of new interest groups and increased activity by existing groups but also inspired elected officials on both the state and national levels to further action as they attempted to formulate new abortion policies. Before being appointed to the U.S. Supreme Court, Ruth Bader Ginsburg perhaps overstated the situation when she noted that the abortion cases "prolonged divisiveness and deferred stable settlement of the issue"—specifically, by shortcutting the more traditional legislative efforts that had begun to occur in the late 1960s and early 1970s throughout the United States (Ginsburg 1993, p. 1198).

The Framers clearly never intended the federal judiciary to be a policymaker. Yet, in *Roe*, that is exactly what the Supreme Court became. "Traditional legislative efforts" were eschewed by feminists and abortion repeal advocates as being too long and offering the possibility of only more limited options for most women. Given the relatively weak organization of women's rights groups at the state level, as later evidenced by the nonratification of the proposed equal rights amendment (an idea embraced by far more Americans than those who supported an absolute legal right to an abortion under unlimited circumstances), their decision to litigate in all likelihood only provided a flashpoint for anti-abortion activity and accelerated the placement of the issue on the national agenda.

The actions of interest groups after *Roe* highlight the basic policy dilemma presented by the abortion issue. But once the Supreme Court spoke, the nature of the debate was altered. That is, some aspects of abortion became an issue of national concern when the Supreme Court declared in *Roe* that the right to an abortion could be derived from a federal constitutional right to privacy. Thus, the dilemma was resolved—at least for the time being. Now that abortion was recognized as a national issue, anti-abortion groups quickly mobilized to work on the national level, where their actions could have the most immediate impact. But these groups also lobbied on the state level, where they were far better organized, given their strong ties to various churches. Since *Doe* had left open many questions as to how far states could go to regulate abortions, some anti-abortion activists looked to state legislatures as possible sources of new abortion restrictions, all the while pressing for a constitutional amendment to overrule *Roe*.

Interest-Group Responses to *Roe*

Roe and *Doe* were met with enthusiasm by women in the abortion and women's rights movements. But they also provided the catalyst for major organizational efforts of the anti-abortion movement, which was caught off guard by the magnitude of the Court's decision as well as by the rapidity with which the policy process had been exploited by abortion reform/repeal groups. One month after the ruling, the executive director of NARAL remarked: "We really haven't gotten over it. It was such a shock. We didn't expect it to be so sweeping. It's just superb" (Malloy, quoted in Rubin 1994, p. 144). Activist Lawrence Lader concurred, saying that the decision "came like a thunderbolt" (quoted in Rubin 1994, p. 140). Meanwhile, although public reaction was mixed, the Roman Catholic Church quickly denounced the decision, and the National Conference of Catholic Bishops (NCCB) issued a statement in which it described the decision as "a flagrant rejection of the unborn child's right to life, . . . bad morality, bad medicine and bad public policy" and called on Americans to oppose and reject the Court's opinion (United States Catholic Conference 1974, pp. 59–60). The Catholic Church was quick to see the importance of immediately pressuring state legislatures and the Congress to act to restrict abortion.

In many respects, the development, growth, and respective successes of the pro- and anti-abortion movements are quite illustrative of what political scientist David B. Truman (1951) called "disturbance theory." He argued that interest groups (or social movements) arise in response to threats. Thus, when one group or interest appears to be able to change the social order or a governmental policy position, other groups will spring up to protect their interests. And, indeed, anti-abortion groups coalesced to form a movement in 1973 in response to the Court's abortion decision. The movement's major goal was reversal of that decision or ratification of a constitutional amendment to give full legal rights of personhood to the fetus from the moment of conception (English 1981).

The Roman Catholic Church and the National Right-to-Life Committee

Most opposition to the abortion law reform or repeal movements in the states prior to *Roe* and *Doe* was led by the U.S. Catholic Conference through its subordinate NCCB, its Family Life Division, and its lay advisers, informally referred to as the National Right-to-Life Committee. Thus, it is not surprising that the first anti-abortion groups to be formed were largely Catholic in composition. In fact, the **National Right-to-Life Committee (NRLC)** was formally organized after the abortion decisions in 1973 with extensive organizational and financial support from the NCCB.

In the spring of 1973, shortly after *Roe* and *Doe*, the NCCB met and made four recommendations concerning abortion:

1. Right-to-life groups should be organized in every state.
2. Local Catholic dioceses should help fund anti-abortion educational activities in their respective localities.
3. The National Right-to-Life Committee should be helped in any way possible.
4. One day each month should be set aside for "prayer and fasting in reparations for abortions" performed (Faux 1988, pp. 328–329).

These recommendations were adopted wholeheartedly by the NCCB, which made ending legalized abortion its number-one priority.

The Roman Catholic Church and the National Right-to-Life Committee were so closely tied that they had an agreement in New York allowing the committee to take up collections from parishioners after Sunday Mass (English 1981). And in 1975, the church itself announced an unprecedented major political campaign. In its "Pastoral Plan for Pro-Life Activities," detailed in Box 4.1, the National Conference of Catholic Bishops declared that it would undertake a major public-information campaign to encourage Catholics to support candidates opposed to abortion (National Conference of Catholic Bishops 1975).

The NCCB plan was extraordinarily broad in scope. It not only called on local churches to target legislators who did not support the anti-abortion position but also explained how to identify, support, and elect like-minded representatives. In essence, the plan "was a brilliant blueprint [for political action], essentially combining in a legal way the efforts of the already existing right-to-life offices of the National Conference of Catholic Bishops and the National Committee for a Human Life Amendment" (Paige 1983, p. 73). Thus, the abortion issue was clearly identified by Roman Catholic elders as a political as well as a moral issue.

BOX 4.1

Key Points from the NCCB's Pastoral Plan for Pro-Life Activities

Legislative Efforts

1. The 1973 abortion decision violates the moral order. Therefore, a pro-life legislative program is essential that includes the following elements:
   A. Passage of a constitutional amendment
   B. Passage of federal and state laws and adoption of administrative policies to restrict abortion
   C. Continual research about *Roe*
   D. Support for legislative alternatives to abortion
2. Support for the plan will require "well-planned and coordinated political action. . . . " Means of action include:
   A. State Coordinating Committees
   B. The Diocesan Pro-Life Committee
   C. The Parish Pro-Life Committee
   D. Creation of Pro-Life Groups in Congressional Districts
3. Duties of the Congressional District Pro-Life Groups include:
   A. Continuing public information efforts to persuade all elected officials and potential candidates that abortion is wrong and should be legally restricted
   B. Counterbalancing "propaganda efforts opposed to a constitutional amendment"
   C. Persuading all residents that a constitutional amendment is necessary
   D. Convincing all elected officials that the issue "will not go away"
   E. Electing members to political party office
   F. Maintaining the positions of all candidates and elected officials on abortion
   G. Working for qualified candidates who oppose abortion

The Stop ERA Movement

The Roman Catholic Church was not the only preexisting group that provided leaders and supporters of the right-to-life movement, as we shall see. The moral issues underlying the abortion debate as captured by *Roe*, and its opponents' depiction of abortion as murder, immediately catapulted the abortion issue into the national headlines. *Roe* and *Doe*, and the attendant publicity they received, quickly attracted the attention of women already involved in the effort to stop state ratification of the proposed equal rights amendment (ERA). And just as the women's rights movement had provided an organizational base for pro-choice forces, anti-abortion advocates were helped when Phyllis Schlafly, an outspoken conservative Republican anti-feminist, publicly attacked the Supreme Court's decision. Schlafly, as head of the Eagle Forum, the largest anti-ERA group, effectively linked abortion rights to the proposed ERA, which had come before the states for their ratification (Mansbridge 1986). Schlafly charged that *Roe* and *Doe* were but two examples of the damage that would be wreaked on traditional values if the ERA were ratified. She tied the ERA's possible removal of some state powers—especially over family relations—to the Supreme Court's removal of the states' right to regulate abortion. She and others opposed to abortion also blamed the Court's abortion decisions on what they saw as the increasing decline in morals and destruction of the family personified by the women's rights movement.

Fundamentalists

Schlafly was not the only one who tied *Roe* and *Doe* to the ERA. So did many conservative fundamentalist churches, including the Church of Jesus Christ of Latter-Day Saints (Mormons) in Utah and the West as well as the Protestant sects in the South. The Mormon Church went so far as to excommunicate members who spoke in favor of the ERA; it also provided a base for the anti-abortion movement, particularly in the West. For example, Mormon Rex E. Lee, a prominent conservative law professor at Brigham Young University who was later to become U.S. solicitor general, linked the ERA to abortion and used *Roe* as an example of how the federal courts could justify regulating personal relationships (Lee 1974).

It took evangelical Christians a bit longer to mobilize against abortion. The first evangelical Christian anti-abortion group was founded in 1975 by the Reverend Billy Graham and Dr. C. Everett Koop, who was later appointed U.S. surgeon general by Ronald Reagan. The creation of the Christian Action Council by Graham and Koop was among the first indications that the evangelical right would not only politically align itself with the more conservative Republican Party but also prove to be a more potent political force than even the Roman Catholic Church in the abortion debate *and* in party politics (Byrnes and Segers 1992, p. 158). Evangelical Christians were quick to tie their opposition to abortion to myriad other social positions, including support for prayer in schools and resistance to the ERA (which was viewed as threatening to the family unit)—positions also ultimately embraced by the Republican Party.

Throughout the middle to late 1970s, however, Roman Catholics, Mormons, evangelicals, and others opposed to the ERA provided a sufficiently large base for the relatively quick mobilization of an anti-abortion movement. Not only were they united in opposition to abortion, they also opposed liberalized abortion statutes, prenatal testing, and homosexuality. Agreement on these issues widened the base of the anti-abortion movement. And because the churches were so well organized on the local level, the anti-abortion movement was effectively positioned to lobby legislators on both the state and national levels. Both the anti-ERA forces and the Roman Catholic Church, in particular, had well-organized units throughout the country on the national, state, and local levels—units that were soon to be joined by evangelical Christians.

Targeting State Legislatures

Soon after *Roe* and *Doe*, as anti-abortion forces became better organized, state legislatures around the nation were deluged with anti-abortion bills. Within six months of *Roe*, for example, 188 anti-abortion bills were introduced in 41 state legislatures (Faux 1988, pp. 318–319). And anti-abortion forces, having interpreted *Doe* as allowing some forms of *state* regulation, vowed to test the limits on "reasonable" state regulations that would be permitted by the federal courts. Proposed laws included provisions to regulate clinics and to require parental or spousal consent, waiting periods, or even the viewing of aborted fetuses before a patient could give her "informed" consent for the abortion procedure. Typical was the law passed in 1974 in Missouri, where anti-abortion sentiment was strong. This law soon became a model for other states and localities. Among its stipulations were the following:

1. Written consent provisions
2. Spousal consent provisions
3. Parental consent provisions
4. Hospitalization requirements for abortions performed after the twelfth week
5. Physician certification of nonviability of the fetus
6. Criminal penalties for physicians who failed to comply
7. Prohibition of fetal research
8. Informed consent
9. Record-keeping provisions

The constitutionality of this Missouri law, and others like it, was soon to be tested in court by advocates of liberalized abortion laws. Nevertheless, anti-abortion activists basically followed what civil rights activists in the 1950s and 1960s had called a "legislate and litigate" strategy. Throughout the segregationist South, state legislators passed laws of very questionable constitutionality and provoked their opponents to spend the time and money to fight them in court. The same tactic was used by those in the anti-abortion movement. But unlike segregationists, anti-abortion activists were largely motivated by religious concerns. It was in this context that they viewed the Constitution as a protector of rights for the unborn rather than of women's right to privacy.

The Liberal Reaction

The passage of new state abortion restrictions like those specified by the Missouri law immediately placed abortion rights advocates on the defensive, but many failed to see the need for overt political action to preserve the rights outlined in *Roe* and *Doe*. Still getting over their unexpected victory, they were perhaps foolishly optimistic in underestimating the power, or potential power, of their opponents. In fact, as NARAL's executive director said after *Roe*: "Before you know it this will be past history and abortion will just be another medical procedure. People will forget about this whole thing" (Malloy, quoted in Rubin 1994, p. 147). Given attitudes such as this, it is easy to see how abortion law repeal advocates were caught off guard by the quick mobilization of the anti-abortion movement. Soon, however, they were forced to expend large sums of money and considerable energy to challenge the constitutionality of new state and national laws in court that restricted or interfered with a woman's right to an abortion. Those opposed to abortion continued to lobby the U.S. Congress for national abortion restrictions and a constitutional amendment to protect human life, and pressured state and even local governments for further restrictions at those levels as well.

Further distracting pro-abortion rights groups was the concerted effort that many women's rights groups were making to win ratification of the proposed ERA in the states. Indeed, many abortion rights advocates believed that *Roe* was the end of their struggle, not just the beginning. They were also slow to recognize the importance of political mobilization for abortion rights and thus neglected to recognize how well organized the anti-abortion forces had become. Moreover, some groups, such as Planned Parenthood, which might have been expected to play an early leading role, were prohibited from engaging in political—as opposed to legislative—efforts because of their tax-exempt status. Planned Parenthood was also harmed by its attitude. Said Alfred F. Moran, executive director of Planned Parenthood of New York City, "We see this as a fundamental human rights issue. It is not a political issue to us. This is an issue that deals with the Constitution and the Bill of Rights" (Herman 1980, p. 8). Sentiments like these prompted Karen Mulhauser, the executive director of the National Abortion Rights Action League (NARAL), to lament about its potential allies: "It's been hard to convince them that in order to take politics out of abortion, we have to get political" (Herman 1980, p. 8). For example, even though the ACLU had specifically created a **Reproductive Freedom Project (RFP)** in 1974 to ensure compliance with *Roe,* most women's rights and abortion rights organizations were surprised by the success of Representative Henry Hyde (R.–Ill.), the congressional sponsor of the Medicaid abortion restrictions, and the state groups that lobbied successfully for the enactment of numerous restrictions and conditions on women's access to an abortion.

Groups Clash in Court

After passage of the Hyde Amendment in 1976, federal funds were cut off for abortions. (The Hyde Amendment is discussed in greater detail later in the chapter.) Well-organized members of the National Right-to-Life Committee and other anti-abortion groups then turned their attention to the sixteen state legislatures that continued to permit free, elective abortions for those women receiving Medicaid. Local anti-abortion groups targeted their state legislatures by offering "model" abortion-restriction statutes dealing with issues that the Supreme Court had not addressed in *Doe*, in particular. They also assisted state officials when challenges to those laws arose. For example, a Virginia law passed at the urging of anti-abortion activists, making it illegal to advertise abortion services, was eventually ruled unconstitutional by the U.S. Supreme Court because it violated free speech and press rights (*Bigelow v. Virginia,* 1975). But, by contrast, the Court upheld the constitutionality of a newly enacted Connecticut law mandating that only physicians could perform abortions, thereby banning the use of some drugs used to induce abortions (*Connecticut v. Menillo*, 1975).

Planned Parenthood of Central Missouri v. Danforth (1976) was the first major post-*Roe* abortion case to reach the Supreme Court. There, Planned Parenthood challenged the 1974 Missouri law enacted at the urging of right-to-life forces. The ACLU's Reproductive Freedom Project, joined by an amicus curiae brief from the National Organization for Women (NOW), successfully challenged the Missouri abortion statute that required informed written consent prior to an abortion. And in a 7-to-2 decision, the Court rejected the right of a man who shared responsibility for a pregnancy (or, in the case of a minor, the right of her parents) to veto an abortion. The U.S. Supreme Court nevertheless also upheld various record-keeping requirements of the law, strongly suggesting that abortion rights supporters could not take all abortion-related rights for granted.

The Right-to-Life Party

In 1970, the **Right-to-Life Party** was founded in New York State. Although its initial energies were largely directed against liberalization of New York's law concerning abortion, its efforts would later grow quickly in scope. Note that, under the federal system, each state is responsible for establishing its own rules concerning political parties and elections. New York is unique in that it has several political parties, and candidates are often cross-endorsed or run under more than one party label. Moreover, since all votes cast for a candidate are added together, most candidates actively seek the endorsements of lesser third parties. Thus, it is not unusual to see a candidate in New York running on both the Republican and Conservative Party lines, for example. For that matter, in 1970 it took only twenty thousand valid signatures on a petition for a candidate to get on the New York State ballot for the first time as a new party candidate (see Figure 4.1).

In 1972 the Right-to-Life Party ran several candidates in New York State. It also endorsed several anti-abortion candidates already running for office on the Republican or Democratic Party lines, giving those candidates an additional line on the ballot and providing some conservative candidates with their margin of victory. (The Democrats it supported were often Roman Catholics.) This impact on state election outcomes did not go unnoticed by others in the anti-abortion movement. In fact, the Right-to-Life Party soon drew more votes than New York's Liberal Party and actually threatened to make the Conservative Party "obsolete" (Crawford 1980, p. 35). But for the time being, most other anti-abortion groups focused their efforts on legislative lobbying.

Targeting Congress

The combined forces of the burgeoning anti-abortion movement quickly descended on Capitol Hill. Its first legislative goal was congressional passage of what was called the **Human Life Amendment;** its second, more modest goal was passage of funding restrictions to end federal payment of abortions for indigent women or those in military service.

The Human Life Amendment

Immediately after *Roe* and *Doe*, the NCCB created the National Conference for a Human Life Amendment (Craig and O'Brien 1993, p. 44). Its purpose was to

FIGURE 4.1

New York State Ballot

	1	2	3	4	5	6	7	8	9
OFFICES	1 GOVERNOR AND LIEUTENANT GOVERNOR (Vote ONCE)	2 COMPTROLLER (Vote for ONE)	3 ATTORNEY GENERAL (Vote for ONE)	4 UNITED STATES SENATOR (Vote for ONE)	5 JUSTICE OF THE SUPREME COURT 9th Judicial District (Vote for any THREE)	6	7	8 REPRESENTATIVE IN CONGRESS 20th District (Vote for ONE)	9 STATE SENATOR 38th District (Vote for ONE)
DEMOCRATIC A	1A Democratic Mario M. Cuomo FOR GOVERNOR Stan Lundine FOR LIEUTENANT GOVERNOR	2A Democratic H. Carl McCall	3A Democratic Karen S. Burstein	4A Democratic Daniel Patrick Moynihan	5A Democratic Doris T. Friedman	6A Democratic John DiBlasi	7A Democratic Ellen B. Holtzman	8A Democratic Gregory B. Julian	9A Democratic VJ Pradhan
REPUBLICAN B	1B Republican George E. Pataki FOR GOVERNOR Elizabeth McCaughey FOR LIEUTENANT GOVERNOR	2B Republican Herbert I. London	3B Republican Tax Cut Now Dennis Vacco	4B Republican Tax Cut Now Bernadette Castro	5B Republican Kenneth W. Rudolph	6B Republican Howard Spitz	7B Republican Matthew F. Coppola	8B Republican Benjamin A. Gilman	9B Republican Joseph R. Holland
CONSERVATIVE C	1C Conservative George E. Pataki FOR GOVERNOR Elizabeth McCaughey FOR LIEUTENANT GOVERNOR	2C Conservative Tax Cut Now Herbert I. London	3C Conservative Dennis Vacco	4C Conservative Bernadette Castro	5C Conservative Kenneth W. Rudolph	6C Conservative John DiBlasi	7C Conservative Matthew F. Coppola		9C Conservative Joseph R. Holland
RIGHT TO LIFE D	1D Right To Life Robert T. Walsh, Sr. FOR GOVERNOR Virginia E. Sutton FOR LIEUTENANT GOVERNOR	2D Right To Life Herbert I. London	3D Right To Life Alfred J. Skidmore	4D Right To Life Henry F. Hewes	Right To Life John J. Barry, J[illegible]	[illegible] nning	Right To Life [illegible] thew F. Cop[illegible]	8D Right To Life Lois M. Colandrea	
LIBERAL E	1E Liberal Mario M. Cuomo FOR GOVERNOR Stan Lundine FOR LIEUTENANT GOVERNOR	2E Liberal H. Carl McCall	3E Liberal Karen S. Burstein	4E Liberal Daniel Patrick Moynihan					
TAX CUT NOW F	1F Tax Cut Now George E. Pataki FOR GOVERNOR Elizabeth McCaughey FOR LIEUTENANT GOVERNOR								
SOCIALIST WORKERS G	1G Socialist Workers Lawrence A. Lane FOR GOVERNOR Mary Nell Bockman FOR LIEUTENANT GOVERNOR	2G Socialist Workers Brock Satter	3G Socialist Workers Nancy H. Rosenstock	4G Socialist Workers Naomi L. Craine					
INDEPENDENCE FUSION H	1H Independence Fusion Thomas Golisano FOR GOVERNOR Dominick A. Fusco FOR LIEUTENANT GOVERNOR	2H Independence Fusion Laureen A. Oliver	3H Independence Fusion James M. Hartman	4H Independence Fusion Ismael Betancourt Jr.					
LIBERTARIAN I	1I Libertarian Bob Schulz FOR GOVERNOR Stanley H. Dworkin FOR LIEUTENANT GOVERNOR	2I Libertarian Richard L. Geyer	3I Libertarian Daniel A. Conti, Jr.	4I Libertarian Norma Segal					

This portion New York State ballot from the general election on November 8, 1994, shows the state's unique variety of political parties and cross-listed candidates. For example, George Pataki, who won the New York governor's race that year, ran under the Republican, Conservative, and Tax Cut Now parties.

negate *Roe* through passage of a constitutional amendment banning abortion. Because the Supreme Court had already interpreted the U.S. Constitution, *Roe* could be changed only (1) if the Court were to overrule itself (an unlikely prospect in light of the 7-to-2 vote in *Roe*); or (2) through a constitutional amendment in Congress that would have required a two-thirds vote in both houses of Congress and then a positive vote in three-fourths of the state legislatures. Thus, a constitutional amendment would settle the issue decisively without the need for more litigation or lobbying for abortion restrictions. Again, the nature of the federal system is evident even in the way that changes can be made to the Constitution.

Through the efforts of the National Conference for a Human Life Amendment and other anti-abortion groups, more than fifty different kinds of constitutional amendments to ban or limit abortions were introduced in Congress by early 1976. Proposed constitutional amendments came in all varieties, including one intended to extend due process protections to the fetus "from the moment of conception," another giving back to the states the power to regulate abortion, and yet another defining the word *person,* as used in the language of the Fourteenth Amendment, to include fetuses. Still, the anti-abortion movement was unable to get both houses of the U.S. Congress to agree on any of these amendments. (See Box 4.2 for the text of a proposed federalism amendment and right-to-life amendment.)

Abortion Funding Restrictions

More successful than the efforts to secure passage of a Human Life Amendment was Senator Jesse Helms's (R.–N.C.) attempt to amend the Foreign Assistance Act to ban the use of federal funds for abortion services or research. This provision, which was passed unanimously by the U.S. Senate, not only affected all military personnel and their families but also restricted research on abortion. Because the U.S. Supreme Court had nationalized the privacy rights that guaranteed women access to abortions, this action by the federal government to refuse to allow abortions in military facilities offshore effectively denied to military personnel and their dependents civil liberties that they would have enjoyed had they been stationed in the United States.

The Hyde Amendment

One possibly unanticipated policy consequence of *Roe* and *Doe* was that poor women, already eligible for free medical assistance under the Medicaid program, could qualify for federal funds to cover the costs of their abortions so long as they were deemed "medically necessary." The majority of the Court in *Doe* had spelled

BOX 4.2

Proposed Constitutional Amendments

Federalism Amendment

The right to an abortion is not secured by this Constitution. The Congress and the several States shall have the concurrent power to restrict and prohibit abortions; *Provided*, That a law of a State more restrictive than a law of Congress shall govern.

Right-to-Life Amendment

Section 1: Neither the United States nor any State shall deprive any human being, from conception, of life without due process of law; nor deny to any human being, from conception, within its jurisdiction, the equal protection of law.

Section 2: Neither the United States nor any State shall deprive any human being of life on account of age, illness, or incapacity.

Section 3: Congress and the several States shall have power to enforce this article by appropriate legislation.

out what it considered to be factors to be taken into account by physicians in determining what were medically necessary abortions. Specifically, the physician's medical judgment was to be exercised in "the light of all factors—physical, emotional, psychological, familial, and the woman's age—relevant to the well-being of the patient." The breadth of these factors made it quite easy to justify the medical necessity of an abortion. Thus, after *Roe* and *Doe*, the number of reported abortions in the United States rose dramatically, as did the number paid for by the federal government. In 1973, for example, approximately 270,000 federally funded abortions were performed at a cost of nearly $50 million (Craig and O'Brien 1993, p. 10).

Although most anti-abortion activists wanted to ban abortions altogether, some, as political pragmatists, opted to pursue legislation at least to limit *Roe*. This view—that elimination of federal funding for abortions for indigent women should be a first step in the process of cutting back on legalized abortion—was not surprising. Since it was assumed by most lawyers that Congress had no authority to legislate about abortion (such authority was the province of the states under their police powers), Congress used its powers to limit the use of tax dollars for abortion and to prevent the use of federal funds for any federal programs that included abortion. Indeed, Congress historically has often used the budget process by underfunding or not funding certain programs as a means of implementing its policy preferences.

In 1976, after several unsuccessful tries, the House of Representatives passed a rider to an appropriations bill banning federal funding of abortions *for any reason.* The version passed by the Senate allowed for federal funds for indigent women to save a woman's life. After a conference committee met to reconcile the House and Senate versions of the bill, both Houses voted to accept less restrictive language, much to the chagrin of the rider's sponsor, Representative Henry Hyde (R.–Ill.), who believed that the new language was far too liberal.

The Hyde Amendment did nothing to change *Roe,* but it limited poor women's access to abortion by prohibiting the use of federal Medicaid funds for abortions except "where the life of the mother would be endangered if the fetus came to term." Each year Congress has wrangled over the language of subsequent riders; at times, depending on the number of pro-choice legislators in the Congress, the Hyde Amendment has banned spending of federal funds in all but three circumstances: (1) when the mother's life was in danger; (2) when two physicians certified that a woman would suffer "severe and long-lasting damage" if she carried to term; or (3) when the pregnancy was the result of rape or incest, as reported to the proper authorities.

Letter-Writing Campaigns and Marches

Letter-writing campaigns have traditionally played a key role in interest-group politics in the United States. To draw attention to its legislative efforts, the anti-abortion movement orchestrated one such letter-writing campaign in the spring of 1973. Churchgoers were encouraged to send letters to their members of Congress urging them to support the Human Life Amendment; the president was also targeted. In fact, as revealed in a memorandum to President Nixon from his aide Patrick J. Buchanan (now a perennial Republican presidential candidate), immediately after *Roe* the president received almost 150,000 letters of protest, along with 2,000 petitions bearing about 1 million names. As one midwestern Republican representative noted, in reference to the anti-abortion movement, "If their ability to generate mail is at all indicative of their political power, we are in trouble" (Liebman and Wuthnow 1983, p. 34). The potential political impact of this movement—specifically, its religious component—was clearly beginning to be recognized, as Buchanan's 1973 memo to Nixon illustrates (see Figure 4.2).

Letter-writing campaigns are not the only means by which interest groups and concerned citizens try to win legislators' attention. Highly publicized marches such as the civil rights movement's March on Washington in 1963, which culminated in Reverend Martin Luther King, Jr.'s "I Have a Dream" speech, also send clear messages to Congress and other elected leaders—as well as to a group's opponents. Since 1974, anti-abortion advocates have marched on Washington every year on the anniversary of *Roe v. Wade*, both to draw attention to abortion and to keep their position and goals on the public agenda.

The 1976 Campaign

Gerald R. Ford became president in 1974, when Richard Nixon was forced to resign just one year after *Roe* had been decided. As president, Ford seemed uncomfortable with the abortion issue, or so his inconsistent actions suggested. Indeed, it wasn't until his wife, Betty Ford, publicly announced her support for *Roe* that he made any comments at all about abortion. In his first public utterance on the issue he voiced support for a constitutional amendment intended to allow the individual states to regulate abortion policy. However, in defense of the Hyde Amendment—and on behalf of the Ford administration—Solicitor General Robert H. Bork filed an amicus curiae brief at the invitation of the U.S. Supreme Court. Ironically, Ford had actually vetoed the Hyde Amendment, but his veto was overridden by Congress. Ford, however, had explained that veto by noting in a press release: "I agree with the restrictions on the use of federal funds for abortions. My objection to this legislation is based purely and simply on the issue of fiscal integrity" (Devins 1995, p. 67).

At no time did Ford publicly voice support of an amendment to outlaw abortions on a national basis. Yet abortion became one of the major issues of the 1976 presidential campaign—some say because there were so few other issues. Ford continued to stress his support for the right of states to restrict abortions but argued for some flexibility, declaring his belief that abortion should be permitted in situations such as rape, incest, or the illness of the mother. Widely criticized for what many perceived to be his "waffling" on the issue, he lost some Republican votes in the November election when anti-abortion activist Ellen McCormack was able to attract voters who supported her single-issue campaign and direct considerable attention to the abortion issue.

FIGURE 4.2

Buchanan Memo to Nixon

THE WHITE HOUSE

WASHINGTON

September 6, 1973

C. F.

MEMORANDUM TO THE PRESIDENT

FROM: PATRICK J. BUCHANAN

In the last eight months, in the mail room, there have arrived 15,900 letters remarking upon the state of the economy, which we consider Issue No. 1. Issue No. 2, the Watergate, has garnered some 75,000 letters this year, prior to the speech on August 15.

However, since January 22, the President has been the recipient of almost 150,000 letters on the Supreme Court decision on abortion -- among them some 2,000 petitions, with names running up toward 1,000,000. This of course is a deeply committed constituency, which was strong for the President, which has expanded far beyond the original "Catholic" base, which is one of the more potent grass roots movements in the country.

Given that the Preisdent has already expressed his view on this score, would recommend strongly a letter to Senator James Buckley, endorsing his Constitutional Amendment, on the same lines and grounds as that letter to Cardinal Cooke, which even Teddy White (opposed to abortion) hailed as a major political stroke in his new book.

Unquestionably, the women's libbers would moan and groan about this -- but, this group we never had, and never will have. We simply cannot hope to match what the Left will promise.

Further, the issue is a "moral" one; it will engage us on the "moral" side of an issue -- and place us into a controversy which would be both politically advantageous and advantageous from the standpoint of legitimate controversy, other than Watergate.

Buchanan

Memo sent to President Richard Nixon from presidential aide Patrick Buchanan in 1973 concerning the amount of mail received at the White House about *Roe v. Wade*.

Ellen McCormack and the Right-to-Life Party

Indeed, the well-organized anti-abortion movement made abortion the focus of the 1976 presidential campaign—the first presidential race after *Roe*. Ellen McCormack's bid for the presidency, in particular, drew attention to the anti-abortion cause and elevated the importance of the issue in the election. It also cast the debate as right-to-life versus murder, stressing the selfishness of women who chose abortion over the sanctity of the family.

Unable to secure passage of a Human Life Amendment, anti-abortion groups became frustrated. Educational campaigns and conventional lobbying, as exemplified by the NCCB's goals (see Box 4.1), were not working. Thus, the 1976 elections were believed to present a unique opportunity for anti-abortion forces. Running first in the Democratic Party primary and then as the candidate of the Right-to-Life Party, McCormack was able to garner tremendous amounts of attention to the anti-abortion cause. When she qualified for federal matching campaign funds, she was viewed as a legitimate candidate. Her graphic television campaign, which included spot ads showing a fetus being aborted, vividly brought the abortion issue into living rooms around the nation.

Abortion as a Campaign Issue

McCormack's presence in the 1976 campaign also forced the major party candidates, Jimmy Carter (Democrat) and Gerald R. Ford (Republican), to address the abortion issue—although neither met the issue head on in the absolutist fashion that had become the hallmark of the McCormack campaign. Meanwhile, McCormack's run for office foreshadowed the potential for electoral activity on behalf of the anti-abortion movement; specifically, it was a harbinger of later efforts to target U.S. senators who opposed the proposed Human Life Amendment.

Changes in Democratic Party rules required that women constitute at least 40 percent of the delegates to the Democratic Party's national convention in 1972. The liberal National Women's Political Caucus (NWPC) held training sessions around the nation to encourage women to run as delegates committed to the inclusion of women's issues in the party's platform. "Disregarding conventional political wisdom, NWPC members even introduced a minority plank calling for a women's right to an abortion" (McGlen and O'Connor 1983, p. 72). A lengthy floor fight ensued, and the provision lost by only a narrow margin. By 1976, the NWPC was able to garner enough votes for a provision in the platform endorsing *Roe v. Wade*, although the party's nominee, Jimmy Carter, opposed it.

Carter specifically disavowed the Democratic Party platform (which labeled as "undesirable" efforts for a constitutional amendment to overturn *Roe),* saying that he believed "abortion is wrong" and that the Democratic Party platform was also wrong. In addition, he repeatedly denied charges from the National Catholic Office for Information, which asserted that the platform language was drafted by Carter's advisers. Yet on July 11, 1976, in an appearance on *Meet the Press,* Carter noted that "we had a major input into the exact wording [of the platform] and into the principles expressed therein." (See Box 4.3 for a comparison of the Republican and Democratic Party platforms in 1976.)

BOX 4.3

The 1976 Party Platforms Compared

Republican Party Platform

The question of abortion is one of the most difficult and controversial of our time. It is undoubtedly a moral and personal issue but it also involves complex questions relating to medical science and criminal justice. There are those in our party who favor complete support for the Supreme Court decision which permits abortion on demand. There are those who share sincere convictions that the Supreme Court's decision must be changed by a constitutional amendment prohibiting all abortions. Others have yet to take a position, or they have assumed a stance somewhere in between polar positions.

We protest the Supreme Court's intrusion into the family structure through its denial of the parents' obligation and right to guide their minor children. The Republican Party favors a continuance of the public dialogue on abortion and supports the efforts of those who seek enactment of a constitutional amendment to restore protection of the right to life for unborn children.

Democratic Party Platform

We fully recognize the religious and ethical nature of the concerns which many Americans have on the subject of abortion. We feel, however, that it is undesirable to attempt to amend the U.S. Constitution to overturn the Supreme Court decision in this area.

Ford often was equally vague about his position on abortion. For example, in a meeting at the White House with the six-member Executive Committee of the National Conference of Catholic Bishops, Ford reiterated his belief that government has "a responsibility to protect life—and indeed to provide legal guarantees for the weak and unprotected"; but elsewhere he was quoted as saying that "the law of the land must be upheld as interpreted by the Supreme Court . . . in *Roe v. Wade* and *Doe v. Bolton*" (Ford 1976, p. 522).

Ford lost votes to McCormack and his Democratic challenger Jimmy Carter, although his position on abortion was not that different from Carter's. However, Carter, a born-again Christian evangelical from the Deep South, generally appeared to be against any kind of constitutional amendment to ban abortions. His generally weak pro-choice position and his weak stance on women's rights would later lead the National Organization for Women to avoid making any presidential endorsement in 1980 when Carter, the incumbent, was challenged by Ronald Reagan.

The Jimmy Carter Years

Jimmy Carter, who defeated Ford in the November 1976 election, refused to support an amendment to restrict abortion, but he did far more than Nixon or Ford to encourage alternatives to abortion. He supported the Hyde Amendment, which opposed federal funding for abortions (although the Democratic Party platform on which he ran supported federal funding for abortions), and his administration even defended the constitutionality of the Hyde Amendment in the Supreme Court. Moreover, Carter's victory "gave evangelicals their first taste of political organization and probably initiated the largest number of interorganizational contacts and coalitions formed since prohibition" (Blanchard 1994, p. 73). Indeed, the 1976 election reenfranchised southern conservatives, many of whom were evangelical Christians. Beginning with the New Deal, through the civil rights era, these southerners believed that they and their ideas were unwelcome in Washington. Carter and his administration's handling of abortion provided an impetus for further anti-abortion organization in the South. The personal became political, and the evangelical Christian right's opposition to abortion was embraced in the highest places in Washington.

During the Carter years, two major types of abortion rights cases came to the Supreme Court after *Roe* and *Doe*. The first type involved abortion restrictions passed by state legislatures or city councils in response to *Doe*; the second type was in response to the Hyde Amendment. Both types of lawsuits were battlegrounds for pro- and anti-abortion forces.

Abortion Restrictions

Soon after *Roe* and *Doe,* several states acted to pass parental consent laws for minors seeking abortions. Massachusetts' parental consent law was ruled unconstitutional in *Belliotti v. Baird* (1979). But it was ruled as such only because the state failed to provide an adequate mechanism through which a woman under the age of eighteen could petition a court for permission to obtain an abortion if both of her parents refused to give their consent. (Today, this mechanism is called a **judicial bypass provision.**) As in *Doe*, the Supreme Court provided the states with a sample of the legislation that might be used to restrict a minor's right to an abortion. The text of this "suggested" legislation noted

> that if the State decides to require a pregnant minor woman to obtain [parental] consent to an abortion, it also must provide an alternative procedure whereby authorization for the abortion may be obtained. A pregnant minor is entitled in such a proceeding to show either: (1) that she is mature enough and well enough informed to make her abortion decision [independently] of her parents' wishes; or (2) that even if she is not able to make this decision independently, the desired abortion would be in her best interests. [This proceeding that must be offered by the state] must assure that a resolution [will] be completed with anonymity and [expedition].

Meanwhile, abortion rights forces, caught off guard by congressional passage of the Hyde Amendment, were forced to go to court to challenge its constitutionality—the only recourse for them since they had been unable to fend off its passage in Congress. In their fight to save continued Medicaid funding for indigent women's abortions, they sued to block implementation of the Hyde Amendment. Initially, they charged that the Medicaid program's refusal to pay for abortions was unconstitutional because it discriminated against poor women. Their arguments were dealt a stunning blow in 1977 by a series of Supreme Court decisions. In three separate challenges by women's rights groups and Planned Parenthood to state Medicaid programs that financed childbirths but not abortions, the Court concluded that these practices did not violate a woman's constitutional right to secure an abortion, even though some women could not afford the procedure (*Maher v. Roe,* 1977; *Beal v. Doe,* 1977; *Poelker v. Doe,* 1977). As a result, the number of publicly funded abortions declined precipitously.

In the aftermath of decisions upholding the constitutionality of the Hyde Amendment and its limits on federal funding of abortions, President Jimmy Carter was asked if he believed it was fair that women who could not afford to get an abortion would be precluded from doing so whereas those who could afford to were not precluded. "There are many things in life that are not fair," Carter replied; he then added, "I don't believe that the federal government should take action to try to make these opportunities exactly equal, particularly when there is a moral factor involved" (quoted in Bonafede 1980, p. 865). These words were music to the ears of right-to-life activists, who would nevertheless soon find a stronger advocate than Carter.

Interest-Group Activity

The Hyde Amendment and the aforementioned three cases decided by the Supreme Court in 1977 had not limited states' ability to fund abortions if they wished, so states that did fund abortions were the next targets of the anti-abortion movement. The growing power of the anti-abortion movement, along with these three Court decisions, finally mobilized some women's rights groups—just as *Roe* had mobilized the anti-abortion movement. Although new groups were not created, the ACLU's Reproductive Freedom Project launched a "Campaign for Choice" that was supported by most other women's rights groups. Thus, the dilemma was now being framed as one of "pro-life" versus "pro-choice."

At the first National Women's Conference in Houston in 1977, pro-life and pro-choice activists went head-to-head. Among the delegates present, 20 percent described themselves as pro-life and/or pro-family and argued strongly against inclusion of a plank on the women's agenda guaranteeing reproductive rights. When it became clear that the pro-choice delegates (who constituted the majority) were going to pass a resolution supporting abortion rights and opposing "the exclusion of abortion . . . from Federal, State, or local funding of medical services," anti-feminists including Schlafly and the presidents of the National Right-to-Life Committee, March for Life, and the National Council of Catholic Women held a rally on the other side of town to protest the conference actions. But their efforts were to little avail, given that the pro-choice plank was adopted (National Women's Conference 1979, p. 160). Thus, many pro-choice activists left Houston believing that, having won this showdown, they had the upper hand. They were mistaken.

In an effort to implement the abortion resolutions passed in Houston, NARAL began a grassroots lobbying campaign modeled after those conducted by the NRLC to help it lobby not only state legislatures but also Congress to pass broad reproductive rights for all women—including medically indigent women. It also founded NARAL-PAC, a committee whose goal was to raise money for pro-choice candidates. Again, this move was a reactive one designed to counter the growing political forces of the anti-abortion movement. But the political winds were blowing in another direction. In 1978, right-to-life forces, aided by growing conservative sentiment in the United States, targeted and then defeated several pro-choice

U.S. senators and members of the House of Representatives who had voted against the Hyde Amendment. Like the women's rights groups that had targeted legislators who failed to support suffrage in 1910–1920, those opposed to abortion in 1978 believed that the successful targeting of vulnerable lawmakers would make other politicians stand up and take note. As noted earlier, Patrick Buchanan, in his 1973 memo to Richard Nixon (see Figure 4.2), clearly foresaw the potential political impact of anti-abortion forces. Indeed, the stage was now set for the right-to-life movement to begin its all-out assault on *Roe* and abortion rights (see Figure 4.3).

The defeat of long-time pro-choice supporters in the Senate shook not only pro-choice activists but other senators and representatives as well. Hit lists were again drawn up, and senators up for reelection in 1980 were concerned because pro-choice activists were not nearly so well organized as the right-to-life movement.

This lack of mobilization was partly attributable to the composition of the pro-choice movement itself. Its potential members included largely young, well-edu-

FIGURE 4.3

Symbols of the Pro-Choice Movement and the Pro-Life Movement

The coat hanger has become a widely used symbol of the pro-choice movement.

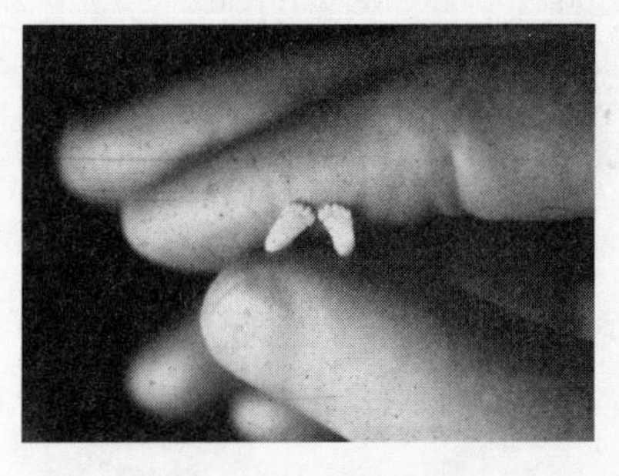

Right-to-life advocates often use photos like this one to illustrate their view that life begins at conception. Photo from John C. Willke, *Abortion Questions & Answers* (Cincinnati: Hayes Publishing Co., 1978). Used by permission.

cated, and professional women—who had the funds to secure an abortion should one become necessary (Craig and O'Brien 1993, p. 136). They were *not* the poor, pregnant women who were being adversely affected by the Court's (and Congress's) continued actions to limit access to abortions to only those women who could afford them. In stark contrast were pro-life advocates, who, convinced that abortion was morally wrong, had the momentum they had gained through the Hyde Amendment and the 1978 elections. Abortion was still legal, but the specter of defenseless fetuses kept their fervor high.

Conclusion

By the dawn of 1980, the right-to-life movement was fully mobilized—having been energized, ironically, by the Carter presidency in 1977 and its judicial and electoral successes in 1978. On the other side of the abortion dilemma, however, pro-choice forces were playing catch-up. They had failed to recognize that *Roe* and *Doe* were but the beginning of the abortion battle and repeatedly found themselves on the defensive and losing ground. Anti-abortion forces were now shaping the debate and having their perspective on the dilemma articulated by Congress, the courts, and the president. As a result of these successes, the political atmosphere was ripe for the emergence of the Moral Majority, which would play a major role in defining and setting the agenda in the November 1980 elections and throughout the Reagan years.

5

The Politics of Abortion, 1980–1988

Each views the perception of the other as not simply false, but wildly, madly false—nonsense, totally unintelligible and literally unbelievable.

—Roger Wertheimer, in "Understanding the Abortion Argument"

THE SUPREME COURT'S DECISIONS in *Roe v. Wade* and *Doe v. Bolton* not only left the abortion dilemma unresolved but actually escalated debate over the issue. Pro-choice forces rejoiced when the Court made it clear that the right to have an abortion was based on a privacy right found in the U.S. Constitution. The Court's opinion in *Doe,* however, was sufficiently vague to inspire anti-abortion activists to try to lessen the impact of the Court's pronouncements—specifically, by urging national and state legislators to formulate restrictive abortion policies so as to frustrate full implementation of the abortion decisions.

As discussed in Chapter 4, soon after *Roe* and *Doe*, several states and the U.S. Congress enacted a variety of abortion restrictions. Perhaps, at least in part, because many abortion restrictions initially dealt with federal funding of abortions for poor women, pro-choice activists were slow to organize against the very effective multifaceted strategies of what had become known as the **right-to-life movement.** Consequently, by 1980 this movement was poised to help elect a pro-life president, Ronald Reagan, who pledged to do everything in his power to overrule *Roe.*

The abortion issue still constituted a very real dilemma for many lawmakers—some of whom saw new abortion restrictions (such as the Hyde Amendment) as a compromise, whereas others viewed them only as a first step toward total eradication of legal abortion. It did not, however, present any kind of moral or religious dilemma for the **Moral Majority,** a pro-life, fundamentalist, and evangelical ministry mobilized by the televangelist Reverend Jerry Falwell. The Moral Majority had the defense of religious practices and the family—as well as an end to legalized abortion—as its major goals. As it turned out, the 1980 elections, the first after the Moral Majority's founding, provided its first opportunity to employ the ballot and political pressure to secure those goals, and eventually it was credited with playing an important role in the election of Ronald Reagan.

The Rise of the Christian Right and the Moral Majority

The Supreme Court's rulings concerning abortion, busing for racial integration, affirmative action and religion in schools, congressional passage of the Civil

Rights Act of 1964, the proposed equal rights amendment (ERA), the **Federal Campaign Financing Act of 1974,** and the rise of the women's rights movement all played key roles in fostering the emergence of a powerful conservative **Christian right** (also called the religious right). The election of Jimmy Carter in 1976 as the first fundamentalist Christian to sit in the White House further mobilized this group, as did the Right-to-Life Party's impact on the 1976 elections, the defeat of several pro-choice senators and representatives in 1978, and a long series of major constitutional cases in which the U.S. Supreme Court handed down decisions that were perceived by the conservative religious right as a threat to their way of life. These cases included the following:

- *Engle v. Vitale* (1962), whereby school prayer in public schools was ruled unconstitutional.
- *Epperson v. Arkansas* (1968), whereby a provision prohibiting the teaching of evolution was ruled unconstitutional.
- *Swann v. Charlotte-Mecklenburg Board of Education* (1971), whereby busing to eliminate vestiges of de jure racial discrimination was ruled an appropriate constitutional remedy.
- *Roe v. Wade* (1973), whereby the constitutional right to privacy was ruled to include the right to terminate a pregnancy.

Likewise, Southern conservatives were threatened not only by congressional passage of sweeping civil rights laws in 1964 and 1965 that made discrimination on the job, at school, and in the election process illegal, but also by the proposed ERA, which many on the right viewed as abolishing the traditional role of women in society. The combined impact of these factors was to provide the catalyst for formation of a strong religious right social movement, of which the anti-abortion movement was just one part.

Interestingly, however, another act of Congress, passage of the Federal Campaign Financing Act of 1974, was to have the unintended policy consequence of fostering the creation of **political action committees (PACs).** Although the purpose of the law was to prohibit individuals from making large contributions to individual candidates, it allowed for the creation of PACS, which were soon used to pour large numbers of dollars into candidate campaign coffers. And, indeed, one of the first groups to use PACs effectively to secure the election of sympathetic legislators was the religious right.

In 1974, one year after *Roe*, only 516 PACs were registered with the Federal Election Commission, the agency charged with monitoring campaign financing. But by 1976, the year after the new rules went into effect, 650 *new* PACs had been registered. Many of these were created to advance the conservative agenda (Crawford 1980, p. 44).

In 1977, however, the Christian right was still a "sleeping giant" (Moen 1989, p. 2). According to the first operations manager of the Moral Majority, "Abortion, pornography, homosexuality—those are hard for average Christians to relate to. They don't read *Playboy*, their daughters aren't pregnant, and they don't know any queers" (Moen 1989, p. 3). Thus, the Christian right needed to be awakened and led to understand how public morals could affect their Christian faith. Pat Robertson, another televangelist, was one of the first of the religious right to acknowledge this fact. Said Robertson, "We used to think that if we stayed home and prayed it would be enough. Well, we are fed up. We think it's time to put God back in government" (Moen 1989, p. 9).

The development of the Christian right as a political force actually had its roots in an organization founded shortly after *Roe v. Wade* was decided. In 1973, the newly elected Senator Jesse Helms (R.–N.C.), a long-time right-wing radio and television personality, founded the Congressional Club along with Richard Vigurie, who later was to become the direct-mail campaign finance guru of the religious right. Vigurie was responsible for the growth of the anti-abortion movement in at least two key ways. First, as the granddaddy of conservative direct-mail solicitation, Vigurie was able "to by-pass the liberal media, and go directly into the homes of conservatives in the country," tapping "the silent majority" (Vigurie, quoted in Crawford 1980, p. 45)—thus allowing conservative leaders to raise millions for the anti-abortion cause and to support the candidacies of conservative candidates pledged to pass legislation to limit *Roe*. Second, Vigurie, along with Helms, helped found the Campus Crusade for Christ in 1974, with the goal of forming a network of young, well-educated conservatives across the nation. These young people, in particular, would later provide an important source of supporters and members for the Christian Voice and Jerry Falwell's Moral Majority.

Christian Voice, which was founded in 1978, had close ties to Pat Robertson, head of the Christian Broadcast Network (CBN) and minister of the *700 Club*. The *700 Club*, a daily religious and news program, was carried to millions on CBN, providing an instant publicity mechanism for the new group. Christian Voice, in an attempt to alert Christians to the evils in Washington, D.C., quickly initiated a "Congressional Report Card," which it used to rate the morality of members of Congress (Liebman and Wuthnow 1983, p. 52). Like other congressional watchdog groups, such as the liberal Americans for Democratic Action and the citizens' group Common Cause, Christian Voice rated all members of Congress based on key votes of concern to the organization. In the case of Christian Voice, moral issues were the focus of concern. And among the key votes included in its rating system were members' votes on a constitutional amendment to prohibit abortion and on the Hyde Amendment in its annual reauthorization bill. Thus, a wide array of secular political issues became religious ones, too, allowing interested voters the opportunity to monitor the performance of their elected representatives.

The Reverend Jerry Falwell

As early as 1956, one week after he opened the Thomas Road Baptist Church in Lynchburg, Virginia, the Reverend Jerry Falwell was using the radio to broadcast his views about God and country. Falwell was one of the first members of the Christian right to recognize the importance of new technologies such as mass media and computer-generated mass mailing and to use these technologies effectively in the expansion of his religious and political goals. By 1965, he was publicly speaking out against the federal expansion of civil rights laws and the activities of anti-war activists. One of the first televangelists, Falwell was also among the first to see how fundamentalists could be moved to action by governmental decisions such as the Supreme Court's rulings on abortion or civil rights.

An effective, charismatic speaker, Falwell won early recognition when he increased the membership of his church from 35 to more than 17,000 members. By the mid-1970s this feat, along with his radio and television broadcasts, had brought him attention in conservative circles. His televised *Old Time Gospel Hour* gave him a receptive audience for his political goals and allowed him to begin creating a mailing list of conservative donors who supported his ideas with the mother's milk of politics—cash.

In 1976, Falwell decided to bring some of his political ideas to the general public. This he accomplished by launching a national *I Love America Campaign* that consisted of patriotic rallies held on statehouse steps around the nation. At these well-publicized rallies, Falwell and conservative state and local politicians spoke about the decaying moral fiber of America. Often joined by a chorus of gospel singers in the background, Falwell was able to focus national attention on hot-button conservative issues including busing, affirmative action, and abortion. By 1980, these rallies were a major source of publicity for candidates endorsed by the Moral Majority. Falwell was also able to join forces with Phyllis Schlafly's Stop ERA movement, which further increased his potential political base.

Having founded the Moral Majority in June 1979, Falwell took to the airwaves in November of that year to initiate a major fundraising effort. His own personal mailing list of more than 250,000 supporters formed the initial base for this computer-generated direct-mail fundraising effort as he sought to create a potent political force consisting of those who wished to get evangelicals back into politics and morals back into government. At the time the Moral Majority was founded, only 55 percent of evangelicals were registered to vote, in contrast to 72 percent of nonevangelicals (Sawyer and Kaiser 1980, p. 37; Liebman and Wuthnow 1983). No longer was the Christian right to be the "silent majority," as Falwell worked to register voters.

The Moral Majority

Four separate entities made up what the public knew as the Moral Majority: (1) Moral Majority, Inc., was its tax-exempt, but not tax-deductible, lobbying arm; (2) the Moral Majority Foundation was its tax-deductible educational foundation, which also engaged in massive voter registration efforts; (3) the Moral Majority Legal Defense Fund was modeled after the American Civil Liberties Union to be the Moral Majority's legal counterpart on the right; and (4) the Moral Majority PAC was created to provide financial support and other forms of assistance to conservative political candidates, especially those who were pro-life.

The mobilization of the Moral Majority occurred swiftly. By exploiting Falwell's access to the media and to advancing computer technologies, it became the best-known Christian fundamentalist political organization in the United States. A December 1980 Gallup poll revealed that more than 40 percent of all Americans had heard of the Moral Majority; by May 1981 that proportion had risen to 49 percent—and in the Bible Belt it reached 75 percent. By contrast, fewer than 25 percent of the population could identify the Speaker of the House of Representatives.

The Moral Majority quickly became a massive enterprise; it was the nation's largest evangelical group, and at the height of its popularity Falwell was heard on 373 local television stations a week. Its *Moral Majority Report* quickly grew to a circulation of 840,000, and Falwell's commentary, which featured a mixture of gospel and politics, was broadcast daily on more than 300 radio stations. In fiscal year 1979, the Moral Majority raised in excess of $35 million from 2.5 million contributors; by 1980 it was reporting an income of more than $1 million per week. Thus, in a very short period of time, Jerry Falwell was able to mold a latent group of voters into a potent political force. In its first two years, for example, the Moral Majority registered thousands of voters around the nation but did especially well in the conservative Bible Belt. This political clout was used to its full advantage in the 1980 national election. Further fueling the Moral Majority's belief in the rightness of its cause were two Supreme Court decisions handed down in 1980: *Harris v. McRae* (1980) and *Williams v. Zbaraz* (1980). In *McRae* the constitutionality of the Hyde Amendment was upheld by a five-man majority, and in

Zbaraz the right of indigent women to obtain abortions was severely restricted. In each of these cases, groups on both sides of the issue had filed amicus curiae briefs urging the Supreme Court to adopt their respective positions on abortion. Seemingly as a harbinger of the November 1980 elections, right-to-life forces again were victorious.

The 1980 National Elections

Capitalizing on its new base in the southern, conservative tradition, the pro-life movement, with Jerry Falwell's Moral Majority and the Christian right now at its helm, made its power known in the 1980 elections. Abortion and congressional passage of the ERA were the most salient issues of the elections. Interest-group forces mobilized around both issues, and candidates were forced to take a stand on abortion. Ellen McCormack ran again as the presidential candidate of the Right-to-Life Party, which refused to endorse Ronald Reagan because he was not opposed to abortion if it was necessary to save the life of the mother (Lynn 1980). Although Reagan, as governor of California, had signed into law the most liberal abortion law in the nation in 1967, by the time he ran for president in 1980 his position on abortion had changed dramatically. Now, as just noted, he supported abortion only if it was necessary to save the life of the mother. This stance allowed him to win the endorsement of most other right-to-life groups, including the National Right-to-Life Committee, which criticized McCormack as a "purist" unable to accept any compromises to obtain her political goals (Lynn 1980).

In banding together for the 1980 elections, the Christian right sought to tie together the anti-abortion movement, the anti-feminist movement, the anti–gun control movement, the anti-pornography movement, and the anti-union movement into one large umbrella social movement. All of these disparate but related movements, moreover, were particularly popular in the Deep South, a region that Jimmy Carter, a native southerner, should have been able to carry in the 1980 election but was unable to do.

Reagan's support from the Christian right was not merely public endorsement or financial assistance in the form of PAC contributions. Members of Reagan's campaign team, such as Robert Billings from the Christian Voice and later the Moral Majority, were also major forces in the organization and growth of the Christian right. In addition, the Christian right organized two major rallies prior to the election in 1980. The first rally, called "Washington for Jesus," was held April 28–29 on the Mall in Washington, D.C., and was based on Falwell's "I Love America" rallies of the late 1970s. At this rally, the Christian right distributed its platform, endorsed candidates, and inspired political activism among its supporters. Reagan was one of many candidates who benefited from this rally. The "National Affairs Briefing" was the second Moral Majority event. Held in August 1980, it attracted 15,000 attendees. Reagan and Falwell were among the speakers who advocated grassroots mobilization and espoused religious conservative ideology about abortion and creationism.

The presidency was not the only goal of right-to-life activists and the Christian right. As a result of the "Deadly Dozen"—a hit list of congressional supporters of abortion rights identified by pro-life activists—five pro-choice Democratic senators were successfully targeted for defeat. The Moral Majority and right-to-life groups not only poured millions of dollars into the campaigns of those senators' opponents but also directly attacked the senators in print advertisements and on radio and television. In addition, the political arm of the anti-abortion Life Amendment Political Action Committee endorsed sixteen Republicans and five Democrats running for the Senate, as well as seventy-eight Republicans and forty-four Democrats seeking election in the House of Representatives. Criteria for selection included a race close enough for the right-to-life movement's impact to be felt; that is, the difference in opposing candidates had to be marked, and the movement had to have enough supporters in the area to get its message across. In short, the Moral Majority and the Life Amendment Political Action Committee wanted to be able to make a difference in elections where the candidate was sure to recognize and, later, reward those groups for their support (*The Economist* 1980).

Some elected advocates of legal abortion, however, managed to hang on despite strong electoral challenges. Planned Parenthood, for example, finally realized that it had to act and took up the cause to defend its allies in Congress and in the state house. In New York City, alone, the Planned Parenthood affiliate spent $297,000 on ads urging voters to back candidates who supported legal abortion (Herman 1980). In spite of efforts like those made by Planned Parenthood, many hailed the 1980 elections as a tremendous victory for right-to-life forces.

The numerous electoral successes of the pro-life movement clearly were fueled by the emergence of the Moral Majority. Falwell threw his organization's support behind the 1980 candidacy of Ronald Reagan by helping to register and mobilize millions of conservative voters throughout the nation—especially in the South, where voters formerly had voted Democratic. The long-lasting consequences of this electoral realignment continues today as more and more Republicans win elections in the South.

The 1980 presidential election also marked the first time since passage of the Nineteenth Amendment in 1920 that women voted differently from men in a presidential election. In what political scientists and members of the media now label the **gender gap,** 8 percent fewer women (46 percent) than men (54 percent) voted for the conservative Republican candidate Ronald Reagan. As white males all over the nation voted Republican in large numbers in support of that party's increasingly conservative agenda, many women cast their ballots for Democrats, but not in sufficient numbers to reelect Jimmy Carter, whose presidency was never embraced with any enthusiasm by feminists. The National Organization for Women (NOW), for example, refused to endorse any candidate in the 1980 presidential election.

Support of Reagan proved to be a successful strategy for opponents of abortion rights. Having earlier been labeled an "extremist" on the abortion issue by Gerald R. Ford, Reagan was avowedly against abortion. He ran for president on a Republican Party platform that by now was much more specific about abortion. One plank, for example, contained the 1976 platform language calling for passage of a "constitutional amendment to restore protection of the right to life for unborn children"; another called for the president to appoint to the federal courts only judges who "respect traditional family values" and the "sanctity of innocent human life." In sharp contrast, the Democratic Party platform that year—though rejected by its candidate, incumbent president Jimmy Carter—recognized "reproductive freedom as a human right." Not only did the Democratic Party platform "oppose government interference in the reproductive decisions of Americans," it also advocated federal funding of abortion, thus making quite clear the differences between the two major parties.

In only a few years, abortion's importance as a clear difference between the two political parties was evident. The influx of religious conservatives into the Republican Party prompted it to solidify its opposition to abortion. In contrast, the Democratic Party's position on abortion became even more liberal at the insistence of women party delegates who became the core movers behind the inclusion of several women's issues in the party's 1980 platform. Thus, as both parties solidified their positions on the abortion issue, neutral ground became more elusive.

The Reagan Years and Abortion

Ronald Reagan's position on abortion in the 1980 presidential election was certainly clear. He opposed it on any grounds except to save the life of the mother and vowed to do everything in his power to end legalized abortion, whether it meant passing an amendment or returning to the states the power to regulate abortions. As a former state governor, Reagan believed strongly in the states' power to regulate (and ban) abortions.

His election in 1980 focused new attention on the abortion issue as it became an increasingly unsettling dilemma for policymakers at all levels, especially since the Supreme Court, the Congress, and the president all appeared to have widely divergent views about the scope of *Roe* and *Doe*. Compounding and exploiting this confusion were interest groups on both sides working toward their goals on both the state and national levels. Many pro-choice advocates had been ousted from Congress by the efforts of the right-to-life movement and the Moral Majority. These members were replaced with pro-life conservatives, and Congress became a prime target for the Christian right.

The Congress

The defeat or near-defeat of several abortion rights advocates in the Congress led many members to hope that the issue would just go away. But the Republican victory in November 1980 gave conservatives a working majority in the Senate—an advantage they and their supporters, especially those in the Moral Majority, planned to exploit. In the Senate, for example, Orrin Hatch (R.–Utah) introduced a new anti-abortion constitutional amendment to give Congress and the states concurrent, or co-equal, authority to restrict or prohibit abortion. (This was the kind of amendment that Gerald R. Ford had said he supported.) Soon, the National Conference of Catholic Bishops—which shared an office in Washington, D.C., with the National Right-to-Life Committee—threw its support behind the Hatch proposal, believing that it would overturn *Roe v. Wade* and give each state the right to recriminalize abortion. The Roman Catholic Church—no longer the leader of the anti-abortion movement, having been upstaged by the successes of the Moral Majority—continued to advocate abortion restrictions but now did so as a general rule in conjunction with the Moral Majority and Christian right.

More encompassing than the abortion restrictions proposed by Hatch was legislation introduced simultaneously in the Senate and House by Senator Jesse Helms (R.–N.C.) and Representative Henry Hyde (R.–Ill.) to define life as beginning at fertilization. This legislation was also supported by President Reagan, who believed that it would negate the need for a constitutional amendment because it would guarantee that fetuses were considered human beings and therefore due all constitutional protections available under the Fourteenth Amendment. But Ronald Reagan's support and a Republican-controlled Senate were not sufficient to muster enough votes for either proposal. Congress, however, did cut Title X of the Public Health Services Act, which provided funding for family planning, and passed the Adolescent Family Life Act (AFLA) in 1981.

Three years earlier, in 1978, Congress had passed the Adolescent Health Services and Pregnancy Prevention and Care Act, sponsored by Senator Edward Kennedy (D.–Mass.) to address the increasing problem of teen pregnancy by funding family planning programs targeted at teenagers. Some saw passage of this type of pregnancy-prevention program as a compromise over the abortion issue: If fewer people got pregnant, there'd be fewer abortions. But members of the Christian right were appalled by the act. Its leaders, including Phyllis Schlafly, charged that the government, especially the federal government, had no business dealing with teen pregnancy. To them, this was a family problem that indicated the precipitous decline in national morals.

Once conservatives had won control of Congress, the Adolescent Health Services and Pregnancy Prevention and Care Act was refunded in 1981 as the Adolescent Family Life Act, often dubbed "the Chastity Act" by liberals. This revised legislation had four new sections. It (1) required the active involvement of religious groups in the family planning process; (2) prohibited the provision of federal funds to any organization (such as Planned Parenthood) involved in abortion counseling or services; (3) instructed providers to counsel pregnant teens to choose adoption over abortion; and (4) required all providers to emphasize premarital abstinence. The media labeled the new act "an eleven million dollar concession to the right" (Devins 1995c, p. 249).

Despite passage of this kind of legislation favored by the Christian right, the 1982 midterm congressional elections saw the defeat of twenty-six Republicans. Although it is common for the president's party to lose seats in the House and Senate in off-year elections, pro-choice activists worked hard to elect more pro-choice representatives to Congress. Hence, as the working majority for pro-life issues was no longer in place, the Human Life Amendment was defeated in the Senate in 1983. Although Reagan campaigned on a right-to-life platform in 1984, Republicans had lost control of the Senate by 1986. Thus, even though Reagan continued to call on Congress to "come together to find positive solutions to the tragedy of abortion" (Reagan 1988), little action to restrict abortion came out of Congress during this period.

The Executive Branch

Ronald Reagan moved quickly to fulfill his campaign promises to pro-life advocates to make abortion restrictions part of his institutional agenda. He not only announced his support of the most extreme version of a pro-life constitutional amendment that would ban abortion, intrauterine devices (IUDs), and some forms of the birth control pill, but also set out to appoint pro-life members to his administration to carry out his anti-abortion policies within the constraints of existing law.

Anti-Abortion Policy Through Bureaucratic Control. Through control of the bureaucracy, the president can effectuate policies—specifically, by enforcing (or not enforcing) the law. The president can also get around congressional statutes that he or his administration does not like by issuing regulations that implement a particular law in a manner different from that intended by Congress. Most of President Reagan's appointees took this approach in dealing with abortion-related issues. For example, he chose as his solicitor general Rex E. Lee, a prominent Mormon law professor from Brigham Young University. Lee took the job at least in part because he viewed it as his responsibility to try to convince the Supreme Court to overrule *Roe*. Another notable pro-life appointment was that of Dr. C. Everett Koop as surgeon general of the United States. A pediatrician and the co-founder of the Christian Action Council, Koop was an outspoken member of the anti-abortion movement who also opposed some methods of birth control. As the nation's top physician in charge of the Public Health Service, the National Institutes of Health, and the Food and Drug Administration, he was believed by pro-life advocates to be "a friend in high places." Throughout his nine-year tenure as surgeon general, Koop remained steadfastly opposed to abortion and even withheld from publication a long-awaited study that concluded that there was little scientific evidence to buttress administration claims that abortion causes women significant psychological or physical harm. Other examples of highly placed right-to-life movement appointees included the former head of the Life Amendment PAC, Donald Devine, to head the Office of Personnel Management (where he removed Planned Parenthood from the list of approved charities to which federal employees could contribute); Centers for Disease Control Director James Mason, who as head of Utah's state health department had opposed abortion rights; and Marjorie Mecklenburg, a founder of the National Right-to-Life Committee (NRLC), as head of the Title X family planning program.

Through promulgation of regulations, selective enforcement of existing laws and regulations, and the appointment of key personnel who agree with him on policy direction, a president can exercise real clout in the lawmaking process. And indeed, soon after President Reagan appointed long-time abortion foe Richard Schweiker, one of the original supporters of the pro-life amendment, as his first secretary of the Department of Health and Human Services (HHS), the department began to investigate Planned Parenthood for several alleged illegalities.

These included (1) the use of federal money to finance abortions in violation of PP's federal contracts to provide family planning services (but not abortion) to low-income women, and (2) pro-abortion lobbying in violation of its tax-exempt status. After an unprecedented series of audits, which were costly to Planned Parenthood but ultimately found no violations of the law, Faye Wattleton, its president, formally complained to the secretary about HHS's harassment campaign. Such uses of bureaucratic power can divert an opponent's energies from abortion rights, for example, to issues of group survival; indeed, bureaucratic power was used effectively by both the Reagan and Bush administrations to harass and divert pro-choice activists.

Schweiker also used his position to limit the reporting to Congress of any data that could be interpreted as pro-choice. When the chief of abortion surveillance at the Centers for Disease Control (CDC) in Atlanta, Georgia, notified the secretary that he intended to testify before a Senate Judiciary subcommittee that legalized abortion had reduced deaths and abortion-related diseases among American women *and* significantly reduced the number of teenage marriages and out-of-wedlock births, Schweiker had him replaced. The new chief then gave an abbreviated report to the subcommittee omitting the positive consequences of abortion.

When Schweiker resigned in 1983, he was replaced by former Representative Margaret Heckler, a long-standing abortion foe. She was replaced in 1985 by Dr. Otis R. Bowen, a former two-term governor of Indiana, who actively sought to limit access not only to abortion and contraceptives but also to abortion clinics.

Roe v. Wade created a market for abortion clinics, where abortions could be performed much more cheaply than at hospitals. These clinics also provided increased access for rural women and the urban poor in areas where public hospitals refused to perform abortions. Between the time *Roe* was decided and Secretary Bowen was appointed, the percentage of abortions performed in clinics rose every year (see Table 5.1).

Thus, although the number of abortions continued to increase throughout the years of the Reagan administration despite its right-to-life rhetoric, regulations affecting clinics and their funding stood to significantly reduce the number of abortions performed each year. Planned Parenthood, for example, received more than $145 million each year in federal funds for medical services, allowing it to serve 4.3 million women annually (Craig and O'Brien 1993, p. 190).

To reduce funds to such organizations, Bowen (unsuccessfully) lobbied Congress on behalf of the administration to revise federal law to ban funding for abortions and abortion counseling in clinics like those operated by Planned Parenthood. And in 1985, after Reagan's landslide reelection, Bowen defended the Adolescent Family Life Act's authorization of funds for religious organizations to teach about contraception. He also defended its restrictions on abortion counsel-

TABLE 5.1

Abortions and Abortion Facilities, 1973–1992

Year	Number of Abortions	Percentage of All Abortions Performed	
		Hospitals	Nonhospital Facilities
1973	744,600	52	48
1975	1,034,200	40	60
1977	1,316,700	30	70
1979	1,497,700	23	77
1980	1,553,900	22	78
1982	1,573,900	18	83
1985	1,588,600	13	87
1987	1,559,100	–	–
1989	1,566,900	–	–
1991	1,556,500	–	–
1992	1,528,900	–	–

Sources: Gerald Rosenberg, *The Hollow Hope* (Chicago: University of Chicago Press, 1991), pp. 180, 197; and Stanley K. Henshaw, et al., "Abortions Services in the United States, 1991 and 1992," *Family Planning Perspectives*, vol. 26, no. 3 (May/June 1994), p. 101.

ing. The Reagan administration successfully appealed a federal district court decision that held that the AFLA was unconstitutional because its advancement of religion violated the First Amendment's establishment clause. In *Bowen v. Kendrick* (1988), a challenge initiated by both the ACLU's Reproductive Freedom Project and the American Jewish Congress, the Rehnquist Court upheld the constitutionality of AFLA on a 5-to-4 vote.

Family Planning. Prior to the administration's narrow victory in *Bowen v. Kendrick*, Secretary Bowen became frustrated when he was unable to convince Congress to revise the Public Health Service Act to limit abortion services and counseling at clinics receiving federal funds. Accordingly, in 1987 Bowen and other members of the Reagan administration decided to go around Congress. Bowen simply announced new administrative regulations reinterpreting the Public Health Service Act, which a deadlocked Congress had been unable to change to bar funding of any organizations that performed or provided counseling about abortions. In the same year, believing that the conservative Rehnquist Court would uphold restrictive regulations, Bowen announced that "[a]bortion has no place in the Title X family planning program" (*Congressional Quarterly Weekly*

Report 1987). Issuing regulations has been a forceful means by which the executive branch can formulate policy or hinder the implementation of a congressional policy. And these new regulations were indeed contrary to congressional intentions. Yet the pro-choice majority in Congress was not sufficiently large to permit it to reassert itself in the policy formulation process.

Beginning as early as 1970, during the Nixon administration, Congress authorized the secretary of the Department of Health, Education, and Welfare to make grants to public and private organizations engaged in family planning projects (Craig and O'Brien 1993, p. 189). (In 1979, the Department of Health, Education, and Welfare split into the Department of Health and Human Services and the Department of Education.) Since that time, public health clinics and private groups—most notably, the Planned Parenthood Federation of America—had received funds under Title X. Although initial regulations issued by Secretary Schweiker to implement Title X limited the scope of counseling to "non-directive counseling" and abortion "referrals" on the request of the patient only, Secretary Bowen's new regulations prohibited even these kinds of assistance. The stipulations of the new regulations were as follows:

1. Title X projects could not "provide counseling concerning the use of abortion as a method of family planning or provide referral for abortion as a method of family planning."
2. Grant recipients could not "encourage, promote, or advance abortion as a method of family planning" in their clinics, either through speakers or by lobbying for liberalized legislation to increase the availability of abortion, using legal action to support abortion rights, or paying dues to any group that supports abortion rights.
3. Funded organizations must be "physically and financially separate from prohibited abortion activities."

These regulations, which collectively became known as the **gag rule,** were immediately attacked by pro-choice groups and some members of Congress as unconstitutional. For groups like Planned Parenthood and many hospitals, which were dependent on Title X funds for continued operations, the new regulations immediately threatened the continued operations of their family planning services, a consequence foreseen by right-to-life proponents in HHS.

The Judicial Branch

Ronald Reagan enthusiastically ran for president on the Republican Party platform that called on him to appoint federal judges who opposed abortion. But

The "gag rule"—a series of regulations stating that family planning clinics receiving federal funds could not offer abortion counseling—drew instant opposition from hospitals and pro-choice groups such as Planned Parenthood and the ACLU's Reproductive Freedom Project. Cartoon used by permission.

when he announced his first appointment to the Supreme Court, Arizona Court of Appeals Judge Sandra Day O'Connor—a woman, as he had promised in his campaign—right-to-life activists were dismayed because they feared that O'Connor was not avowedly pro-life and would not vote to overturn *Roe.* In the first nationally televised judicial confirmation hearings, representatives from the Moral Majority and the National Right-to-Life Committee attacked her nomination. They cited her support as a state legislator of a family planning bill that would have repealed existing state laws banning abortions. Further distressing right-to-lifers was O'Connor's refusal to answer any questions on the issue, although some conservative Republican senators tried to quiz her regarding her views on abortion. Nevertheless, her appointment as the first woman on the Court was confirmed by a 99-to-0 vote of the U.S. Senate, much to the chagrin of those in the right-to-life movement who opposed her confirmation.

Interest-Group Challenges to State Laws in Court

The Issue of Consent. While interest groups were pressuring the president, members of his administration, and members of Congress to end abortions on the national level, local and national right-to-life groups were very active and effective on the state level. Taking their cue from *Planned Parenthood of Central Missouri v. Danforth* (1977), in which the Supreme Court had suggested that some forms of state abortion regulation might be permissible, scores of anti-abortion lobbyists urged state and local lawmakers to consider parental notification or permission provisions as well as informed consent laws requiring women to be given detailed information on the various stages of fetal development prior to undergoing an abortion procedure (Halva-Neubauer 1993).

Right-to-life groups were aided by their ability to build on preexisting networks of conservatives who had successfully fended off state approval of the proposed equal rights amendment. Many of them refocused the debate; it was no longer over the right to abortion per se. Instead, in states where little attention had been given to abortion, anti-abortion supporters lobbied for parental consent laws. These bills were widely supported in most public opinion polls and could be framed not as abortion restrictions but, rather, as parental rights legislation (Halva-Neubauer 1993, p. 171). Soon, however, the abortion dilemma was focused on issues involving consent and how and where abortions were to be performed. Eventually, the consent issue was to include provisions dealing with a woman's informed consent as well as spousal and parental notification and consent. Right-to-life interest groups were especially interested in seeing how Ronald Reagan's first appointee to the Supreme Court, Sandra Day O'Connor, would decide.

Akron v. Akron Center for Reproductive Health, Inc. One of the first and most famous post-*Roe* laws sponsored and drafted by the right-to-life movement involved a series of abortion restrictions enacted by the City Council of Akron, Ohio. The Akron ordinance was a regulation drafted by right-to-life groups as part of their effort to restrict abortions at the state and local levels. Also challenged, at the same time that *Akron* was before the Court, was Missouri's requirement that second-trimester abortions be performed in hospitals.

Right-to-life interest groups were not content simply to secure some restrictive pieces of legislation at the state level. They immediately recognized that they would be called upon to defend their restrictions' constitutionality in court. Thus, they took a keen interest in Reagan's appointments to the federal bench, especially those to the Supreme Court.

The fears of right-to-life activists that Justice O'Connor would not overrule *Roe* were borne out, at least in part, by her key dissent in *Akron v. Akron Center for Reproductive Health, Inc.* (1983), a case challenging the Akron ordinance. *Akron* was also important in that it attracted significant pro- and anti-abortion interest-group involvement at all levels. On the one hand, the ACLU's Reproductive Freedom Project represented clinics that were challenging the constitutionality of the ordinance; on the other, the U.S. government filed an amicus curiae brief and participated in oral arguments to urge the Court to reconsider *Roe*. It was in *Akron v. Akron Center for Reproductive Health, Inc.*, that a U.S. president, for the first time, used the Justice Department to advance a pro-life position in a case where no federal issues were at stake. The government's amicus curiae brief (see Figure 5.1) claimed that "the time has come to call a halt" to judicial limitation on state regulation of abortion. And U.S. Solicitor General Rex E. Lee, in his amicus brief in support of the city of Akron, urged the Court to adopt a new test to replace *Roe v. Wade*'s trimester approach. Specifically, Lee asked the Court to go beyond *Roe*'s rigid framework and instead adopt what he called an "unduly burdensome" test that would allow states to regulate abortions at any stage of a woman's pregnancy so long as those regulations were not unduly burdensome on a woman's right to an abortion. (This issue is discussed later in the section.) Many right-to-life activists, however, were angered by Lee's failure to ask the Court *directly* to overrule *Roe*.

Yet in spite of that anger, it is unlikely that the Supreme Court, as composed, would have had much sympathy with a request to overrule *Roe*. In a 6-to-3 decision, the Court struck down as unconstitutional the vast majority of the city's abortion restrictions at issue in *Akron*. Among the restrictions not permitted by the majority were these:

- a ban on performing second-trimester abortions in outpatient clinics rather than in hospitals;
- a requirement that physicians provide detailed information about abortion to women before they signed consent forms; and
- a twenty-four-hour waiting period between giving consent and having the abortion.

The Court concluded that the hospital requirement unnecessarily increased the cost of an abortion without significantly increasing a woman's safety, that the information requirement was designed to persuade a woman not to get an abortion, and that the waiting period requiring two separate trips to the facility was unnecessarily inflexible. None of these requirements met the Court's definition of reasonable state regulation envisioned in *Roe*. O'Connor, Reagan's lone appointment to that date, however, joined the dissenters in *Akron*, noting her belief that *Roe* "was on a collision course with itself" because the trimester approach was "unworkable" in light of rapidly changing medical technology. Moreover, perhaps borrowing language from the solicitor general's brief, she proposed that *state* regulation of abortion be

FIGURE 5.1

Cover of the U.S. Amicus Curiae Brief, 1982

In The Supreme Court of the United States

OCTOBER TERM, 1982

CITY OF AKRON, PETITIONER

v.

AKRON CENTER FOR REPRODUCTIVE HEALTH, INC., ET AL.

JOHN ASHCROFT, ET AL., PETITIONERS

v.

PLANNED PARENTHOOD ASSOCIATION OF KANSAS CITY, MISSOURI, INC., ET AL.

ON WRITS OF CERTIORARI TO THE UNITED STATES COURTS OF APPEALS FOR THE SIXTH AND EIGHTH CIRCUITS

BRIEF FOR THE UNITED STATES AS AMICUS CURIAE IN SUPPORT OF PETITIONERS

REX E. LEE
Solicitor General

J. PAUL MCGRATH
Assistant Attorney General

KENNETH S. GELLER
Deputy Solicitor General

RICHARD G. WILKINS
Assistant to the Solicitor General

Department of Justice
Washington, D.C. 20530
(202) 633-2217

permitted unless those regulations presented an **undue burden** on a woman's decision to terminate her pregnancy. This position, however, fell far short of the position advocated by the right-to-life movement.

Akron and the Missouri case, *Planned Parenthood Association of Kansas City v. Ashcroft* (1983), were not close decisions, as revealed in Table 5.2; yet well-organized right-to-life groups continued to convince state legislatures to pass restrictive abortion laws, sensing that the Supreme Court—if Reagan got the opportunity to appoint more justices—could be convinced to restrict *Roe* severely, if not overrule it altogether. And, eventually, through Reagan's appointment of several justices to the Supreme Court as well as the elevation of conservative William H. Rehnquist (one of the two dissenters in *Roe*) to the position of Chief Justice, the scope of *Roe* was limited and right-to-life forces appeared to move closer to reaching their goals.

Although some right-to-life groups were disheartened by *Akron* and *Ashcroft*, the movement redirected itself, much as it had after *Roe*. Many right-to-lifers gave up on the idea of a constitutional amendment, devoting their energies instead to the passage of restrictive state laws and then to litigation to protect these victories.

TABLE 5.2

Votes in Abortion Cases: The Effect of the Supreme Court's Changing Composition

	1973 Roe *vote*		*1983* Akron *vote*		*1986* Thornburg *vote*	
Justices	*Pro-choice*	*Anti-abortion*	*Pro-choice*	*Anti-abortion*	*Pro-choice*	*Anti-abortion*
Burger	x		x			x
Brennan	x		x		x	
Marshall	x		x		x	
Stewart	x		–	–	–	–
Blackmun	x		x		x	
Powell	x		x		x	
Douglas	x		–	–	–	–
Stevens	–	–	x			x
Rehnquist		x		x		x
White		x		x		x
O'Connor	–	–		x		x

Note: Two of the majority justices in *Roe* were replaced: As Douglas's replacement, Stevens supported abortion rights ten years later; and O'Connor, who was more conservative than Stewart, voted against the majority.

In a move similar to that of the NAACP in 1939, when it decided that the time was ripe to go to court to challenge pervasive racial segregation, many pro-life advocates decided to litigate in an effort to convince the Court to limit or overrule *Roe v. Wade,* sensing that the Court would be increasingly receptive to state limits on abortion. One prominent pro-life legal center, Americans United for Life, mimicked earlier NAACP strategies by holding a conference in Chicago in 1984 to bring together various right-to-life groups. This conference was attended by more than five hundred individuals, and its goal was to "devise a coordinated strategy for developing cases for court challenges to abortion" (Craig and O'Brien 1993, p. 55).

A litigation strategy, however, requires cases to bring the issue (or issues) to court. Thus, attendees of the conference were advised to lobby for state laws to add new limits on abortions. But *Akron* appeared to limit the range of options open to state legislators. Accordingly, many pro-life activists lobbied for more unusual restrictions such as wrongful life/wrongful birth statutes, and fetal disposal and fetal pain laws or regulations not addressed by the Supreme Court in *Akron* (Halva-Neubauer 1993, p. 176). States with strong pro-life movements, however, appeared undaunted by *Akron* and continued to press for restrictive legislation—whether or not it was unconstitutional. Meanwhile, some pro-lifers, upset with the whole process, began picketing clinics to pressure women not to seek abortions, at times resorting to other, more radical forms of mental or physical intimidation of clinic staffers and patrons. These actions immediately led to a backlash against pro-lifers in some state legislatures as anti-harassment laws and resolutions condemning violence were passed.

It was continued pro-life pressure in state legislatures, however, that resulted in the greatest gains for the movement. As restrictive laws were passed, their constitutionality had to be challenged by pro-choice advocates in court. But the further these controversies extended into the Reagan years, the more conservative federal judges there were to uphold the constitutionality of restrictions regardless of *Roe, Akron,* and *Ashcroft.*

Changes in the Composition of the Supreme Court

Two years after his reelection, in 1986, Reagan was given the opportunity to appoint a new chief justice when Warren Burger—one of the members of the seven-man majority in *Roe*—retired to head the U.S. Bicentennial Commission. Reagan nominated Associate Justice William H. Rehnquist to replace him and then nominated conservative, Roman Catholic, U.S. Circuit Court of Appeals Judge Antonin Scalia to replace Rehnquist. Not only were both nominees avowed conservatives, but their conservative approach was wedded to a well-considered conservative legal philosophy that Reagan and his advisers hoped would intellectually steer the Court in a new direction.

In spite of Scalia's well-defined conservative views on issues ranging from affirmative action and abortion to federalism and the role of the states, his hearings were quick and without much controversy—unlike Rehnquist's, which generated considerable liberal complaint. Of Rehnquist, Senator Edward M. Kennedy (D.–Mass.), who led the attack, said: "[He's] too extreme on race, too extreme on women's rights, too extreme on freedom of speech, too extreme on separation of church and state, too extreme to be Chief Justice" (Green 1986). Nevertheless, Rehnquist was confirmed by a vote of 65 to 33. Scalia, whose Senate Judiciary Committee final report contained a mere 76 words compared to Rehnquist's 114 pages, was confirmed on a 98-to-0 vote (Craig and O'Brien 1993, p. 180).

Thornburgh v. American College of Gynecologists and Obstetricians. By the mid-1980s, state legislatures were willing to pass new restrictions on abortion, pro-choice groups were willing to challenge those restrictions in federal court, and staunchly right-to-life state attorneys general were willing to defend the constitutionality of the restrictions in federal court. The states of Missouri and Pennsylvania, where pro-life forces were especially powerful, quickly became sites of major challenges to the continued viability of *Roe.*

In 1985, before Chief Justice Burger retired, the U.S. Supreme Court decided to review a challenge to the constitutionality of the Pennsylvania Abortion Control Act, which had been ruled unconstitutional by a U.S. circuit court. The state law at issue in *Thornburgh v. American College of Gynecologists and Obstetricians* (1986) included numerous restrictions sought by right-to-life activists, among them the following:

1. A woman seeking an abortion must receive information from her physician about the details of fetal development and be told of the availability of printed materials before giving her informed consent.
2. Abortion providers must file detailed reports with the state, including identities of providing and referring physicians, methods of payment, and so on.
3. Postviability abortions must be done with the "degree of care" required to save the life and health of the child.
4. A second physician must be present if it is possible for the fetus to survive the procedure.

Pennsylvania's position was supported by an amicus curiae from Reagan's acting solicitor general, Charles Fried, who urged the Court to "reconsider [*Roe*] and on reconsideration abandon it" based on its "so far flawed . . . textual, doctrinal and historical basis." Fried became solicitor general only after agreeing to urge the Court to overrule *Roe.*

This argument continued to fall on deaf ears with a majority of the justices. Although Justice Blackmun conceded that Fried and the administration would most likely always get four votes to hear challenges to *Roe* (appeals need to muster the votes of four justices in order to be accepted for review), he remarked that "the other five of us heave a deep sigh and wish we didn't have to go through this traumatic experience again" (Simon 1995, p. 125).

Although *all* restrictions were again ruled unconstitutional as a violation of *Roe*, this time four justices dissented—including Chief Justice Burger, who had voted with the majority in *Roe*. Thus, many anti-abortion activists believed that they were but a vote away from overruling *Roe*.

More Appointments. Shortly after the *Thornburgh* (1986) decision, Justice Rehnquist replaced Chief Justice Burger and U.S. Circuit Court of Appeals Judge Antonin Scalia was added to the Court to replace Rehnquist. Scalia was expected to help solidify a strong anti-abortion wing on the Court.

Justice Louis Powell, one of the justices continuing to support *Roe*, then resigned on the last day of the 1986–1987 term, setting off more alarms with liberals than the Rehnquist/Scalia nominations had done the year before. Thus, when Ronald Reagan announced his nomination of Judge Robert H. Bork of the D.C. Circuit Court of Appeals, pandemonium broke out among liberals, who organized to orchestrate a stunning defeat of the conservative nominee. Bork, a former U.S. solicitor general, had written extensively about constitutional issues and, on more than one occasion, had criticized the Supreme Court's ruling in *Roe*, arguing that a privacy right could not be supported by the U.S. Constitution.

In response to the Bork nomination, Planned Parenthood took out a full-page newspaper advertisement claiming that "Robert Bork is an extremist who believes you have no constitutional right to personal privacy" (Bork 1990, p. 291). Other liberal groups lobbied hard against the nomination. After Bork's 58-to-42 defeat in the Senate, President Reagan nominated U.S. Circuit Court of Appeals Judge Anthony Kennedy, who, though a sitting federal judge, had a more limited paper trail on controversial issues. NOW president Molly Yard opposed his nomination, citing concerns with his privacy decisions among others; but Kennedy's hearings, in which he told senators that he accepted a constitutional right to privacy, ultimately led the Senate to confirm his nomination with few dissenters.

"How to Disrupt an Abortion Clinic"

As the stakes increased with each new appointment to the Court, interest groups on both sides of the abortion dilemma fought vigorously. Although traditional right-to-life groups continued to use conventional lobbying methods to end or limit abortion, others in the movement became frustrated over the time it was taking to end legal abortion.

As early as 1976, at the annual meeting of the National Right-to-Life Committee, a seminar entitled "How to Disrupt an Abortion Clinic" was held. According to NARAL, this seminar instigated an onslaught of widely ranging tactics, including picketing and sit-ins at abortion clinics. The executive director of NARAL voiced her fear that, from this series of incidents, "it was but a short jump to violence" (Boeth et al. 1978, p. 33). How right she was.

Some anti-abortion activists, believing that abortion was tantamount to murder, quickly turned to violence to stop what they viewed as the ultimate criminal act. Frustrated by Congress's failure to pass a constitutional amendment, they believed that traditional lobbying tactics were unlikely to produce quick or satisfactory results. Nevertheless, in 1980 Friends for Life, a Chicago-based anti-abortion group, expelled its director and co-founder, Joseph Scheidler, a former Roman Catholic Benedictine monk, for his "guerrilla tactics"—which included many types of clinic violence and harassment (Carabillo, Meuli, and Csida 1993, p. 94):

> [P]icketing clinics and physician's offices, . . . appealing to women entering them not to kill their babies, . . . [placing] epoxy cement . . . in clinic locks; stink bombs were ignited inside clinic bathrooms by bogus patients; bomb threats were called in to the clinics; clinic employees received threatening calls at home; patients were followed home or traced through license tags and loudly denounced in their own neighborhoods or before their family; judges conducting trials for anti-abortion activists who had violated the law were threatened; court trials of arsonists and bombers were picketed; . . . [and] several clinic personnel were injured during incursions by protestors. (Blanchard 1994, pp. 53–54)

Scheidler's expulsion did not stop his anti-abortion activities. On the contrary, he founded the Pro-Life Action League, which was among the first groups to advocate violence as a political strategy to thwart implementation of existing laws.

Resort to violence is not an uncommon feature of the American political system. Frustration over the political system's inability or refusal to accommodate all viewpoints—especially those of uncompromising extremists—has historically led to violence, destruction of property, and even bloodshed. The Boston Tea Party, John Brown's raid on Harper's Ferry, and campus bombings in protest against the Vietnam War all illustrate this continuing fact of political life.

In the case of abortion, as with so many other controversial issues involving deeply rooted views, interest groups on both sides resorted to numerous tactics to advance their positions. From the conventional to the unconventional, such interest groups were key players in defining how abortion would be played out in the media and dealt with by elected officials and the courts (see Figure 5.2).

FIGURE 5.2

Pro-Life and Pro-Choice Ads

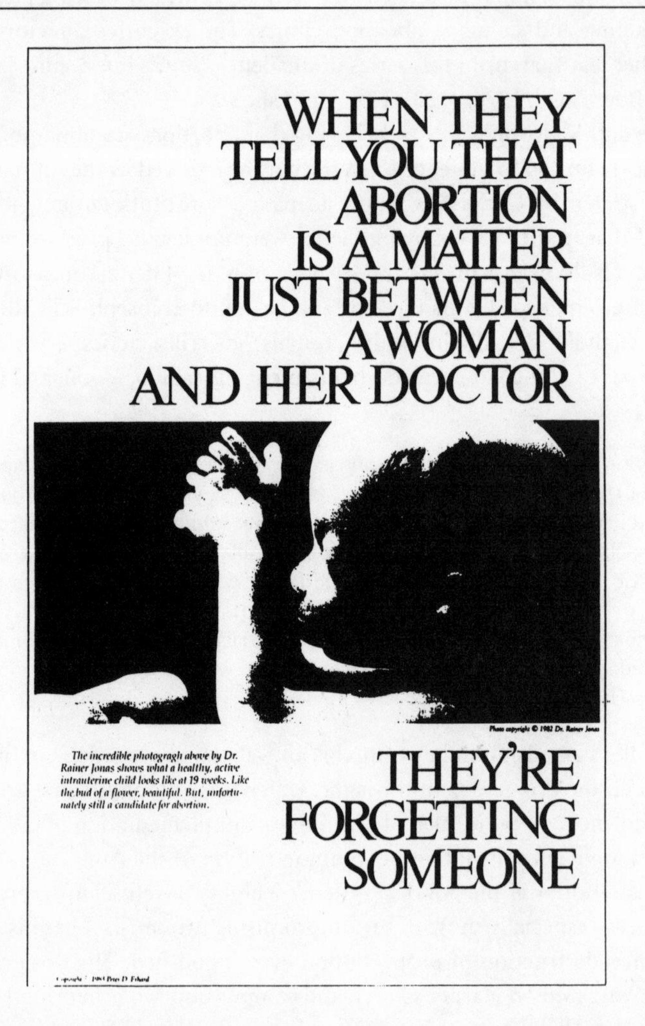

Advertisements such as these from (a) the National Right-to-Life Committee, (b) Planned Parenthood, and (c) NARAL are among the more conventional strategies used by interest groups on both sides of the abortion issue.

This is what they mean by planned parenthood

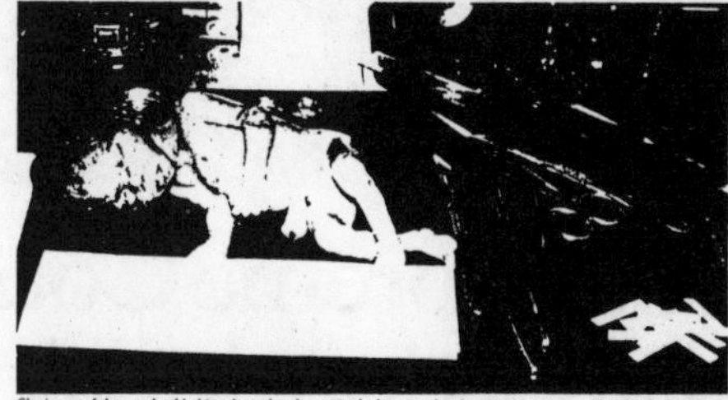

She is one of thousands of babies aborted each year in the late months of pregnancy *Photo by Dr. Wm. Jones*

They mean abortion is now used for birth control.

They mean that unborn babies shouldn't have the right to live . . . not even in the ninth month of pregnancy.

Thousands of unborn children are being aborted even after five months in the womb![1] The chief of the federal Center for Disease Control's Abortion Surveillance Branch recently estimated that 400 to 500 live births follow late-term abortion attempts each year![2] Most of these survivors are severely injured in the process and soon die.

At the same time, medical researchers are rapidly developing wonderful new life-saving surgical techniques for treating unborn babies in the womb.

We now know that at 18 days from conception the unborn child's heart begins to beat. At 40 days, brain waves have been recorded. By 6 to 7 weeks, unborn babies will pull their heads back if you touch their noses!

Yet, in America, abortion is legally available at any time during the nine months of pregnancy in all 50 states for almost any reason![3]

Abortion advocates focus on "hard case" pregnancies. However, rape and incest-related abortions represent only a fraction of 1% of the abortions performed. Girls under 15? Only 1%![4]

And, no more than 1% of abortions are performed for physical health reasons, a leading "pro-choice" medical expert recently stated in testimony before a U.S. Senate Subcommittee![5]

One-third of the women obtaining abortions each year are coming back for their second, third, or fourth abortion![6]

The legalization of abortion-on-demand has promoted the development of a nationwide abortion delivery system. As a result, the number of abortions performed annually has exploded -- increasing six- to seven-fold since the prelegalization era![7]

We need to pass laws to halt this abortion madness and save hundreds of thousands of innocent lives annually.

[1,6,7] *Center for Disease Control: "Abortion Surveillance 1978," 1980.*

[2] *Philadelphia Inquirer, August 2, 1981.*

[3] *The Supreme Court forbids states from restricting abortions even in the third trimester if an abortionist decides that a woman's "health" is at stake. The Court stated that the abortionist may define "health" in terms of "all factors — physical, emotional, psychological, familial, and the woman's age — relevant to the well-being of the patient."* Doe v. Bolton, 1973.

[4] *Testimony of Irwin M. Cushner, M.D., of the UCLA School of Medicine, before the Senate Judiciary Subcommittee on the Constitution, October 14, 1981.*

[5] *Testimony of Professor Thomas A. Hilgers, M.D., of the Creighton University School of Medicine, before the Senate Judiciary Subcommittee on the Constitution, October 14, 1981.*

Abortion. You pay for it with your tax dollars. Women pay for it with their bodies. Unborn babies pay for it with their lives.

FIGURE 5.2 *continued*

Will the Supreme Court's next abortion decision be carved in stone?

Before the 1973 Supreme Court ruling in *Roe v. Wade* made abortion legal, accessible, and safe, countless women were maimed and killed in illegal back-alley abortions.

Different states had different rules about who could obtain an abortion. As a result, women of all ages suffered — teenagers, young working women, mothers who couldn't cope with another unintended pregnancy.

Denied a safe choice, they were forced to sacrifice their health and their lives.

Now, nearly 20 years after this butchery ended, the Bush Administration has asked the Supreme Court to use a Pennsylvania abortion case to overturn *Roe v. Wade*, letting states go so far as to ban abortion outright.

But women are in danger even if *Roe* is left standing.

Recent Supreme Court rulings have already started giving states back the power to interfere with a woman's private choices. And in *Planned Parenthood of Southeastern Pennsylvania v. Casey*, the Court may greatly expand that power.

Pennsylvania's so-called "Abortion Control Act" isn't meant to protect a woman's health or her privacy. It has been designed to add hardship, expense, and delay:

- Parental involvement requirements intimidate and endanger teens in troubled families.
- Waiting periods are a roadblock for rural women who must travel long distances to a clinic, and for working mothers who must arrange child care and time off for two clinic visits instead of one.
- Husband notification rules target only those women who fear for their safety or their family's integrity if the state forces them into a confrontation.

Pennsylvania's law is no "middle ground." Opponents of a woman's right to choose have deliberately set up these barriers in the path of the most desperate women — the young, the poor, the isolated and abused, women in crisis — to drive them away from the option of a safe, legal, early abortion.

If the Supreme Court permits this kind of frightening interference, *any* state can pass laws designed to deepen the suffering of women already forced to confront the tragedy of an unwanted pregnancy.

The lesson of the past is painfully clear: the more restrictions on safe, legal abortion, the more women are killed and injured.

We must preserve a *national* standard assuring every woman's right to choose a safe, legal abortion without interference — no matter what state she lives in.

Unless this protection is carved in stone, the tragic consequences surely will be.

☐ I'm calling my representatives on Capitol Hill at 1-202-224-3121 and telling them to do everything they can to keep abortion safe and legal. ☐ I'm enclosing my contribution to all your activities and programs, including education and contraception programs that reduce the need for abortion: __$15 __$25 __$35 __$50 __$75 __$100 __$500 or $______.

NAME

ADDRESS

CITY STATE ZIP

Planned Parenthood Federation of America
810 Seventh Ave., N.Y., N.Y. 10019-5882

Don't wait until women are dying again.

A copy of our latest financial report is available from the New York Department of State, Office of Charities Registration, Albany, New York 12231, or from Planned Parenthood Federation of America, 810 Seventh Avenue, New York, New York 10019. Please write PPFA for a description of our program and activities and/or a list of the organizations to which PPFA has contributed in the last year. © 1992 PPFA, Inc. This ad was paid for with private contributions.

WHEN WOMEN HAD NO CHOICE . . . THEY TOOK A TERRIFYING WALK INTO THE BACK ALLEYS OF AMERICA.

The right to choose is in great danger. On April 26, the Supreme Court will hear arguments in a Missouri case, Webster v. Reproductive Health Services.

The Court's ruling on the Webster case could give state politicians the power to determine whether or not women can obtain safe and legal abortions. The Court could give politicians the power to make your most personal decision for you.

The danger is real. The Webster case is the first time the Supreme Court, with its new conservative majority, will consider the question of who decides this most private matter.

President Bush and his Justice Department believe that now is the time to overturn the decision that legalized abortion and now is the time to let judges and politicians determine your ability to obtain a safe and legal abortion.

The Attorney General of the United States formally petitioned the Court to use its decision in this case to end legal abortion. The Attorney General's argument raises this question: who will decide whether or not a woman can have an abortion? You or 7,461 state politicians?

If we lose the right to choose, America will go back to the terrifying days when women risked their lives in back alleys.

DO WE WANT OUR DAUGHTERS TO FOLLOW IN THEIR FOOTSTEPS?

You can keep our daughters from using alleys as operating rooms. You can keep the government out of your personal life. You can keep the politicians from taking away your right to decide. Call us at 1-900-988-8888 or clip the coupon and add your voice to the majority of Americans who believe private decisions should be in the hands of the people, not the politicians.

The National Abortion Rights Action League was founded in 1969 to win the right to a safe and legal abortion. NARAL, a non-profit, non-partisan advocacy organization with more than 250,000 members and local affiliates in 34 states, works in conjunction with the NARAL Foundation. It is the only organization dedicated solely to protecting a woman's right to choose whether or not to have an abortion. Contact NARAL now, while you still have the choice.

NARAL

I agree. The decision whether or not to have an abortion is a private one. I do not want politicians determining the most personal choice a woman can make. I support the National Abortion Rights Action League's Campaign to protect my right to choose.

Name:
Address:
City:
State: Zip:
Phone:

Enclosed tax deductible donation of:

$15 $25 $50 $100 $ more

Please return coupon to:
National Abortion Rights Action League
PO Box 336, 2040 Polk Street
San Francisco, CA 94109

National Abortion Rights Action League, 1101 14th Street, N.W., Suite 500, Washington, DC 20005

Paid for by NARAL and the NARAL Foundation.

Clinic harassment and violence, though practiced or advocated by only a small segment of the right-to-life community, created their own dilemma within that community. How could the violence of abortion be reconciled with the violence of these anti-abortion tactics? Beginning in 1983, abortion providers were wracked by a series of fires, bomb blasts, and other violent activities. In the same year, the Justice Department and the Bureau of Alcohol, Tobacco, and Firearms created special clinic violence teams to deal with the rash of bombings and other forms of clinic violence. Traditional anti-abortion activists, who felt their cause was injured by the upswing in violence, even offered rewards for information on the bombings. One radical anti-abortion group known as the Army of God actually kidnapped a prominent gynecologist who performed abortions and his wife. It also took credit for several bombings. The group even threatened Justice Louis Powell and took credit for shooting into the apartment of Justice Harry A. Blackmun, the author of *Roe v. Wade*.

As shown in Figure 5.3, clinic bombings began in 1977; in fact, eight such bombings were reported between 1977 and 1983. This activity skyrocketed in 1984, just a year after the right-to-life movement's defeat in *Akron*. While groups like Americans United for Life were meeting to plan further litigation in spite of *Akron*, Scheidler and many of his supporters began forming a national network of small organizations dedicated to taking any action necessary to stop abortions from being performed. In 1984, Scheidler also published *Ninety-Nine Ways to Close the Abortion Clinics*. In it he offered suggestions for harassing, intimidating, and interfering with abortion providers and their clients. These suggestions would eventually provide the blueprint for other groups seeking to stop abortions.

As violence against clinics increased, abortion rights advocates became angered by President Reagan's refusal to classify it as terrorism and the FBI's refusal to add clinic bombings to its list of terrorist activities. In January 1985, however, the president finally condemned such violence, and the Bureau of Alcohol, Tobacco, and Firearms assigned fifty of its two hundred employees to its clinic violence team. Then, in April 1985, NARAL began its grassroots campaign to track and combat clinic violence, and Planned Parenthood launched its own "Stop Clinic Violence" campaign.

Yet the violence and other forms of protest against clinics did not subside. Using what Scheidler called "nonviolent action to protect babies" (Craig and O'Brien 1993, p. 57), the Pro-Life Action League and several other new anti-abortion groups soon began trying to shut down abortion clinics by blocking access with hundreds of dedicated demonstrators. In 1986, NOW filed a lawsuit to end clinic violence, charging that Scheidler's Pro-Life Action League and several other militant groups violated a federal law that was originally intended to deter Ku Klux Klan activity.

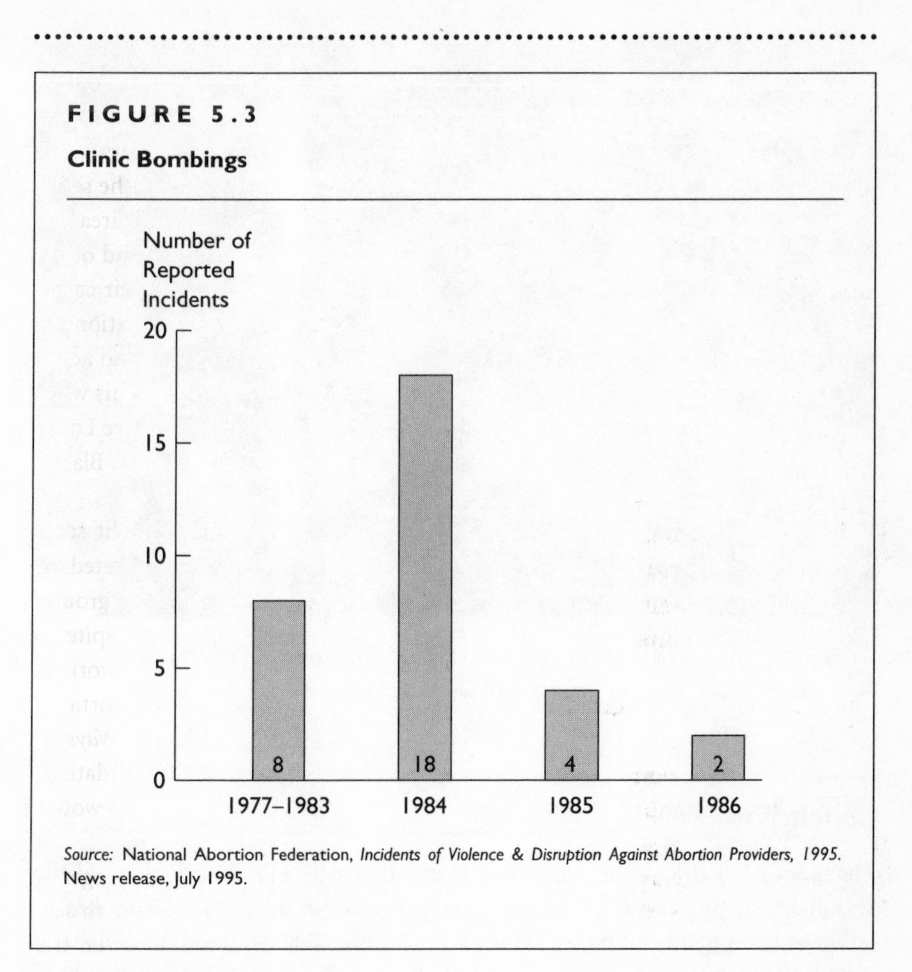

Source: National Abortion Federation, *Incidents of Violence & Disruption Against Abortion Providers, 1995.* News release, July 1995.

The efforts of the Pro-Life Action League were the model for "We Will Stand Up," a series of clinic "rescues" planned to correspond with Pope John Paul II's 1987 tour of the United States and Randall Terry's **Operation Rescue**'s actions. The latter, a national group created by pro-lifers frustrated by the slow, piecemeal effort to end abortions through traditional lobbying tactics, used more aggressive methods such as barring access to the clinics in which they were performed. It first made its presence known in 1988, when it launched a series of demonstrations in New York City. Participants physically blockaded entrances to abortion clinics to force them to close their doors. More than 1,500 arrests were made. Shortly thereafter, Operation Rescue blasted onto the national scene when it demonstrated at the 1988 Democratic National Convention in Atlanta, Georgia. There, it blockaded several clinics and health centers.

Dallas police arrest a member of Operation Rescue at a protest on the anniversary of *Roe v. Wade*. Photo used by permission of Operation Rescue.

Conclusion

The election of Ronald Reagan was a triumph for the Moral Majority and the anti-abortion movement. Reagan successfully ran for president in 1980 on the Republican Party platform that called for a constitutional amendment to end abortion. Despite the Reagan administration's efforts to urge Congress to pass abortion restrictions or the Court to overrule *Roe*, little progress was made until a series of resignations from the Court allowed Reagan to appoint pro-life justices to the Court.

The specter of the potential reversal or severe limitation of *Roe v. Wade* mobilized groups on both sides. Some pro-life activists turned their attention to the states, where their strength at the grassroots level allowed them to convince state legislatures to enact abortion restrictions; others, frustrated by the long, drawn-out process and the lack of change, adopted more unconventional tactics including "rescues" and clinic violence. Meanwhile, pro-choice activists, who were better organized on the national level, went to federal court to challenge the constitutionality of those restrictions. The Court's near-reversal of *Roe* in *Thornburgh* reenergized pro-choice activists while also giving to right-to-life forces fairly clear directives about how to draft further state abortion restrictions to limit *Roe.*

While pro-choice forces were invigorated by their defeat of Robert H. Bork, the religious right, nevertheless, was heartened by the close (5-to-4) vote in *Thornburgh.* This decision, moreover, emboldened members of the Reagan Justice Department to talk to Missouri's attorney general, William Webster, about appealing a federal court's invalidation of that state's restrictive abortion law. The Reagan administration believed that it was likely to get the opportunity to name yet another justice to the Supreme Court by the time the next abortion case could reach the Court. Webster, in turn, believed that the state law should be defended as "nothing more than regulat[ing] abortions within the parameters allowed by *Roe v. Wade*" (Craig and O'Brien 1993, p. 187). But Webster was persuaded to repeat language directly from Fried's amicus curiae brief in *Thornburgh* urging the Court to overrule *Roe.* Again, the Reagan administration filed a brief asking the Court to overrule *Roe.*

By the end of his second term in office, then, President Reagan had not only given more attention to abortion issues than any of his predecessors but had also legitimized the right-to-life movement through his enthusiastic support of its opposition to abortion. Not only did many of his Cabinet-level appointees take an active role in advancing pro-life positions, his appointments to the U.S. Supreme Court increased the likelihood that *Roe* would be limited, if not ultimately overruled.

During the Reagan years, the abortion policy process came full circle. At the same time, however, right-to-life forces played a far larger role in defining the issue and shaping the public agenda than they had previously. Abortion was viewed both by the president and by many conservative members of Congress as morally wrong, whereas pro-choice advocates were put on the defensive in their efforts to redefine the issue. Although the Supreme Court continued to uphold the essence of *Roe*, actions by the White House and the Court chipped away at *Roe* as abortion policy was being formulated on the national level.

6

The Politics of Abortion, 1988–1992

Becky Bell, a seventeen-year-old Indianapolis girl, died in an illegal abortion in 1988 after she was refused a legal operation because she was too afraid to ask her parents' permission. . . . In Missouri, women seeking abortions were traveling all day across the state and camping in the parking lot of the lone family planning clinic in St. Louis that performs second trimester abortions. . . . By 1990, the National Center for Health Statistics was reporting an increase in teenage birthrate, reversing an eighteen-year decline.

—Susan Faludi, *Backlash: The Undeclared War Against American Women* (1991)

SINCE *ROE V. WADE* WAS DECIDED in 1973, abortion has shaped both the American domestic and foreign policy agendas. The abortion issue continues to illustrate the dilemma faced by the polity when there is no clear compromise on a public policy. Not only has resolution of the dilemma often pitted elected versus appointed officials against each other, it has also stirred vehement feelings on both sides of the debate. The 1988 presidential election and, especially, the Supreme Court's decision in *Webster v. Reproductive Health Services* (1989) appear to have been a turning point in the abortion wars. The nature of the tactics used by those in the pro-life movement seemed to change as some groups resorted more and more often to civil protest and at times, outright violence. Drawing parallels with the liberal civil rights movement, particularly Reverend Martin Luther King, Jr.'s use of marches and nonviolent sit-ins, leaders of the anti-abortion movement increasingly resorted to protests at clinics to stop abortions and to focus media attention on their cause while those in the ultraconservative wing of the movement resorted to threats, violence, and even murder.

Unlike other policy issues such as the environment, whereby most citizens agree on the need for clean air or water though not necessarily on the best way to meet that need, the abortion arena affords no consensus regarding the *right* to an abortion, making agreement on policy impossible. This lack of agreement, compounded by both sides' inability to compromise, heightened the stakes for all concerned. Nevertheless, pro- and anti-abortion groups have made every possible effort to win policy concessions from all levels and branches of government, preferring half a loaf, or even a slice, to none at all. In short, abortion is an interesting issue by which to view and understand the dynamic nature of the national policymaking process. The interchanges and exchanges between the federal courts—staffed by unelected judges—and Congress and the president—elected by the people—highlight not only the system of separation of powers created by the Framers but also the dilemma that occurs when unelected judges appear to make policy in an area where compromise is difficult.

The fact that abortion has become an issue only nonelected officials seem able to moderate—if not resolve—leads conservatives to argue that the political system has failed because such an issue should be handled by the legislative branch, and liberals to argue that abortion is an individual decision properly made apart from government. But the nature of abortion did not keep it from being an important issue—and, some would argue, a defining issue—in the electoral process. Now was the time for pro-life forces to build on their successes by heightening their activity in the 1988 presidential election and *Webster,* and for pro-choice forces to plan their apparently uphill battle to save *Roe.*

The 1988 Presidential Election and *Roe*

The 1988 elections offered an opportunity for both pro-life and pro-choice forces to present the American public with clear choices on the abortion issue. During the 1988 presidential primaries, Vice-President George Bush tried to shed his label as the "candidate of the Wall Street wing of the Republican Party" by moving to the right on social issues (McKeegan 1992, p. 150). Distrusted by the conservative right, which included right-to-lifers, Bush was well aware of a 1987 poll in the *Conservative Digest* reporting that only 9 percent of those polled favored Bush as the candidate of the Republican Party (McKeegan 1992, p. 150). Accordingly, Bush tried to recast himself as an ardent foe of abortion to win the support of these new conservative Republicans.

The Republican National Convention

In 1988 the abortion debate permeated the Republican Party's National Convention as a "feminist presence re-emerged" (Freeman 1988, p. 9). At the same time, the growing force of the right-to-life movement was clearly evident. Before evangelicals under Reverend Jerry Falwell and others had been mobilized as a political force, the Republican Party had been largely dominated by eastern bankers and business interests. Now, the full force and impact of the Christian right could be seen. Ignoring testimony from Republican pro-choice women that the party's anti-abortion crusade was damaging its image in the eyes of women voters and that the gender gap could make the difference in a close race and had already accounted for the loss of up to seven Senate races in 1986, the Republican Party chose to add several new anti-abortion planks to its platform after "Bush operatives made it clear that they didn't want any minority reports or floor debate" on issues like abortion (Freeman 1988, p. 10). The new planks included calls to end funding for pro-choice population organizations; parental consent requirements for minors regarding the use of *birth control;* and prohibitions on the use of aborted fetuses in scientific research.

In an effort to shore up support for his candidacy, Bush named U.S. Senator Dan Quayle (R.–Ind.) as his vice-presidential running mate. Quayle, a young conservative with a strong pro-life record, had a "deeply evangelical wife, who discounted the theory of evolution and believed in Noah's Ark" (McKeegan 1992, p. 150). These views were widely accepted by many evangelicals active in the right-to-life movement. Moreover, the popularity of the Quayles helped Bush ward off attacks by Pat Robertson, the conservative televangelist who had launched a strong primary challenge against Bush, especially in the South.

The Democratic National Convention

The Democratic National Convention in 1988 could not ignore the abortion issue, inasmuch as Operation Rescue was staging massive demonstrations around Atlanta, the site of the Democrats' meeting. But feminist organizations were unfazed by this activity, because they had made electing a Democratic president their number-one priority. Indeed, as Jo Freeman has pointed out, "There was universal agreement that the Reagan years had been disastrous for women and that four more years of Republican rule would, at the very least, result in a Supreme Court that would limit women's options for decades to come" (Freeman 1988, p. 12).

Feminists quickly became alarmed, however, when the National Committee chair voiced his opinion that he wanted a short platform that "softpedalled" controversial issues such as abortion (Freeman 1988, p. 13). Thus, in spite of strong lobbying from women activists, the first draft of the platform made only casual reference to "freedom of choice regarding childbirth." However, Massachusetts Governor Michael Dukakis, the Democratic Party's nominee, insisted on stronger language. As finally adopted, the platform declared the party's support of "the fundamental right to reproductive choice [which] should be guaranteed regardless of ability to pay"—a platform directly rejecting an entreaty from the pro-life United States Catholic Conference, which urged Democrats to support an amendment ensuring "legal protection for the lives of the unborn."

To capitalize on the hordes of media representatives who were gathered in Atlanta to report on the 1988 Democratic National Convention from around the nation, Randall Terry, the leader of Operation Rescue, announced a "Siege on Atlanta." Terry had labored for two years prior to the convention to plan and orchestrate the actions of several pro-life groups. His efforts ultimately brought nearly two thousand protestors to Atlanta for the purpose of blockading the entrances to several abortion clinics located near the convention center. Modeling the nonviolent actions of Reverend King in the heart of the South just minutes away

FIGURE 6.1

The Operation Rescue Pledge

A Pledge for Non-Violence

I UNDERSTAND the critical importance that this Mission be unified, peaceful, and free of any actions or words that would appear violent or hateful to any witnesses of this event.

I REALIZE that some pro-abortion elements of the media may seek to discredit this event and focus on a side issue in order to avoid the central issue at hand; MURDERED CHILDREN AND EXPLOITED WOMEN.

HENCE, I UNDERSTAND that for the children's sake, this gathering must be orderly and above reproach. THEREFORE:

As an invited guest, I will cooperate with the spirit and goals of this Mission, as explained to me.

I commit to be peaceful, prayerful, and non-violent in both word and deed.

Should I be arrested, I will not struggle with police in any way (whether in word or deed), but remain polite and passively limp, remembering that mercy triumphs over judgment.

I will listen and follow the instructions of the Mission's leadership and crowd control marshalls.

I understand that certain individuals will be appointed to speak to the media, police, and to women seeking abortion. I will not take it upon myself to yell out to anyone, but will continue singing and praying with the main group, as directed.

I SIGN THIS PLEDGE, having seriously considered what I do, with the determination and will to persevere by the grace of God.

Pro-life Rescuer ______________________ Date ______________

The Operation Rescue Pledge for Non-Violence. Used by permission.

from the church where King had preached his message of nonviolence, these protestors were not only schooled in the politics of protest but media-savvy as well. (See Figure 6.1 for a reprint of the pledge signed by all Operation Rescue protestors.) The nonviolent sit-ins they engaged in were designed to prevent those seeking abortions from gaining access to clinics. To that end, "rescuers" were instructed not to push or shove but also not to budge or allow clinic patrons to pass. The "Siege on Atlanta" was broadcast on every nightly news station and network, bringing incalculable attention to the pro-life movement. It also helped Operation Rescue itself, whose contributions rose from $5,000 a month before the convention to more than $60,000 a month just four months afterward (Wills 1989).

Public Opinion, Abortion, and the 1988 Election

After Vice-President Bush was selected as the Republican Party's nominee, he frequently urged "adoption not abortion" as a solution to unwanted pregnancies and resurrected the conservative call for passage of a constitutional amendment to ban abortions. In contrast, Michael Dukakis, the Democratic Party standard-bearer, repeatedly called for protection of *Roe v. Wade*. This stance prompted the appearance of pro-life picketers at nearly every campaign stop, as Joseph Scheidler's Pro-Life Action League repeatedly disrupted Dukakis's campaign speeches and those of his running mate, Senator Lloyd Bentsen (D.–Tex.).

At the same time that the presidential campaign was focusing attention on abortion and on the clear choice presented by the two major party candidates, public opinion polls continued to reveal little change in the public's attitudes since the Court's decision in 1973. In late October 1988, for example, 57 percent of those polled favored legal abortions in only some circumstances, whereas 24 percent supported abortion in all circumstances. Only 17 percent preferred an outright ban on all abortions (Gallup and Gallup 1988). George Bush's opposition to abortion, however, dealt him no fatal blows in the national election. Bush won with 53 percent of the popular vote at a time when, according to an *ABC News* poll, abortion was being cited as the number-one issue by nearly one-third of the voters. But those who cited abortion as their major issue overwhelmingly voted for Bush. Thus, in just one year, Bush was able to convert conservative skeptics by transforming his pro-life stand into a campaign asset—a feat that confounded many political commentators. Nevertheless, the gender gap persisted inasmuch as men favored George Bush by 7 percent and women were divided equally between the two candidates.

Pro-Choice Groups React. The pro-choice movement saw the need to act quickly. The election of George Bush as president signaled to pro-choice activists the precariousness of *Roe*. Bush, like Reagan before him, was avowedly pro-life, and four more years of a Republican in the White House meant the likelihood of more conservative, right-to-life justices on the Supreme Court. The cumulative impact of *Thornburgh* (1986), increased "rescue" activity, clinic violence, and the election of another avowedly pro-life president drove home the point that the tides had turned. As if this were not enough, just two days after the election the U.S. Justice Department filed an amicus curiae brief in *Webster v. Reproductive Health Services* (1989) urging the Court to use the case as an opportunity to overrule *Roe*. Molly Yard, president of the National Organization for Women (NOW), and Ellie Smeal, president of the Fund for the Feminist Majority (and former president of NOW), immediately called a press conference to denounce the move, charging that the administration had waited until after the election to file the controversial brief.

In response to the growing threat to abortion rights posed by right-to-life groups and at least four more years of a Republican administration, Kate Michelman, the executive director of NARAL, decided to launch a major national campaign to let women know that *Roe* and access to safe, legal abortions were in jeopardy. Working closely with other groups, including Planned Parenthood (PP), NOW, and the Fund for the Feminist Majority, NARAL designed a two-part strategy. In the first part it would let women know about *Webster v. Reproductive Health Services*, the case that the Reagan administration actually had urged the state of Missouri to appeal. And in the second part it would educate the public to understand that even if *Roe* was not overturned, *Webster* could be a major setback if the Supreme Court was no longer willing to preserve a woman's right to an abortion using the *Roe* framework. Asking the same question posed by Judge Bork during his unsuccessful Supreme Court nomination hearings, NARAL's scheme was to get Americans to think about "Who decides?" in an effort to alter the way the debate was being framed by changing the way abortion was being dealt with on the public agenda (see Figure 6.2).

For the first time, NARAL launched a massive print and television campaign using a series of well-crafted ads. One television ad included photos of a young girl growing up. As the photos stop abruptly in the girl's late teens, an announcer intones, "She grew up in the '50s and died in the '60s, a victim of illegal abortion" (Tribe 1992, p. 174). By stressing the possibility that abortion could soon revert to being illegal, NARAL and pro-choice forces brilliantly turned the right-to-life's own message on itself, thereby reshaping the public debate. When Judge Bork had asked "Who decides?" during his unsuccessful Supreme Court nomination hearings, he was focusing attention on the debate between the Supreme Court and the big federal government. As the debate was now refocused, pro-choice activists were essentially "out-anti-governmenting" conservatives. Accordingly, the question had become, Who makes this intimate, personal decision about abortion—the states or the individual?

Even though the justices themselves could not be the object of conventional lobbying techniques, the pro-choice movement brought its "Who Decides" campaign to the Supreme Court. A record number of amicus curiae briefs were filed on both sides of the issue in *Webster*, as illustrated in Table 6.1. Pro-choice leaders also set out to inform the Court that women were concerned that their reproductive rights were being threatened. An unconventional letter-writing campaign was

FIGURE 6.2

Pamphlet and Brochure Covers from Both Sides

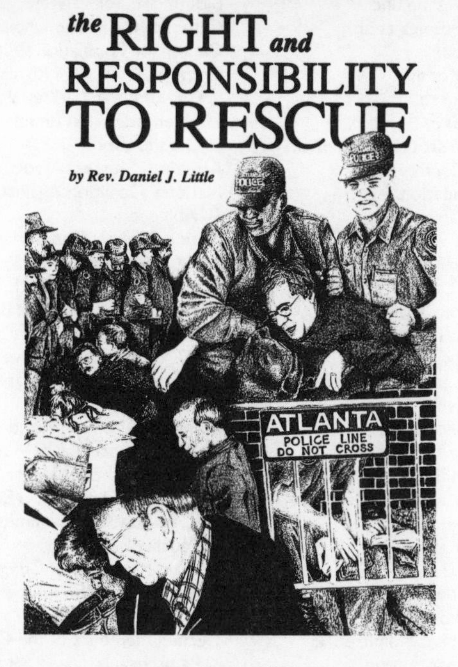

Floods of pamphlets and brochures are used by pro-choice and right-to-life groups alike in their media campaigns.

TABLE 6.1

Interest-Group Participation in *Webster*

For Missouri	For Reproductive Health Services
Counsel: William L. Webster, Attorney General of Missouri	*Counsel: Frank Susman*
Supported by Amicus Curiae from:	Supported by Amicus Curiae from:
Charles Fried, on behalf of the U.S.	American Civil Liberties Union et al.
Alabama Lawyers for Unborn Children, Inc.	American Jewish Congress et al.
American Association of Prolife Obstetricians and Gynecologists	American Medical Association et al.
American Family Association, Inc.	American Psychological Association
American Life League, Inc.	American Public Health Association et al.
Catholic Health Association of the United States	Americans for Democratic Action et al.
Catholic Lawyers Guild of the Archdiocese of Boston, Inc.	Americans United for Separation of Church and State
Center for Judicial Studies et al.	Association of Reproductive Health Professionals et al.
Covenant House et al.	Bioethicists for Privacy
Focus on the Family et al.	Catholics for a Free Choice et al.
Holy Orthodox Church	Center for Population Options et al.
Knights of Columbus	Committee on Civil Rights of the Bar of the City of New York et al.
Lutheran Church–Missouri Synod et al.	22 International Women's Health Organizations
Missouri Catholic Conference	American Nurses' Association et al.
National Legal Foundation	National Coalition Against Domestic Violence
Right to Life Advocates, Inc.	National Family Planning and Reproductive Health Association
Rutherford Institute et al.	National Association of Public Hospitals
Southern Center for Law and Ethics	Population-Environment Balance et al.
Southwest Life and Law Center, Inc.	281 American Historians
United States Catholic Conference	2,887 Women Who Have Had Abortions
127 Members of the Missouri General Assembly	California National Organization for Women et al.
American Academy of Medical Ethics	Canadian Abortion Rights Action League
American Collegians for Life	National Association of Women Lawyers et al.
Association for Public Justice	National Council of Negro Women, Inc., et al.
Catholics United for Life et al.	NOW Legal Defense and Education Fund et al.
Christian Advocates Serving Evangelism	77 Organizations Committed to Women's Equality
Doctors for Life et al.	Certain Members of Congress
Feminists for Life et al.	Congressman Christopher H. Smith et. al.
Free Speech Advocates	608 State Legislators
Human Life International	Certain Members of the Commonwealth of Pennsylvania
International Right-to-Life Federation	Briefs of amici curiae were filed for the States of California, New York, Massachusetts, Colorado, Texas, Vermont, Louisiana, Arizona, Idaho, and Pennsylvania
National Right-to-Life Committee, Inc.	
New England Christian Action Council, Inc.	
Right-to-Life League of Southern California, Inc.	
Birthright, Inc.	

launched, and the justices' chambers were inundated with mail from irate women. Although the Court normally receives about one thousand pieces of mail a day, the volume soon reached forty thousand per day, effectively stalling the Court's communications system. Said Toni House, the Court's public information officer, "I hope they [the letter writers] understand this is not a popularity contest. We are not keeping score of who favors abortion and who does not. While people have a right to write the court I hope that they do not expect that the enunciation of their opinion will have any effect on the justices" (quoted in Craig and O'Brien 1993, p. 65).

At the same time, these pro-choice groups and others were preparing for a march on Washington, D.C. to show the Supreme Court and the nation that women did not want to see abortion rights put in jeopardy by the Court. On April 9, 1989, more than 300,000 marchers showed up, overwhelming organizers but making an effective statement. Evidently the very real threat of a return to pre-*Roe* days had reenergized the movement. Reenergized it was, and it would become even more so after the Court's decision in *Webster*.

***Webster:* The Tides Keep Turning.** On April 26, 1989, the day *Webster* was to be argued orally before the Court, pro-choice and pro-life demonstrators were out in full force in front of the Court, as if to underscore the division on the issue that existed in the polity. At the normally quiet Court, "[p]assions ran high as competing protestors squared off at the courthouse steps, chanting, singing and screaming at each other" (Simon 1995, p. 128). Division over abortion was also highlighted by the record number of amicus curiae briefs submitted—seventy-eight, many written on behalf of numerous other groups, individuals, and organizations (see Table 6.1).

William Webster, the Missouri attorney general, argued the case along with Harvard law professor Charles Fried. And Fried, who as solicitor general had argued the Reagan administration's position in *Thornburgh*, was asked by the Bush administration to repeat his arguments in support of the constitutionality of a wide array of abortion restrictions, including the following:

1. a preamble declaring that the "life of each human being begins at conception";
2. a prohibition on the use of public facilities or employees to perform abortions;
3. a ban on public funding of abortion counseling; and
4. the requirement that a doctor, prior to performing an abortion on a woman whom he or she believes to be twenty or more weeks pregnant, ascertain whether the fetus is "viable" by performing such examinations and tests as are necessary to determine the gestational age, weight, and lung maturity of the fetus.

During oral arguments, Fried urged the Court to overrule *Roe* but to preserve the constitutional right to privacy fashioned by the Court in *Griswold v. Connecticut* (1965). Then, on behalf of the Bush administration—in expanding on his amicus brief, where he argued that the right to privacy was limited to freedom from bodily restrictions—Fried told the Court: "[W]e are not asking the Court to unravel the fabric of unenumerated and privacy rights which this Court has woven in cases like . . . *Griswold*. Rather we are asking the Court to pull this one thread."

While the nation waited to see if the fabric of *Roe* would remain unaltered, the intense publicity that surrounded oral arguments in *Webster* as well as the wait for the Court's decision continued to focus public attention on the abortion debate. When *Webster* was finally announced on the last day of the term in July 1989, network news media broke into all regularly scheduled programs to announce the decision. But the Court's decision in *Webster* was not an easy one to condense into soundbites. Four justices—Reagan appointees Antonin Scalia and Anthony Kennedy, along with Chief Justice William H. Rehnquist and Byron White (both of whom had dissented in *Roe*)—formed a four-justice **plurality** that seemed willing to overrule *Roe*. Much to their chagrin, however, they were unable to muster the support of a fifth justice. In fact, Justice Scalia was especially outraged by Justice O'Connor's refusal to join the four conservatives in overruling *Roe*. Not only did he appear "to lecture O'Connor in the intricacies of constitutional law," but he did so "as a senior law professor might speak to an undergraduate" (Simon 1995, p. 137).

Although O'Connor refused to provide the fifth, key vote to overrule *Roe*, she did agree with her conservative brethren that all of the Missouri statute's provisions were constitutionally permissible. (Since the preamble declaring that life began at conception was not being enforced, the Court declined to address its constitutionality.) She came to this conclusion by again applying her "undue burden" standard. In this context, O'Connor, a strong supporter of states' rights in the federal system, found that none of the state's regulations unduly burdened a woman's right to obtain an abortion. Thus, she concluded that Missouri's regulation of abortion was reasonable under its state police powers, as reserved under the Tenth Amendment. *Roe*, then, was not overturned, but Missouri's restrictions on abortions in public hospitals and, more important, its required tests for fetal viability were upheld. The fetal viability tests, in particular, allowed the states to push back the point of state interest by four weeks—from the end of the second trimester announced in *Roe* to the beginning of the second half of the pregnancy.

The three justices in dissent—Harry A. Blackmun (the author of *Roe*), William Brennan, Jr., and Thurgood Marshall—were visibly upset with the plurality decision. Indeed, the portions of their dissent reprinted in Box 6.1 reveal the emotional tone of their joint dissent. Said Blackmun, who was writing now for only two of his brethren, *Roe* and "the fundamental constitutional right of women to decide whether to terminate a pregnancy, survive but are not secure." It was this portion of the dissenters' opinion, moreover, that many news commentators, in their effort to analyze more than a hundred pages of judicial opinion quickly, turned to feverishly as their starting point in telling the public what the Court had done.

As Blackmun stated, *Roe* had survived—but its framework was largely abandoned. Furthermore, the ultimate decision of the Court, said Blackmun, "implicitly invite[d] every state legislature to enact more and more restrictive abortion regulations in order to provoke more and more test cases, in the hope that sometime down the line the Court will return the law of procreative freedom to the severe limitations that generally prevailed in the country before January 22, 1973."

The Impact of *Webster v. Reproductive Health Services*

Webster had several immediate consequences. The decision dramatically brought home not only how divided the polity was about abortion but also how badly fractured the Court was concerning a woman's constitutional right to an abortion. Four justices—Rehnquist, White, Kennedy, and Scalia—appeared ready to overrule *Roe*. Four others—Blackmun, Brennan, Marshall, and Stevens—continued to believe that *Roe* had been correctly decided. The only woman on the Court, Justice O'Connor, took the position that the states had the right to regulate abortion in some circumstances, so long as those restrictions did not place what she called an "undue burden" on a woman's right to an abortion and did not prohibit it altogether. Moreover, her opinion built on her *Akron* dissent by indicating her continued discomfort with late-term abortions in light of medical advances that continued to push back the point of fetal viability.

Although the Supreme Court was making policy when it decided *Webster*, the exact nature of that policy was not clear. What the badly divided nature of the Court did make clear to those on both sides of the issue—as well as to those who opted for some sort of a midpoint solution to the dilemma—was that the nation was far from reaching any kind of widely accepted compromise.

Webster also highlighted the problems that can occur when the Supreme Court—composed of nine diverse, unelected individuals—attempts to make policy in a controversial issue area. Unlike its earlier decision in *Brown v. Board of Education of Topeka* (1954) and many of its decisions concerning racial integration,

BOX 6.1

Excerpts from *Webster v. Reproductive Health Services*

Legal citation: 492 U.S. 490
Argued: April 26, 1989
Decided: July 2, 1989
Opinion by: Chief Justice Rehnquist

In announcing the judgment of the Court, after ruling that the various provisions of the Missouri statute were constitutional and declining to overrule *Roe v. Wade*, Chief Justice Rehnquist wrote:

> . . . In *Roe v. Wade*, the Court recognized that the State has "important and legitimate" interests in protecting maternal health and in the potentiality of human life. . . . During the second trimester, the State "may, if it chooses, regulate the abortion procedure in ways that are reasonably related to maternal health." After viability, when the State's interest in potential human life was held to become compelling, the State "may, if it chooses, regulate, and even proscribe, abortion except where it is necessary, in appropriate medical judgment, for the preservation of the life or health of the mother." . . .
>
> Stare decisis is a cornerstone of our legal system, but it has less power in constitutional cases, where, save for constitutional amendments, this Court is the only body able to make needed changes. . . . We have not refrained from reconsideration of a prior construction of the Constitution that has proved "unsound in principle and unworkable in practice." . . .
>
> We think the *Roe* trimester framework falls into that category. In the first place, the rigid *Roe* framework is hardly consistent with the notion of a Constitution cast in general terms, as ours is, and usually speaking in general principles, as ours does. The key elements of the *Roe* framework—trimesters and viability—are not found in the text of the Constitution or in any place else one would expect to find a constitutional principle. Since the bounds of the inquiry are essentially indeterminate, the result has been a web of legal rules that have become increasingly intricate, resembling a code of regulations rather than a body of constitutional doctrine. As Justice White has put it, the trimester framework has left this Court to serve as the country's "ex officio medical board with powers to approve or disapprove medical and operative practices and standards throughout the United States." . . . In the second place, we do not see why the State's interest in protecting potential human life should come into existence only at the point of viability,

and that there should therefore be a rigid line allowing state regulation after viability but prohibiting it before viability. . . .

The tests that [the State] requires the physician to perform are designed to determine viability. The State here has chosen viability as the point at which its interest in potential human life must be safeguarded. . . . It is true that the tests in question increase the expense of abortion, and regulate the discretion of the physician in determining the viability of the fetus. Since the tests will undoubtedly show in many cases that the fetus is not viable, the tests will have been performed for what were in fact second-trimester abortions. But we are satisfied that the requirement of these tests permissibly furthers the State's interest in protecting potential human life.

Justice Blackmun takes us to task for our failure to join in a "great issues" debate as to whether the Constitution includes an "unenumerated" general right to privacy as recognized in cases such as *Griswold v. Connecticut* and *Roe*. But *Griswold v. Connecticut*, unlike *Roe*, did not purport to adopt a whole framework, complete with detailed rules and distinctions, to govern the cases in which the asserted liberty interest would apply. As such, it was far different from the opinion, if not the holding, of *Roe v. Wade*, which sought to establish a constitutional framework for judging state regulation of abortion during the entire term of pregnancy. That framework sought to deal with areas of medical practice traditionally subject to state regulation, and it sought to balance once and for all by reference only to the calendar the claims of the State to protect the fetus as a form of human life against the claims of a woman to decide for herself whether or not to abort a fetus she was carrying. The experience of the Court in applying *Roe v. Wade* in later cases suggests to us that there is wisdom in not unnecessarily attempting to elaborate the abstract differences between a "fundamental right" to abortion, as the Court described it in *Akron,* and a "limited fundamental constitutional right," which Justice Blackmun today treats *Roe* as having established, or a liberty interest protected by the Due Process Clause, which we believe it to be. The Missouri testing requirement here is reasonably designed to ensure that abortions are not performed where the fetus is viable—an end which all concede is legitimate—and that is sufficient to sustain its constitutionality.

Justice Blackmun also accuses us, inter alia, of cowardice and illegitimacy in dealing with "*the most politically divisive domestic legal issue of our time*" [emphasis added]. There is no doubt that our holding today will allow some governmental regulation of abortion that would have been prohibited under the language of [earlier] cases. But the goal of constitutional adjudication is

BOX 6.1 *continued*

surely not to remove inexorably "politically divisive" issues from the realm of the legislative process, whereby the people through their elected representatives deal with matters of concern to them. The goal of constitutional adjudication is to hold true the balance between that which the Constitution puts beyond the reach of the democratic process and that which it does not. We think we have done that today. Justice Blackmun's suggestion, . . . that legislative bodies, in a Nation where more than half of our population is women, will treat our decision today as an invitation to enact abortion regulation reminiscent of the Dark Ages, not only misreads our views but does scant justice to those who serve in such bodies and the people who elect them.

Justice O'Connor concurred with the judgment of the Court but felt it was important to forestall a reexamination of *Roe*. Said O'Connor:

. . . When the constitutional invalidity of a State's abortion statute actually turns on the constitutional validity of *Roe v. Wade*, there will be time enough to reexamine *Roe*. And to do so carefully. . . .

Finally, and rather halfheartedly, the plurality suggests that the marginal increase in the cost of an abortion created by Missouri's viability testing provision may make [the Missouri statute], even as interpreted, suspect under this Court's decision in *Akron v. Akron Center for Reproductive Health, Inc.* (1983), striking down a second-trimester hospitalization requirement. I dissented from the Court's opinion in *Akron* because it was my view that, even apart from *Roe*'s trimester framework which I continue to consider problematic, the *Akron* majority had distorted and misapplied its own standard for evaluating state regulation of abortion which the Court had applied with fair consistency in the past: that previability, "a regulation imposed on a lawful abortion, is not unconstitutional unless it unduly burdens the right to seek an abortion."

It is clear to me that requiring the performance of examinations and tests useful to determining whether a fetus is viable, when viability is possible, and when it would not be medically imprudent to do so, does not impose an *undue burden* [emphasis added] on a woman's abortion decision. On this ground alone I would reject the suggestion that [the Missouri statute] as interpreted is unconstitutional. . . . The second-trimester hospitalization requirement struck down in *Akron* imposed, in the majority's view, "a heavy, and unnecessary, burden," more than doubling the cost of "women's access to a relatively inexpensive, otherwise accessible, and safe abortion procedure." By contrast, the cost of examinations and tests that could usefully and prudently be performed when a woman is 20–24 weeks pregnant to determine whether the fetus is viable would only marginally, if at all, increase the cost of an abortion. . . .

Justice Scalia, concurring in part and concurring in the judgment, reacted angrily by attacking Justice O'Connor in stinging language not often used by justices:

Justice O'Connor's assertion that a "'fundamental rule of judicial restraint'" requires us to avoid reconsidering *Roe* cannot be taken seriously. By finessing *Roe* we do not, as she suggests, adhere to the strict and venerable rule that we should avoid "'decid[ing] questions of a constitutional nature.'" We have not disposed of this case on some statutory or procedural ground, but have decided, and could not avoid deciding, whether the Missouri statute meets the requirements of the United States Constitution. The only choice available is whether, in deciding that constitutional question, we should use *Roe v. Wade* as the benchmark, or something else. What is involved, therefore, is not the rule of avoiding constitutional issues where possible, but the quite separate principle that we will not "'formulate a rule of constitutional law broader than is required by the precise facts to which it is to be applied.'" The latter is a sound general principle, but one often departed from when good reason exists. It is rare, of course, that the Court goes out of its way to acknowledge that its judgment could have been reached under the old constitutional rule, making its adoption of the new one unnecessary to the decision, but even such explicit acknowledgment is not unheard of. . . .

The real question, then, is whether there are valid reasons to go beyond the most stingy possible holding today. It seems to me there are not only valid but compelling ones. Ordinarily, speaking no more broadly than is absolutely required avoids throwing settled law into confusion; doing so today preserves a chaos that is evident to anyone who can read and count. Alone sufficient to justify a broad holding is the fact that our retaining control, through *Roe*, of what I believe to be, and many of our citizens recognize to be, a political issue continuously distorts the public perception of the role of this Court. We can now look forward to at least another Term with carts full of mail from the public, and streets full of demonstrators, urging us—their unelected and life tenured judges who have been awarded those extraordinary, undemocratic characteristics precisely in order that we might follow the law despite the popular will—to follow the popular will. Indeed, I expect we can look forward to even more of that than before, given our indecisive decision today. . . .

BOX 6.1 *continued*

> Of the four courses we might have chosen today—to reaffirm *Roe*, to overrule it explicitly, to overrule it sub silentio, or to avoid the question—*the last is the least responsible*. [emphasis added]

Justices Blackmun, Stevens, and Marshall then dissented from the opinions of the plurality and those of Justice O'Connor, with Justice Blackmun writing:

> Today, *Roe v. Wade* (1973), and the fundamental constitutional right of women to decide whether to terminate a pregnancy, survive but are not secure. Although the Court extricates itself from this case without making a single, even incremental, change in the law of abortion, the plurality and Justice Scalia would overrule *Roe* (the first silently, the other explicitly) and would return to the States virtually unfettered authority to control the quintessentially intimate, personal, and life-directing decision whether to carry a fetus to term. Although today, no less than yesterday, the Constitution and the decisions of this Court prohibit a State from enacting laws that inhibit women from the meaningful exercise of that right, a plurality of this Court implicitly invites every state legislature to enact more and more restrictive abortion regulations in order to provoke more and more test cases, in the hope that sometime down the line the Court will return the law of procreative freedom to the severe limitations that generally prevailed in this country before January 22, 1973. Never in my memory has a plurality announced a judgment of this Court that so foments disregard for the law and for our standing decisions. . . .
>
> I fear for the future. I fear for the liberty and equality of the millions of women who have lived and come of age in the 16 years since *Roe* was decided. I fear for the integrity of, and public esteem for, this Court. I dissent. . . .
>
> Thus, "not with a bang, but a whimper," the plurality discards a landmark case of the last generation, and casts into darkness the hopes and visions of every woman in this country who had come to believe that the Constitution guaranteed her the right to exercise some control over her unique ability to bear children. The plurality does so either oblivious or insensitive to the fact that millions of women, and their families, have ordered their lives around the right to reproductive choice, and that this right has become vital to the full participation of women in the economic and political walks of American life. The plurality would clear the way once again for government to force upon women the physical labor and specific and direct medical and psychological harms that may accompany carrying a fetus to term. The plurality

would clear the way again for the State to conscript a woman's body and to force upon her a "distressful life and future." . . .

Of the aspirations and settled understandings of American women, of the inevitable and brutal consequences of what it is doing, the tough-approach plurality utters not a word. This silence is callous. It is also profoundly destructive of this Court as an institution. To overturn a constitutional decision is a rare and grave undertaking. To overturn a constitutional decision that secured a fundamental personal liberty to millions of persons would be unprecedented in our 200 years of constitutional history. Although the doctrine of stare decisis applies with somewhat diminished force in constitutional cases generally, even in ordinary constitutional cases "any departure from . . . stare decisis demands special justification." This requirement of justification applies with unique force where, as here, the Court's abrogation of precedent would destroy people's firm belief, based on past decisions of this Court, that they possess an unabridgeable right to undertake certain conduct.

Webster was not unanimous. In *Brown*, Chief Justice Earl Warren had labored long to ensure that the Supreme Court presented the American public with a unified front so that the Court would not be put in a position of presenting the nation with an ambiguous decision that southern states, in particular, could use to their advantage. But in *Webster*, Chief Justice Rehnquist, long a foe of abortion rights, was unable to muster enough votes to overrule *Roe*. There was not actually a five-person majority who agreed on *any* of the legal reasoning for upholding *any* of the Missouri abortion restrictions, and the lack of consensus on the Court was widely reported.

Policy implementation works best when there are clear policy formulations or directives. Accordingly, the Court's lack of consensus in *Webster*, as noted by Justice Blackmun in dissent, only muddied the policy issues as states were left wondering how far they could go to restrict abortion. Would Justice O'Connor find their restrictions an undue burden? Or would President Bush be able to appoint a new pro-life justice to the Court before any new legislation could get to the Supreme Court for review, thus giving the plurality their fifth vote without needing to sway O'Connor? In *Roe*, seven members of the Court had agreed to clearly delineated standards. In *Webster*, in sharp contrast, the Court again made policy, but it was fuzzy policy at best and not particularly effective in terms of providing guidelines to policy implementers.

Interest Groups Respond to Webster

After *Webster*, NARAL's executive director Kate Michelman warned, "The Court has left a woman's right to privacy hanging by a thread and passed the scissors to the state legislatures" (Arieff 1989). *Webster* had mobilized forces on both sides, as evidenced by the marches being held around the country; and even sitting justices had begun to voice their fears about a post-*Roe* nation. At this time, pro-choice groups including NARAL, NOW, the Fund for the Feminist Majority, and Planned Parenthood met to devise an effective strategy to use at both the national and state levels.

On the other side, right-to-life activists pursued several new as well as existing strategies. From 1990 to 1992, for example, they formed "life chains" in more than seven hundred communities around the nation. Usually on Sundays, families got together to line major streets as they held placards and signs opposing abortion. This public form of protest was much milder than the "rescue" attempts and clinic violence that nevertheless continued.

Pro-life groups also launched a series of boycotts against nearly fifty large American corporations that contributed funds to Planned Parenthood. Borrowing a page from a strategy that had been used by numerous labor organizations, the Christian Action Council and twenty-four other pro-life organizations urged their members to stop using American Express, AT&T, and several other corporate sponsors of family planning organizations. AT&T, which had supported PP for the past twenty-five years, and ten other large corporations quickly withdrew their support of PP and its family planning clinics. Ironically, most of the AT&T money funded teenage contraceptive services designed to prevent the need for abortions.

Although many groups engaged in or supported these forms of protest activity, all was not rosy in the pro-life movement. In 1989, for example, the Reverend Jerry Falwell closed down the Moral Majority in the face of declining revenues. The **Christian Coalition** (CC), headed by televangelist Pat Robertson, quickly moved to take its place. In the main, however, pro-life forces were heartened by *Webster*. Clearly ebullient, Randall Terry predicted that "*Roe* is going to go down . . . [and] we're going to introduce an avalanche of legislation to protect the children" (Terry 1989). Terry's prediction was correct. By July 1990, 350 abortion-related bills had been introduced in state legislatures, two times the number that had been filed in 1989 (Lacayo 1990, p. 27).

The National Right-to-Life Committee (NRLC) played a leading role in the effort to secure passage of restrictive state abortion laws throughout the country. Yet, despite its impressive ability to convince individual legislators to introduce abortion restrictions, its successes were mixed. In Florida, Republican Governor Bob Martinez was the first to respond by calling a special session of the state legislature to debate model legislation proposed by the NRLC, but it was stalled in committee. In Louisiana, by contrast, the state legislature (which was 98 percent male) voted to enforce a 134-year-old statute that prohibited abortions under any circumstances, including those endangering the life of the mother (*Family Planning Perspective* 1991, p. 82). One of the first states to consider and pass new abortion restrictions was Pennsylvania. Like *Roe*, *Akron*, and *Webster*, these restrictions would serve as defining moments for those on both sides of the abortion issue.

Public Opinion After Webster

Although right-to-life groups hailed *Webster* and several states responded enthusiastically to the opportunity to pass new restrictive laws, Americans in general were not enthralled with what they perceived the Court had done. According to the first Gallup poll taken after the decision was announced, 55 percent disapproved of the decision, whereas 37 percent approved. Moreover, although 71 percent reported that they had strong feelings one way or the other about *Webster*, the poll left open the question as to how much anyone actually understood the decision. Each side, however, does appear to have been able to put its own spin on the decision. In particular, most pro-choice women thought the Court went too far toward regulating abortion rights, whereas most right-to-life advocates believed the Court did not go far enough.

The Gallup poll continues to underscore how difficult it would be for policymakers to reach any compromise about the abortion decision. Although most of the Americans surveyed reported that they opposed a total reversal of *Roe*, a majority also reported that they were quite comfortable with some state restrictions on abortion, particularly parental consent requirements. In addition, women, as a group, reacted more strongly than did men on the subject of abortion and told pollsters that they would now give increased weight to a candidate's position on abortion when they voted.

The abortion issue also appeared to mobilize a relatively apathetic electorate. Women, in particular, apparently saw the abortion issue as a political issue. For example, 58 percent of the women polled reported that they were more likely to call or write an elected official about abortion, and nearly half of them said that they were more likely to give time or money to an organization supporting their point of view—whether liberal or conservative—on abortion. These sentiments were borne out by the huge membership and contribution increases experienced by NOW, NARAL, Planned Parenthood, and Operation Rescue, among others. Planned Parenthood, for example, saw its donations quadruple from $24.5 million in 1980 to $96.4 million in 1990.

The effect of *Webster* was felt more or less equally by pro-choice and pro-life women. Clearly, the Court's decision had acted as a catalyst for more mobilization and debate on both sides of the issue. And the Gallup poll revealed to a startling degree how the division on the Court, though an unelected policymaker, simply mirrored (albeit somewhat more conservatively) the division in the American populace regarding abortion and the various statutory limitations on that right.

Abortion and the Election Process in the Post-*Webster* Era

In 1988, perhaps in anticipation of the outcome of the upcoming national elections, Kate Michelman noted that "even though polls show that most Americans support the right to an abortion the anti-abortion side has in some way won the public debate, captured the terms and framed the issues" (Lewin 1988, p. A20). In the wake of *Webster*, groups on both sides of the issue believed that control of state houses and governor's mansions would soon be the key to their respective successes. The Supreme Court had invited the states to exercise their police powers and decide what, if any, state restrictions should be placed on abortion. But George Bush's 1988 victory, instead of cementing the clout of the pro-life vote, actually appeared to hurt it. In Virginia, for example, African-American Democrat Douglas Wilder made his pro-choice stand the centerpiece of his gubernatorial campaign. Winning the votes of suburban Republicans, especially Republican women, Wilder was victorious in 1989, just months after *Webster* was decided. Similarly, in New Jersey, the pro-choice Democratic candidate for governor, James Florio, openly campaigned on his pro-choice position and received 62 percent of the vote against his pro-life challenger.

In both states, pro-life activists used militant tactics that had worked well for them in earlier campaigns. Relying heavily on churches for an organizational base, they handed out leaflets in an effort to mobilize the pro-life vote. But these tactics—perhaps because they were coupled in the public mind with the headline-grabbing activities of groups like Operation Rescue and the repeated clinic violence and harassment of clinic workers, doctors, and patrons—turned off many voters. By contrast, one Southern Baptist legislator in Virginia noted that pro-choice groups "seem[ed] to take a softer line and [did] not [engage in] any of this calling somebody a murderer" or greeting churchgoers with photos or plastic replicas of dead fetuses (McKeegan 1992, pp. 152–153). This "softer line" in a kinder, gentler America appeared to be working.

So pronounced was the impact of the pro-choice vote that GOP governors were told by some at their 1989 convention that the party should change its position on abortion. One Republican pollster cautioned the governors not to underestimate the power of the phrase that, after *Webster,* had captured the issue on the public agenda: "a woman's right to choose."

As discussed in Chapter 1, the way an issue is defined often determines how well it will play with the electorate. And indeed, in their attempt to cast the debate away from abortion per se and more toward the right to choose, pro-choicers, for the first time since pre-*Roe* days, appeared to have the upper hand—at least in terms of focusing the debate.

Discussions like those at the GOP governors' convention, and the steam of the pro-choice movement, scared many right-to-life advocates. One such advocate, the bishop of San Diego, tried to exercise his influence over voters by taking aim at a pro-choice Catholic running in a special election for a California Senate seat. In a highly publicized and unprecedented action, he barred the candidate from receiving communion. A subsequent poll showed that 71 percent of Catholic voters opposed the bishop's action; indeed, overall voter reaction to this attempt by Roman Catholic officials to further politicize the abortion issue appears to have contributed to the pro-choice candidate's ability to overcome an early 14-point deficit to win the special election.

Pro-choice groups were definitely on a roll, but not just in the state house. The 1990 congressional elections delivered a new crop of pro-choice representatives and senators to the U.S. Congress as well. According to a Harris poll conducted the summer before the election, 30 percent of the voters reported that a candidate's position on abortion would be the critical factor in how they voted in November. But in contrast to the 1988 elections, a pro-choice position now seemed a plus. In six of seven House races where abortion was a major issue, pro-choice advocates won, further unnerving Republicans and right-to-life activists. The final tally after the 1990 elections was impressive: There were two more pro-choice votes in the Senate and nine more in the House, and four more pro-choice governors. Moreover, seven state houses had shifted from the pro-life to the pro-choice position (McKeegan 1992, p. 154).

*The Post-*Webster *Elections as Reflective of Problems in the Right-to-Life Movement*

Although *Webster* had undeniably mobilized pro-life forces, the immediate rush from this "victory" masked growing problems in the movement. The Moral Majority, which had played such a key role in motivating evangelical Christians during the 1980 elections, was gone. And the National Conference of Catholic Bishops (NCCB) had tried to regain its once-dominant role in setting the anti-abortion agenda, but to little avail. Attempts to directly intervene in politics, as Catholics had done in San Diego, turned off many voters—non-Catholic and Catholic alike.

Also adversely affecting the Catholic bishops' ability to mobilize their flocks was their unwavering opposition to abortion in all circumstances, despite the fact that American Catholics were becoming increasingly tolerant of birth control and abortion. In particular, they were upset by the bishops' refusal to modify their adamant opposition to any form of artificial birth control, which many viewed as a means of preventing the need for abortions.

By the dawn of the 1990s, and in the wake of growing charges of pedophilia among Catholic priests, the Catholic Church had lost its ability to dictate the morals of its members. Recall that in 1989 the Catholic bishops of New Jersey had strongly endorsed Operation Rescue. And in 1988 a poll revealed that only 20 percent of Roman Catholics agreed with the church's stand on abortion (Greeley 1990, pp. 98–99). Polls like this one, and the actions of Catholics, did little to deter the church from its absolutist position on abortion.

Despite a clear change in views on morality and abortion in the public at large, and among Catholics more specifically, the Catholic Church stepped up both its internal and external efforts to bring about an end to legalized abortion. In 1990, for example, the NCCB selected Cardinal John O'Connor of New York City to head its Committee on Pro-Life Activities. O'Connor, a prominent conservative, went so far as to hire a well-known New York City public relations firm at a cost of $5 million to promote the pro-life position. Again, many voters—both non-Catholic and Catholic—were appalled by this apparent attempt to intermingle church and state regarding issues of morality.

While the Catholic Church was hardening and publicizing its position on abortion, the National Right-to-Life Committee appeared to waver. It refocused its attention *away* from passage of a Human Life Amendment to prevent all abortions, having recognized that the public, according to polls taken after *Webster*, was not going to buy such a bold reversal of *Roe*. Instead, it turned its energies to drafting model state legislation specifying situations in which abortions could be prohibited by states. These situations included abortion as a means of birth control (a provision that could effectively be used to ban abortions in all cases except those involving rape or incest, fetal abnormality, or pregnancy that posed a threat to the life of the mother) and abortion for sex selection.

The NRLC's model state legislation also required

- that parental or spousal consent or notification be obtained by a woman seeking an abortion;
- that women be given detailed information about the development of the fetus and then wait twenty-four hours before undergoing the procedure; and
- that the performance of abortions be barred in publicly funded hospitals.

Although several states ultimately enacted versions of this model legislation (as discussed below), the NRLC's deemphasis of a total ban on abortions shocked and dismayed the more conservative, far-right wing of the anti-abortion movement. Thus, instead of seeing the NRLC's actions as a first step toward public resolution of the abortion dilemma through compromise, some feared that this effort would derail the movement. Others disgruntled over this change in tactics turned to outright violence, in contrast to the nonviolent forms of protest advocated by Randall Terry and his followers.

During this period, even the activities of Terry and Operation Rescue were coming under increasing public attack. In 1991, during what was called the "Summer of Mercy," Wichita, Kansas, was placed under siege for forty-two days as thousands of pro-life activists converged on the city to blockade its clinics. More than 2,600 "rescuers" were arrested. Although Terry viewed these demonstrations as a success, the reaction they received in the press and among the public was largely negative. The demonstrations cost the city hundreds of thousands of dollars in police overtime, jail, and court costs, and public opinion turned against the participants. A Gallup poll revealed that the "Summer of Mercy" not only failed to change public support for legal abortion but actually generated disapproval among 77 percent of the American public. Even among those who favored the limiting or overruling of *Roe*, 57 percent disapproved of Operation Rescue and its tactics (Hugick 1991, p. 49). A federal judge, Patrick Kelly, eventually issued an injunction ordering Operation Rescue to call off the demonstrations, despite Bush administration efforts to get his order vacated on the grounds that the participants were only exercising their constitutional rights. "Disgusted" by the administration's legal brief, Judge Kelly described the administration's response to his order as "license for mayhem" (Horne 1991, p. 58).

So unpopular was Operation Rescue and the Bush administration's support of it that one GOP pollster said, "Operation Rescue might as well as have been funded by NARAL" (Clift 1991, p. 31). Indeed, in 1991 the Republican Party seemed to be losing the centrist voters it had at the time *Roe* was decided. Bush's close ties to Operation Rescue, though they solidified his support on the right, turned off scores of moderate voters who believed that abortions should be available in a variety of situations.

While the public was voicing disapproval of the "Summer of Mercy" and the Bush administration's actions (only 37 percent of the public had approved of them), other, more radical groups were stepping up their campaign to threaten and intimidate clinics out of existence. As early as 1989, Scheidler's Pro-Life Action League had taken more than four thousand aborted fetuses from a Chicago pathology lab and staged a series of highly publicized "funerals." Meanwhile, splinter groups such as Advocates for Life and Defensive Action were openly encouraging violence, and the number of reported attacks on clinics continued to rise.

In short, by the time the polity began gearing up for the 1992 elections, the right-to-life movement was no longer united in either its goals or its methods of achieving an end to abortion. The Roman Catholic Church had hardened its position, the NRLC had opted to pursue a more politically feasible solution by limiting abortions at the state level, and other groups had stepped up "rescues" and/or the use of violence. This lack of a united front, coupled with well-publicized violence, was to have a negative impact on the right-to-life movement's prospects for legislative success either in a Democratic Congress or with an electorate that was leery of any changes in the wake of *Webster*.

Congressional Politics

Although Republicans had captured the White House in 1988, the House of Representatives and the U.S. Senate remained in the firm control of the Democratic Party. Moreover, many of those Democrats, as well as some liberal Republicans, were pro-choice. Thus, in spite of Bush's threat to veto pro-choice legislation, the Congress—spurred on by the lobbying activities of liberal pro-choice groups, many of whom had been emboldened by their ability to stop Senate confirmation of Judge Bork to the Supreme Court—continued to debate liberalized abortion laws.

The Congress also was not immune to the implications of the election outcomes in 1989 and 1990. There could be little doubt that, for the time being at least, public opinion was on the side of pro-choice forces—a scenario that some members of Congress found encouraging. For example, in 1989 the Senate, in reauthorizing the Hyde Amendment, voted 67 to 31 to allow the use of federal funds to pay for abortions for poor women who had become pregnant as the result of rape or incest. Shortly thereafter, the House of Representatives voted 216 to 206 on the same provision, picking up 50 pro-choice votes from a similar vote a year earlier. Two-thirds of the Republican women voted in favor. This liberalized version of the Hyde Amendment, along with a bill that would fund abortions for poor women in the District of Columbia, was also passed in Congress. Nevertheless, both bills were vetoed by President Bush, and pro-choice supporters were unable to muster enough votes to override those vetoes.

In the meantime, the *Webster* decision and the apparent shifts in the electorate's views on abortion—or, at least, its increased awareness of the issue—prompted one of the more liberal pro-choice supporters in the U.S. Senate, Alan Cranston (D.–Calif.), to introduce the **Freedom of Choice Act (FOCA)** on November 17, 1991. An identical companion bill was introduced in the House by Representative Don Edwards (D.–Calif.). FOCA proposed to prohibit the states from enacting any abortion restrictions before the time of fetal viability or at any time that an abortion was necessary to save the life of the mother. Its supporters argued, as the politicized conservative Court moved farther and farther away from *Roe*, that it was incumbent on the Congress to protect *Roe* through passage of federal legislation.

Executive Politics

Soon after becoming president, George Bush moved to fulfill his commitments to his pro-life supporters. One of his first major appointees was Richard Thornburgh, the former governor of Pennsylvania, who had been the named defendant in *Thornburgh v. American College of Gynecologists and Obstetricians* (1986).

Consistent with his pro-life position, President Bush was ardently opposed to passage of FOCA. Not only did members of his administration speak out against the legality of the proposed law, but Bush himself quickly announced that he would "veto any legislation that weakens current law or existing regulations," just as he had vetoed all four pro-choice bills that had reached his desk in 1989. And even before House subcommittee hearings on the act began, Bush pledged in an address to the Nation of Evangelicals in Chicago that FOCA would "not become law so long as I am president" (Devins 1995a, p. 520). Yet Bush never had the opportunity to fulfill his pledge, because FOCA never actually came to the floor of either the House or the Senate for a vote while Bush was president, thus averting the necessity of a presidential veto.

The Gag Rule. President Bush, however, did instruct his solicitor general, Kenneth Starr, to vigorously defend the gag rule—the Reagan administration's ban on any discussion of abortion in federally funded family planning clinics, even if a woman's life was in danger. Bush's insistence that abortions were wrong under most circumstances made him very popular in the right-to-life community, but his repeated attempts to limit abortions cost him in the moderate center.

In 1990, while judicial challenges to the gag rule were working their way through the judicial system, David Souter was appointed to the Supreme Court by George Bush to replace Louis Powell, one of the original members of the majority in *Roe*. Souter, a federal judge from New Hampshire, was a mystery to many. A quiet, self-effacing bachelor, he led a very private life and had a limited paper trail. Unlike Justice Scalia or Judge Bork, for example, Souter had written no law review articles or delivered any public speeches on controversial issues. Bush's choice of Souter as his first nominee to the Court was viewed by many as an effort to diffuse likely liberal efforts to derail his appointment. During his confirmation hearings, Souter declined to explain his views on abortion to the Senate Judiciary Committee. Fearing that he would soon become the fifth, and deciding, vote to overrule *Roe*, pro-choice forces lobbied hard against Souter's appointment. In spite of Souter's failure to discuss *Roe*, he won easy confirmation from the Senate.

The *Rust v. Sullivan* Backlash. At this point, interest groups were very eager to watch how Souter reacted during oral arguments of his first case involving abortion issues, *Rust v. Sullivan*—a challenge to the constitutionality of the gag rule. Dr. Irving Rust, a physician at a clinic receiving Title X funds now controlled by the gag rule, sued Louis Sullivan, the secretary of the Department of Health and Human Services. (This was the agency that promulgated the restrictive regulations discussed in Chapter 5.) Note that the issuance of rules more restrictive than the original law passed by Congress is an important means by which the president and his administration can affect policy implementation. In this instance, a pro-life president made certain that the regulations to implement the law were drawn to limit the number of abortions performed. Nevertheless, although it could be argued that the gag rule interfered with a woman's ability to exercise all of the rights guaranteed to her under *Roe*, the Bush administration pursued its own policy course, unfazed by the questionable constitutionality of the regulations. And, apparently, rightly so. A federal district court upheld the constitutionality of the regulations, and the Second Circuit U.S. Court of Appeals upheld that decision. By that time, however, several other circuit courts, in which similar challenges had been filed as part of a concerted effort by pro-choice groups to overturn the regulations, had ruled that the regulations implementing Title X were unconstitutional.

Rust then appealed his adverse decision to the U.S. Supreme Court. The Court granted certiorari—at least in part because the case presented an important question of federal law and there was considerable conflict among the federal circuit courts of appeal concerning the constitutionality of the regulations. Again, scores of interested groups filed amicus curiae briefs on both sides of the dispute. Unlike *Webster*, in which the U.S. government had filed an amicus curiae brief, *Rust* involved the U.S. government as a direct party to the case. Moreover, in the first abortion-related case in which Souter participated, he sided with the conservative majority.

In *Rust v. Sullivan* (1991), the Court upheld the constitutionality of the gag rule by a vote of 5 to 4. Despite arguments that the regulation violated not only a poor woman's right to be apprised of her constitutional rights and medical options but also her physician's free speech, the Court also ruled that Title X, as enacted by Congress, was fairly vague concerning Congress's intent to allow or prohibit such funding. Because of this vagueness, said the five-person majority, the lower court should have deferred to the actions of the executive branch in implementing such legislation, as is proper in the scheme of separation of powers intended by the Framers. But in rejecting arguments that the gag rule interfered with free speech rights protected by the First Amendment, Chief Justice Rehnquist, writing for the Court, stated that "Congress has . . . not denied clinics or organizations receiving federal funding the right to engage in abortion-related activities." Instead, Congress, through the executive, simply was not paying for them. Moreover, in responding to pro-choice claims that the Fifth Amendment's due process clause prohibited the federal government from denying women fundamental rights guaranteed by *Roe*, Rehnquist responded: "The difficulty that a woman encounters when a Title X project does not provide abortion counseling or referral leaves her in no different position than she would have been if the government had not enacted Title X."

The Court's decision in *Rust v. Sullivan* outraged many people, including numerous members of Congress, pro-choice activists, and members of the medical community. Groups as diverse as the League of Women Voters and the American College of Gynecologists and Obstetricians launched an all-out legal and media campaign to reverse it. Surprisingly, it was congressional Republicans who led the effort in Congress to minimize the ban on abortion information and counseling. In the House, legislative action to suspend the gag rule as inconsistent with the original intent of Congress won easy passage on a vote of 353 to 74. And in the Senate, a voice vote was taken to avoid public embarrassment of the president (McKeegan 1992, p. 158). But again, President Bush, with "little option but to fulfill his long-standing pledge to veto all pro-choice legislation" (McKeegan 1992, p. 159) vetoed the action—and again, Congress was unable to override his veto.

The Judicial Stakes Get Higher

Again, too, pro-choice activists tried to raise public awareness about the direction in which the Court was going. Soon after *Rust* was announced, on the last day of the 1990–1991 term of the Court, liberal, pro-choice Justice Thurgood Marshall resigned. Soon thereafter, George Bush nominated another African American, Clarence Thomas, the former head of the Equal Employment Opportunity Commission (EEOC), to succeed him. Thomas, unlike Souter, had a lengthy paper trail—and all of it decidedly conservative. In 1986, for example, Thomas had signed off on a White House working paper criticizing *Roe* (McKeegan 1992, p. 140). And in 1987, he had praised a Heritage Foundation report claiming that fetuses had an inalienable right to life (Thomas 1991, p. 17). Despite concerted lobbying by women's rights groups, a low rating of judicial fitness from the American Bar Association, serious charges of sexual harassment, *and* statements to the Senate Judiciary Committee to the effect that he had never before talked about *Roe*, Thomas took his place on the Court after winning narrow Senate confirmation. His appointment gave right-to-lifers an apparent majority on the Court; but in addition, after twelve years of Republican administrations, the lower federal courts, where all federal abortion challenges are first heard, now were largely staffed by Republicans who had been selected, at least in part, for their pro-life views.

In the wake of Thomas's confirmation, in keeping with their strategies announced earlier, pro-choice groups opted to raise the political stakes. At a joint press conference, the heads of Planned Parenthood, NARAL, and the ACLU, along with Kathryn Kolbert, who was set to argue against the constitutionality of Pennsylvania's Abortion Control Act before the Supreme Court, decided to intensify the abortion debate *before* the 1992 elections—specifically, by asking the Court either to reaffirm that abortion was a **fundamental right** (i.e., one that required a compelling reason to justify state infringement) or to overrule *Roe* if this was what it intended to do. As Faye Wattleton of Planned Parenthood explained,

> Even if [the Court's ruling] does not come before the election, it will still be a major issue in this election. This is not whether it's better for us politically, but what is better for women. We will not permit the courts to have the last word ever again, and we will show our strength in the polls because we simply will not go back. (Berke 1991)

Given the makeup of the Court, which now appeared to be dominated by conservative Reagan/Bush appointees, pro-choice groups saw little hope of winning liberal decisions from it.

Abortion and the States

The states and right-to-life groups were quick to pick up on the ambiguity of the Court's decision in *Webster*. Pennsylvania was one of their big successes. In 1989, its governor, Robert Casey, a pro-life Democrat, signed into law a sweeping set of abortion restrictions entitled the Abortion Control Act. Consistent with the model NRLC legislation, it included the following measures:

1. Compulsory anti-abortion lectures by doctors
2. A twenty-four-hour delay in obtaining an abortion after the lecture
3. Reporting requirements that potentially could subject providers to increased harassment
4. Spousal notification
5. More stringent parental consent rules requiring parents to come to a clinic with the minor or, in lieu of parental permission, requiring the minor to obtain judicial approval from a judge

These restrictions were immediately challenged by Planned Parenthood, which, by the time the case came to the U.S. Supreme Court, was being supported by 178 organizations including the Women's Legal Defense Fund, NOW, NARAL, the YWCA, the National Women's Health Network, the Federation of Feminist Women's Health Centers, and the National Women's Political Caucus. Supporting the state in *Planned Parenthood of Southeastern Pennsylvania v. Casey* (1992), as the challenge to the Pennsylvania law had come to be known, was the Bush administration, which again urged the Court to overrule *Roe*. Joining the U.S. government in support of Robert Casey were groups including Feminists for Life, the U.S. Catholic Conference, and the National Right-to-Life Committee.

Given the close nature of *Webster* and *Rust*, as well as Bush's appointment of two new judges, many Supreme Court watchers expected that the Court would use *Casey* to overturn *Roe*. In addition to filing briefs, women's groups sponsored the March for Women's Lives on April 5, 1991. Drawing between 500,000 and 700,000 marchers, it was the largest pro-choice march ever, and it was designed to draw more public and media attention to the issue.

Nearly four months after oral arguments, and as tensions on both sides mounted, a slim majority of the Court reaffirmed *Roe*'s "central holding." This majority stipulated that it would not permit states to enact any laws that "unduly burden" access to abortion or to ban abortions altogether in the early stages of pregnancy. Still, making sense of the 184-page decision was difficult. In a move that surprised many, Justices O'Connor, Kennedy, and Souter announced a joint opinion that, although it upheld a woman's right to an abortion, gave the states even greater leeway than *Webster* to limit abortions. The O'Connor-Kennedy-Souter plurality opinion rejected *Roe*'s trimester approach to balancing the interests of women and the state. It also overturned portions of several other abortion rights cases that had struck down informed consent, parental consent, and abortion counseling requirements. But most important, the plurality opinion (actually, seven justices including Clarence Thomas) rejected the idea that a woman's right to an abortion was a fundamental right. Four justices—Rehnquist, White, Scalia, and Thomas—said they would overrule *Roe;* however, they were unable to muster that fifth, key vote to give their position a majority. Thus, the opinion of O'Connor, Kennedy (who had sided with Rehnquist and White in *Webster*), and Souter—an opinion that redefined the "central principle" of *Roe* and replaced it with a lesser standard, the undue burden standard—became the opinion of the Court (because two other justices, Stevens and Blackmun, agreed that *Roe* should not be overruled). According to the three-justice plurality, states could enact abortion restrictions so long as they did not place an undue burden on a woman's right to an abortion. In *Casey*, none of the state's impediments to abortion noted above, except one requiring spousal consent, was deemed an undue burden.

As with *Webster*, the division on the Court in *Casey* closely paralleled the lack of firm agreement about abortion rights in the polity. As shown in Table 6.2, Gallup polls conducted on the evening following announcement of the decision revealed that fewer than 15 percent of the public believed that abortion should always be illegal, about half thought that abortion should be legal only "under some circumstances," and one-third responded that abortion should "always be legal" (Newport and McAneny 1992).

Casey meant "full employment for reproductive lawyers," said Kathryn Kolbert, inasmuch as it pushed the abortion debate back to the states. Said one National Right-to-Life official, "We're back to where we were in the 1970s and 1980s, testing limits of what the Court will allow" (Marcus 1992). Groups on both sides of the issue again attempted to use the decision as a wake-up call to mobilize their troops. For example, NOW, which claimed that *Roe* was hanging on by only a slim thread, was able to bolster membership renewals and attract new members. On the other side, Randall Terry told his followers that they needed to step up their "rescue" efforts, since *Roe* was still good law. In short, groups on both sides of the issue again tried to put their own spin on the outcome of a Supreme Court case. As one Democratic strategist noted, "Very few Americans will actually read the decision, so we are now in a definitional battle of how people will view [it]"

TABLE 6.2

Gallup Poll After Webster

1. *Do you approve or disapprove of this week's Supreme Court decision allowing states to pass laws that restrict abortion? Do you feel strongly about this or not?*

Approve: 37%	Disapprove: 55%
Strongly: 28%	Strongly: 44%
Not strongly: 9%	Not strongly: 11%
Don't know: 0%	Don't know: 8%

2. *As I read some restrictions on abortions that are being considered in some states, tell me if you would favor or oppose such a restriction in your state.*

   a. *Not allowing abortions to be performed in a public hospital unless the abortion is required to save a woman's life.*

   Favor: 54%
   Oppose: 43%
   Don't know: 3%

   b. *In cases where the mother is five months pregnant, requiring a test to see if the fetus might survive outside of the womb before allowing the abortion.*

   Favor: 52%
   Oppose: 41%
   Don't know: 7%

   c. *Requiring that women under 18 years of age get parental consent before they are allowed to have an abortion.*

   Favor: 67%
   Oppose: 29%
   Don't know: 4%

3. *Do you feel that it is likely or unlikely that laws will be passed in your state that will make it difficult for a woman to get an abortion?*

   Likely: 54%
   Unlikely: 36%
   Don't know: 10%

4. *Which political party better reflects your views on abortion—the Republicans or the Democrats?*

Party	*Total*	*Republican Respondent*	*Democratic Respondent*	*Independent Respondent*
Republicans	34%	66%	13%	24%
Democrats	37	16	63	31
Neither (answer was volunteered)	8	4	3	16
Both (answer was volunteered)	1	1	2	2
Don't know	20	13	19	27

Source: *Gallup Poll News Service*, vol. 54, no. 10a, Wednesday, July 12, 1989.

(Ciolli 1992, p. 4). In the upcoming 1992 state and national elections, this fight over the public agenda would be reflected in attempts by both sides to shape the abortion issue in furtherance of their own cause.

The 1992 Presidential Campaign

Casey was decided on June 29, 1992, just as the presidential campaign was heating up. Many commentators believed that the Court's decision not to overturn *Roe* would help President Bush. But according to several polls, although abortion would eventually be a key to understanding the 1992 elections, George Bush was not the candidate to profit from public opinion on the issue.

Conservative Right-to-Life Groups Mobilize

Pat Robertson's Christian Coalition did not take long to move into the void created by the demise of the Moral Majority. In fact, the CC was able to build upon already mobilized voters—namely, Robertson's *700 Club* viewers, as well as those who had supported his unsuccessful bid for the Republican Party's presidential nomination in 1988. But unlike the Moral Majority, the CC had much more ambitious political goals. In addition to targeting 1992 as "the year of pro-family values," it focused attention on grassroots politics and prepared to launch a slate of candidates in local elections across the United States. In particular, it "relentlessly registered churchgoers, canvassed 'pro-family' voters, [and] prepared campaign literature, . . . striving to mobilize a bloc of 20 million 'pro-family' voters . . . to effect every election" (Conason 1992, p. 541). Included in its mantra, of course, was a call to end abortion and teenager access to contraceptives.

The Christian Coalition's ability to mobilize concerned citizens to run for school boards, town and city councils, and even higher office shocked many as it quickly became a potent political force in many areas of the country. Unlike Scheidler's Pro-Life Action League, Randall Terry's Operation Rescue, and other more radical groups including the Lambs of Christ (which was founded by Operation Rescue members who were upset that OR refused to adopt a philosophy that accepted the violence at clinics as justified), the Christian Coalition was geared toward conventional political action. Yet unlike the Moral Majority, which was heavily focused toward the media, the CC preferred to avoid headlines. Indeed, according to its director, Ralph Reed, Jr., it tried to "fly below radar." Nevertheless, it spent around $10 million to influence the outcome of the 1992 elections (Conason 1992). Included in this total was the cost of distributing an unprecedented 40 million copies of the CC's "Family Values Voter Guide" in more than 100,000 churches the weekend before the elections (Moriwaki 1992).

Around the same time, Roman Catholics were also mobilizing formally in an effort to influence the outcome of the 1992 elections at any level where abortion was or could be an issue. In 1991, for example, the Catholic Campaign for America was launched. Headed by Mary Ellen Bork (the ex-nun wife of former U.S. Supreme Court nominee Robert Bork), conservative commentator Pat Buchanan, former Secretary of Education William Bennett, and the head of the Stop ERA movement, Phyllis Schlafly, the campaign attempted "to activate Catholic citizens, including the Catholic electorates' influence in family policy, and focus the public's attention on the richness and beauty of Catholic teaching," which itself, of course, included staunch opposition to abortion in all circumstances (*Church & State* 1991, p. 16). This effort—coupled with the NCCB's public relations efforts, which had begun a year earlier—was aimed at mobilizing Roman Catholic voters in time for the 1992 elections and at countering the NRLC's new approach to the abortion issue. Catholics were very perturbed over the fact that a group they had founded was now willing to compromise on abortion in some situations. Catholic leaders wanted the electorate to conclude that *any* form of abortion under *any* circumstance was immoral and should be illegal.

The Arthur DeMoss Foundation was another conservative group to add its voice to the anti-abortion chorus. With ties to conservative Senator Jesse Helms (R.–N.C.) and the Reverend Jerry Falwell, it began a nationwide television campaign—called "Life, What a Beautiful Choice"—in an effort to neutralize negative publicity about the pro-life position. The "Life" campaign was also designed to change the way the reproductive freedom issue was being discussed and formulated on the public agenda.

The Republican Party. The Republican Party's 1992 national convention was a well-orchestrated salute to the family and family values. Former Nixon aide-turned-political commentator Pat Buchanan, a Christian Coalition favorite, addressed the convention during prime-time television viewing hours and underscored the need for the party to be at the forefront of the family values campaign. The Christian Coalition had done its homework. Hundreds of its supporters were present at the convention as delegates who wildly cheered Buchanan. Although most CC members preferred Buchanan, the organization eventually, and enthusiastically, supported President Bush.

The Christian Coalition's strength on the convention floor allowed it to weigh in on the way abortion was being treated in the party platform, despite pleas from several pro-choice Republicans. Thus, it was not surprising that the 1992 Republican

Party platform contained a plank supporting a constitutional amendment to ban abortions except in cases where a mother's life was in danger. In that regard, the Republican platform went even further than the views of George Bush, who believed that exceptions for rape and incest should be allowed. Moreover, the party platform was the most conservative one in history, inasmuch as it accused the Democrats of "waging a guerrilla war against American values."

The Democratic Party. During the 1992 Democratic convention, as in 1988, local clinics and abortion providers were picketed by Operation Rescue and Lambs of Christ. But this time, pro-choice activists were prepared. NOW, the Fund for a Feminist Majority, and Planned Parenthood turned out their members in far greater numbers than before to provide escorts for those seeking abortions—again drawing attention to the imminent threat to the exercise of abortion rights.

Pro-choice groups, moreover, were quick to see the potential of electing a Democratic president to halt another four years of President Bush's staunchly pro-life rhetoric and actions. In 1992, all of the candidates for the Democratic Party's nomination were pro-choice, although they varied somewhat concerning their support of federal funding for abortions and/or parental consent. Pro-choice Bill Clinton, however, secured enough votes prior to the convention to ensure his nomination, and he selected the pro-choice Senator Al Gore, Jr. (D.–Tenn.) as his running mate. Clinton and Gore carefully orchestrated the 1992 convention, and Clinton supporters went so far as to deny pro-life Pennsylvania Governor Robert Casey the opportunity to address the convention and present an anti-abortion point of view. The Democrats perceived the pro-choice position as the one to have and were not about to allow the nation to detect any cracks in the party's unified front for abortion rights. Thus, the Democratic Party platform called for strict adherence both to the standards originally set out in *Roe v. Wade* and to support for public funding of abortions in far greater detail than that specified in its 1988 platform. (See Box 6.2 for a comparison of the Republican and Democratic Party platforms.)

The Election of Bill Clinton

Throughout the 1992 presidential campaign, "It's the Economy, Stupid" became the public war cry of the Democratic Party. Yet the abortion issue was probably the deciding factor in the 1992 presidential election. Fewer than 1 percent of those polled in the 1992 American National Election Study, for example, were unable or unwilling to offer an opinion on abortion (Abramowitz 1993, p. 3). Abortion had

BOX 6.2

The 1992 Party Platforms Compared

Republican Party Platform

We believe that the unborn child has a fundamental independent right to life that cannot be infringed. We therefore reaffirm our support for a human life amendment to the Constitution, and we endorse legislation to make clear the Fourteenth Amendment's protections apply to unborn children. We oppose using public revenues for abortion and will not fund organizations that advocate it. We commend those who provide alternatives to abortion by meeting the needs of mothers and offering adoption services. We reaffirm our support for appointment of judges who respect traditional family values and the sanctity of human life.

Democratic Party Platform

Choice. Democrats stand behind the right of every woman to choose, consistent with *Roe v. Wade*, regardless of ability to pay, and support a national law to protect that right. It is a fundamental constitutional liberty that individual Americans—not Government—can best take responsibility for making the most difficult and intensely personal decisions regarding reproduction. The goal of our nation must be to make abortion less necessary, not more difficult or more dangerous. We pledge to support contraceptive research, family planning, comprehensive family life education, and policies that support healthy child-bearing and enable parents to care most effectively for their children.

gone from being a nonissue in the 1972 election to one about which nearly all of the polity could voice an opinion. By a margin of 44 to 33 percent, according to a CNN poll, abortion was a deciding issue in how prospective voters would vote—and indeed, most of those polled believed that the Democrats were doing a better job at handling abortion than the Republicans. It is interesting to recall that Bill Clinton spoke out immediately after *Casey,* criticizing the decision and noting that "only a president committed to maintaining the present law can maintain the constitutional right to choose" (Clinton 1992). On numerous occasions he sought to differentiate his position from that of George Bush, who advocated "adoption not abortion" at every opportunity.

Abortion as a Factor in the Election

The 1992 National Election Study contained a single question about legalized abortion. It asked respondents to select one of four abortion policy alternatives, which ranged from least to most restrictive, and then to state their perceptions of the two major candidates' positions on abortion, using the same four policy options. As shown in Table 6.3, nearly half of those polled opposed any restrictions on abortion. Clearly, then, very few voters agreed with the Republican Party platform concerning abortion. Consistent with studies of the post-*Webster* elections in 1989 (e.g., Cook, Jelen, and Wilcox 1994) that concluded that abortion had been a key factor in those elections, abortion significantly influenced the way many individuals cast their votes in the 1992 presidential and congressional elections. Indeed, as one political scientist noted:

> Approximately one-fourth of all major party voters were aware of the candidates' positions on abortion and mentioned abortion at least once in response to open-ended questions dealing with national problems, party differences, and likes and dislikes about the parties and candidates. Among this subset of "aware and concerned" voters, *abortion had a much stronger influence on candidate choice than any other issue, including the state of the economy.* (Abramowitz 1993, p. 7; emphasis added)

A Pro-Choice President

The election of Bill Clinton in 1992, coupled with a large number of new female pro-choice national and state legislators, sharply altered the abortion horizon.

TABLE 6.3

Public Opinion on Abortion, 1992

Policy	*Percentage of Respondents in Agreement*
1. **Abortion** should never be allowed.	10
2. **Abortion** should be allowed only in cases of rape, incest, or to save the life of the mother.	29
3. **Abortion** should be allowed as long as a clear need exists	14
4. **Abortion** should not be restricted because it is a woman's choice.	47

Source: 1992 National Election Study.

Just two days after his inauguration, on the eve of the twentieth anniversary of *Roe v. Wade*, Clinton—cognizant of the debt he owed his pro-choice supporters—issued several **executive orders** overturning five restrictions on abortion that had been instituted during various Republican administrations. The first of these repealed the Reagan/Bush gag rule on abortion counseling, which had been declared constitutional by the Supreme Court in *Rust v. Sullivan* (1991).

The second executive order lifted the ban on fetal tissue research by federally funded researchers. Instituted by President Reagan, this ban was supported by President Bush, who vetoed a 1992 bill that would have lifted the prohibition. In removing the ban, Clinton said that it had "significantly hampered the development of possible treatments for individuals afflicted with serious disease and disorders, such as Parkinson's disease, Alzheimer's disease, diabetes and leukemia" (Toner 1993, p. 1).

The third executive order directed the secretary of Health and Human Services to review the ban on importation of **RU-486,** the so-called abortion drug. The fourth executive order lifted the ban on abortions in overseas military hospitals, which had been an issue since the days of the Republican Nixon administration. In 1992, President Bush had effectively blocked an effort by the Democratic Congress to repeal the ban; now, abortions were to be allowed so long as they were not paid for by federal funds.

The fifth executive order changed a controversial Reagan/Bush policy, often called the Mexico City policy, that barred U.S. aid to any international family programs that included abortion counseling. The swift announcement of these dramatic changes in executive abortion policy, after twelve years of Republican administrations pledged to do their utmost to end abortions, sent shock waves through the right-to-life movement. So did Clinton's support of abortion services in his proposals for national health care and his quick appointment of two pro-choice justices, Stephen G. Breyer and Ruth Bader Ginsburg, to the U.S. Supreme Court. In fact, Clinton said that he settled on Ginsburg only "after becoming convinced that she was clearly pro-choice" (Devins 1995a, p. xxiv). Thus, for the first time since *Roe v. Wade* was decided by the Court, a pro-choice president with a pro-choice agenda sat in the White House.

Conclusion

By 1992, and the election of Bill Clinton, the abortion issue had come full circle. From the time of Ronald Reagan's election in 1980 until George Bush's defeat in 1992, pro-life conservatives controlled the White House and the rule-making machinery of the executive branch. George Bush, whom conservatives initially had a difficult time trusting fully, attempted to win their support by courting the right-to-life movement and doing everything in his power to ensure that his administration advanced the pro-life position. Moreover, he used his executive and judicial appointments to promote the pro-life agenda both through rule making and in the courts, often urging the Supreme Court to overrule *Roe v. Wade.*

The 1988 presidential campaign had presented the American public with a clear choice about abortion, but few seemed to be listening as the economy took priority. And although Operation Rescue and other, more radical anti-abortion groups stepped up their activities during the campaign season, few seemed to translate their disapproval of these tactics into votes for the Democratic nominee. Shortly after Bush's victory, however, the Reagan/Bush administration filed an amicus curiae brief with the U.S. Supreme Court, asking the Court to overrule *Roe.* Whereas that action was greeted warmly by pro-life activists, it served to galvanize women's and reproductive rights activists who were still angered over the results of the November elections. Anger also seemed to permeate the public, who for the first time appeared to realize that abortion rights were indeed in peril—this time, in the form of a possibly adverse decision in *Webster v. Reproductive Health Services* (1989).

As it turned out, the Court in deciding *Webster* came within a single vote of overturning *Roe,* triggering extensive pro-choice activity such as mass media campaigns, lobbying, and work for pro-choice candidates at all levels—a series of moves necessitated by *Webster*'s clear invitation to the states to enact new abortion restrictions. At the same time, some pro-life activists became frustrated by the slow pace of traditional forms of political activity and stepped up a range of tactics designed to prevent women from securing abortions. The resulting friction culminated in the 1992 elections, which brought a pro-choice president to the White House and added a record number of pro-choice women to the U.S. Senate. Thus, by 1993, liberals believed that they were poised on the brink of codifying *Roe* through passage of a federal statute free from the threat of a presidential veto and with women's reproductive rights ensured by a chief executive committed to appointing pro-choice judges to the federal courts.

The abortion problem as defined by liberals appeared close to being resolved. But liberals underestimated the power of the newly reenergized right, especially that of Pat Robertson's Christian Coalition. As they would soon discover, the CC was a sleeping giant ready and able to turn the public's anger at the federal government to its own purposes.

The up-and-down nature of the abortion issue as it unfolded from George Bush's election to that of Bill Clinton is illustrative of the near impossibility of stable public policymaking in an issue area fraught with emotion. Certainly the two major political parties have held sharply divergent views about how to resolve the abortion dilemma, and each has done its best to move policy in a direction favorable to it.

Interestingly, the political system has worked in the sense that the two political parties have stood for clear alternative policies. Yet few Americans have embraced the absolutist positions of either party. In an era of fifteen-second soundbite campaigning, compromise positions are perhaps too difficult for candidates to articulate. For example, a candidate who expresses support for abortion but includes a laundry list of caveats risks being labeled "anti-choice" by abortion rights advocates. And similarly, a candidate who morally opposes abortion but sees a need for it as an option in one, two, or even five circumstances risks being labeled "pro-choice" by right-to-life advocates. In short, interest groups on both sides of the issue have forced candidates from the two major political parties to adopt *extreme* positions to avoid being labeled as anything less than supporting or opposing abortion. For this reason, the public's attitudes about abortion have not been easily captured in the electoral process and are unlikely to be so in the near future.

It is not surprising that the courts have played such a central role in defining and redefining abortion policies. When Democrats controlled Congress they were unable to get much pro-choice legislation passed; and when they did, George Bush vetoed it. Likewise, efforts of the Republican-controlled Congress to restrict abortion were vetoed by Bill Clinton. This inability to reach compromise in the legislative and executive branches has forced the courts to fill the void, notwithstanding Ruth Bader Ginsburg's lament that "traditional legislative efforts" would have avoided the "prolonged divisiveness" of the abortion issue (Ginsburg 1992, pp. 1185, 1208). In all likelihood, then, the stalemate between Congress and the president over abortion will not be remedied unless and until one political party controls both branches of government.

Recall that George Bush was unable to move resolution of the abortion issue as far as he would have liked because he was eventually ousted from office—a defeat that some political scientists would attribute to his drastic stand on abortion. Thus, it could be argued that the system does indeed work, but that stable policy-making, in some issue areas, is quite difficult, if not altogether impossible.

7

The Clinton Years and Beyond: From Abortion Politics to Abortion Policy

I am sitting here behind my desk, looking out a bullet-proof window. I work in four layers of bullet-proof windows. Death threats are so common they are not remarkable. I went to a pro-choice meeting in Denver recently, and as I walked through the picket line, someone said, "You should die."

—Dr. Warren Hern, medical director of the Boulder Abortion Clinic (quoted in Barringer 1993)

I think, frankly, there has been a philosophical or even moral groundwork laid for assassinating abortionists by certain people in the pro-life movement, and I think they bear some of the blame. . . . You don't win a moral war through force or coercion or intimidation. You win through reason.

—Bill Price, president of Texans United for Life (quoted in Barringer 1993)

ROE V. *WADE* HAD AN INCREDIBLE EFFECT on women's lives. By removing the fear of pregnancy, it changed forever not only the status of women in American society but also the landscape of American politics. Abortion wasn't even on the political radar screen prior to *Roe*, but it soon became a litmus test for candidates seeking office at all levels of government. Said Richard Vigurie, the conservative direct-mail genius, "[A]bortion changed politics forever—Republicans as well as Democrats"—and indeed, each party struggled to come to some consensus on the issue. Moreover, it changed the "look" of each party in a way that the Court or policymakers could never have envisioned, as *Roe* moved social issues to the heart of the Republican Party and feminism to the heart of the Democratic Party (von Drehle 1994). *Roe* also drew organized religion into the political fray, to a greater extent than any other issue before: Evangelical Christians, Roman Catholics, and Orthodox Jews—groups as diverse as these were brought together in their opposition to abortion.

The 1992 election of Bill Clinton, the first truly pro-choice president since abortion leaped onto the public agenda, indisputably put abortion on what political scientists call the **institutional agenda**. Clinton targeted a series of specific policies, including the gag rule and the ban on RU-486, for change. He also nominated Dr. Jocelyn Elders, a strong proponent of *Roe v. Wade*, to be the U.S. surgeon general, further trumpeting a change in administrative policy.

These actions threw right-to-life forces into turmoil and highlighted the dilemma that continued to vex the polity: How can policy be made in an issue area where there is so little consensus around a single middle ground and very strong feelings on the extremes? The flurry that arose in September 1995, when former General Colin Powell announced during a Barbara Walters interview that he was pro-choice, illustrates how this dilemma affects politics at every level. Prior to Powell's announcement, many Republicans were hoping that Powell would seek their party's endorsement. Yet a single comment, "I'm pro-choice," jeopardized his hopes of the Republican nomination and brought legions of protesters out to picket each of his book signings. Remember, Powell at the time was not an announced candidate for president but, rather, a private citizen promoting a new book. The mere specter of a pro-choice Powell candidacy, however, was enough to bring out Operation Rescue members and other protestors in full force.

The Search for a Neutral Ground Continues

Abortion, and its treatment in the polity, has effectively evidenced the full range of the policy cycle. Having bounded onto the agenda in *Roe v. Wade* in 1973, it was then implemented through a variety of state, congressional, executive, and judicial actions. At each stage of the process, the issue was repeatedly defined and redefined by interest groups, the media, and policymakers in the continued search for a neutral ground on which to resolve the conflict. In many ways, the badly divided U.S. Supreme Court decision in *Planned Parenthood of Southeastern Pennsylvania v. Casey* (1992) came the closest of any case to mirroring the general attitudes of the polity about abortion and providing some basis for a neutral, or common, ground. But the Court's "solution" to the abortion dilemma—allowing states to restrict but not ban all abortions—failed to satisfy those on the radical right of the pro-life movement. In fact, *Casey*, when coupled with the National Right-to-Life Committee's apparent willingness to compromise on legislation so as to reduce the number of abortions, the election of Bill Clinton in November 1992, and Clinton's immediate action to liberalize federal policies concerning abortion, appeared to trigger renewed violence on the right.

Violence on the Right

"So close, yet so far away"—such was the general sentiment of those in the right-to-life movement by 1993. "It's amazing," said Walter Webster of the anti-abortion American Center for Law and Justice. "It took us 20 years to get to the brink of where we thought *Roe v. Wade* would be overturned. But it only took a year for everyone to realize that nothing like this is going to happen" (Zremski 1994). In the wake of *Casey*, many in the right-to-life movement stepped up their efforts to convince the states to enact new abortion restrictions, using traditional, well-established lobbying tools, as evidenced by the variety of abortion restrictions listed in Table 7.1. Others, however, leveled increased hostility, harassment, and violence at abortion clinics, providers, and clients, as shown in Table 7.2. Some pundits, moreover, attributed this rise in violence to Clinton's election, a conclusion supported by the "key dates concerning clinic violence" in Table 7.3. As one NARAL official surmised, "opponents haven't won in the political system, so they're apparently determined to shoot, stalk and murder their way to their goal" (Beck 1994, p. 34).

Litigating to Stop the Violence

Pro-choice groups, initially caught off guard by clinic violence, were at a loss for a response. They understood the rules of the conventional political game but had no clear plan for ending or even limiting the violence, which was beginning to take its toll on women's ability to procure abortions. By the end of the Reagan years, although 84 percent of all obstetricians and gynecologists believed that "abortion should be legal and available," only one-third of those who approved of abortions were performing them—and two-thirds of those said that they had performed only a few (Blanchard 1994, p. 66). More and more physicians were opting not to perform abortions at all, and fewer and fewer medical schools were even training medical students in the procedure. It would have been a hollow victory, indeed, if pro-choice activists were able to stop *Roe v. Wade* from being overruled but unable to provide abortions because physicians were too intimidated to perform them. After careful thought, then, and in reaction to the Reagan administration's initial refusal to investigate clinic violence, the National Organization for Women (NOW) decided to seek legal **injunctions** against groups that were attempting to interfere with the daily routine of abortion clinics.

NOW v. Scheidler. As early as 1986, following an upsurge of clinic violence, the National Organization for Women filed suit on behalf of two clinic owners seeking injunctive relief against Joseph Scheidler's Pro-Life Action League (PLAL) and several other militant pro-life groups. NOW argued that activities directed at clinics were part of a massive conspiracy to drive abortion clinics out of business. After a series of legal maneuverings, which included one court's actual dismissal of the lawsuit, NOW petitioned the Supreme Court to reinstate the case against Scheidler and four other "rescue"/protest organizations. The Court agreed to hear the case, and *National Organization for Women (NOW) v. Scheidler* (1994) was slated for oral argument.

Scheidler is a perfect example of how interest groups can be forced into "creative" lawyering to stop practices that they find objectionable but for which no clear statutory remedy exists. For example, it was in this case that NOW attempted to curtail anti-choice activity by alleging that the Racketeer Influenced and Corrupt Organizations Act (RICO), initially enacted by Congress as a prosecutorial tool against mob activity and organized crime, could be applied to anti-choice violence even though the perpetrators were not necessarily trying to interfere with business practices for economic gain.

The litigation before the Court drew an unusual set of allies for the pro-life movement. Arguing before the Court on behalf of Scheidler on December 8,

TABLE 7.1

A State-by-State Review of State Abortion Laws, 1994

	Abortion Specific					
State	*Parental Consent Required*	*Mandatory Waiting Periods (*If Less than 24 Hours)*	*Clinic Violence and Harassment Barred by Law*	*Minor's Access Restricted by Law*	*Public Funding of Indigents' Abortions Prohibited*	*Abortions in Public Facilities or by Public Employees Barred by Law*
Alabama	X			X		
Alaska				X	X	
Arizona				X		
Arkansas	X			X		
California	X		X	X	X	
Colorado			X	X		
Connecticut	X				X	
Delaware	X	X				
District of Columbia						
Florida	X			X		
Georgia				X		
Hawaii					X	
Idaho	X	X		X	X	
Illinois	X			X		
Indiana	X	X		X		
Iowa						
Kansas	X	X*	X	X		
Kentucky	X	X*		X		X
Louisiana	X			X		X
Maine	X			X		

Maryland			X	X		
Massachusetts	X	X	X	X	X	
Michigan	X	X		X		
Minnesota	X		X	X	X	
Mississippi	X	X		X		
Missouri	X			X		X
Montana	X			X		
Nebraska	X	X		X		
Nevada	X		X	X		
New Hampshire						
New Jersey					X	
New Mexico				X		
New York				X		
North Carolina			X		X	
North Dakota	X	X		X		X
Ohio	X	X		X		
Oklahoma						
Oregon			X		X	
Pennsylvania	X	X		X		X
Rhode Island	X			X		
South Carolina				X		
South Dakota	X	X		X		
Tennessee	X	X		X		
Texas	X					
Utah	X	X		X		
Vermont						
Virginia	X				X	
Washington			X		X	
West Virginia				X	X	
Wisconsin	X		X	X		
Wyoming				X		

TABLE 7.2

Growing Clinic Violence

Number of Incidents

Violence	*1977–83*	*1984*	*1985*	*1986*	*1987*	*1988*	*1989*	*1990*	*1991*[a]	*1992*	*1993*	*1994*	*1995*	*Total*
Murder	0	0	0	0	0	0	0	0	0	0	1	4	0	5
Attempted Murder	0	0	0	0	0	0	0	0	2	0	1	8	0	11
Bombing	8	18	4	2	0	0	2	0	1	1	1	3	0	40
Arson	15	6	8	7	4	4	6	4	10	16	9	5	8	100
Attempted Bomb/Arson	5	6	10	5	8	3	2	4	1	13	7	4	0	68
Invasion	68	34	47	53	14	6	25	19	29	26	24	2	1	348
Vandalism	35	35	49	43	29	29	24	26	44	116	113	42	17	602
Assault & Battery	11	7	7	11	5	5	12	6	6	9	9	7	1	96
Death Threats	4	23	22	7	5	4	5	7	3	8	78	59	20	245
Kidnapping	2	0	0	0	0	0	0	0	0	0	0	0	0	2
Burglary	3	2	2	5	7	1	0	2	1	5	3	3	3	37
Stalking[b]	0	0	0	0	0	0	0	0	0	0	188	22	16	226
TOTAL	149	131	149	133	72	52	76	70	95	194	434	159	66	1,780

Disruption														
Hate Mail & Phone Calls	9	17	32	53	32	19	30	21	142	469	628	381	113	1,936
Bomb Threats	9	32	75	51	28	21	21	11	15	12	22	14	26	333
Picketing	107	160	139	141	77	151	72	45	292	2,898	2,279	1,407	315	8,027
TOTAL	125	209	246	245	137	191	123	77	449	3,379	2,929	1,802	461	10,393
Clinic Blockades														
No Incidents	0	0	0	0	2	182	201	34	41	83	66	25	4	638
No Arrests[c]	0	0	0	0	290	11,732	12,358	1,363	3,885	2,580	1,236	217	52	33,717

Notes:

[a]Numbers represent incidents reported to NAF as of 7/01/95; actual incidents are most likely higher [in number].

[b]Stalking is defined as the persistent following, threatening, and harassing of an abortion provider, staff member, or patient *away from* the clinic. Especially severe stalking incidents are noted on NAF Incidents of Extreme Violence fact sheet. Tabulation of stalking incidents began in 1993.

[c]The "number of arrests" represents the total number of arrests, not the total number of *persons* arrested. Many blockaders are arrested multiple times.

Source: National Abortion Federation, *Incidents of Violence & Disruption Against Abortion Providers. News release, July 1995.*

TABLE 7.3

Key Dates Concerning Clinic Violence After Clinton's Election

January 13, 1993	U.S. Supreme Court rules that abortion protests cannot be deterred through application of the KKK Act (*Bray v. Alexandria Women's Health Clinic*).
March 10, 1993	Dr. David Gunn killed in Pensacola, Florida.
March 1993	FACE introduced in both houses of Congress.
August 19, 1993	Dr. George Tiller shot in Wichita, Kansas.
September 29, 1993	PP clinic torched in Lancaster, Pennsylvania.
October 1993	Ruth Bader Ginsburg joins Supreme Court.
December 21, 1993	Physician and escort killed in Pensacola, Florida.
January 24, 1994	RICO Act can be applied to limit protest activity (*NOW v. Scheidler*).
May 5, 1994	House passes FACE 241–174.
May 13, 1994	Senate passes FACE 69–30.
May 1994	Bill Clinton signs FACE into law.
June 30, 1994	U.S. Supreme Court upholds buffer zone around clinics (*Madsen v. Women's Health Center).*
July 1994	Women's clinic firebombed in Falls Church, Virginia.
August 10, 1994	PP clinic firebombed in Brookline, Massachusetts.
December 30, 1994	Two receptionists killed and five people injured in shootings at two Brookline clinics.
December 31, 1994	Twenty-three bullets fired into a clinic in Norfolk, Virginia.
January 1995	American Coalition of Life Activists targets "Dirty Dozen" abortion providers/physicians.
March 1996	U.S. Supreme Court agrees to hear clinic protest case involving a 15-foot buffer zone.
June 19, 1995	U.S. Supreme Court refuses to hear challenge to constitutionality of FACE.
October 3, 1995	U.S. Supreme Court upholds constitutionality of FACE.

1993, for example, was Jay Sekulow. As general counsel of the American Center for Law and Justice, the legal arm of the Christian Coalition, Sekulow routinely appears on the Trinity Broadcast Network (Diamond 1994). He was assisted by Notre Dame law school professor Robert Blakey, the author of RICO, who argued that the law was never intended to regulate this kind of noneconomically motivated behavior. Both Sekulow and Blakey were supported by amicus curiae briefs from People for the Ethical Treatment of Animals (PETA) and the radical environmental group, Earth First! These normally very left-leaning friends of the Court argued that an adverse decision would violate the constitutional rights of protest groups that rely on unconventional tactics to achieve or draw attention to their goals. PETA, for example, believes that its actions to protest animal cruelty, which range from illegal release of laboratory animals to save them from experimentation to break-ins at furriers, could possibly be prosecuted under RICO.

Bray v. Alexandria Women's Health Clinic. *Scheidler*'s arrival at the Supreme Court on appeal could not have been more auspicious for NOW. Just one year earlier, President Clinton had been able to appoint a pro-choice justice, Ruth Bader Ginsburg, to replace Justice Byron White, one of the original dissenters in *Roe.* Only days before Clinton was sworn into office, however, the Court had shocked pro-choice activists with its decision in *Bray v. Alexandria Women's Health Clinic* (1993), which appeared to limit the government's ability to prosecute clinic protestors. In *Bray*, originally filed in 1989, after *Scheidler* had initially been dismissed by a lower court, NOW, Planned Parenthood (PP) of Metropolitan Washington, and several Virginia abortion clinics obtained an injunction against Operation Rescue after it announced plans to shut down several clinics. Frustrated because their RICO suit appeared to be going nowhere, these groups filed suit under what is known as the Ku Klux Klan (KKK) Act, which was enacted by Congress in 1871 to curtail conspiracies designed to deny any members of an identifiable group (in the case of the KKK Act, newly freed slaves) their constitutional rights.

Represented by the NOW Legal Defense and Education Fund, the clinics argued that the KKK Act could be used to bar Operation Rescue and members of the Bray family from blocking the entrance to an Alexandria clinic. Because the lower federal courts had previously been unreceptive to the RICO arguments being used in *NOW v. Scheidler*, women's rights groups now attempted to challenge Operation Rescue's blockades on the grounds that such actions were part of a conspiracy to deprive women of rights protected by the **equal protection clause** of the Fourteenth Amendment to the U.S. Constitution.

Bray was first heard by the Supreme Court in 1991, before Clarence Thomas's appointment to the Court. It was held over for reargument during the next term, leading to speculation that the justices were split 4 to 4 and wanted Thomas to hear the case so as to break the tie. After it was reargued in 1992, however, *Bray* resulted in a 6-to-3 decision against the Alexandria Women's Health Clinic. Writing for the Court, abortion foe Antonin Scalia concluded that the KKK Act did not apply to abortion protestors because their activities were not designed to discriminate against women as a class. This Court opinion called into question the legality of at least twenty injunctions that were in place against clinic protesters around the nation.

Congress Acts

The Court's decision in *Bray* appeared to embolden some in the right-to-life movement. Joseph Scheidler, in fact, called clinic bombers "good citizens" (Blanchard 1994, p. 100). And the month of February 1993 saw a rash of firebombings on clinics nationwide. In response, the Fund for the Feminist Majority offered a $20,000 reward for identification of perpetrators who were picketing the homes of abortion providers and following their children to school. It also urged pro-choice supporters in Congress to enact legislation to outlaw violent protest activity.

Increasing violence and the failure of the Court to uphold the injunctions against "rescuers" around the nation led pro-choice interest groups to lobby the Democratic-controlled 103rd Congress and the fledgling Clinton administration to limit pro-life activity insofar as it affected clinic access and caused physical intimidation. The issue of clinic violence thus provided a way to get abortion on the agenda. But instead of formulating a pro-choice abortion policy, Congress began to formulate a policy to deter clinic violence. Just as pro-choice groups started lobbying for legislation to guarantee clinic safety, Dr. David Gunn was shot and killed on March 10, 1993, outside of the Florida clinic where he worked. His assailant was Michael Griffith, who had been picketing the clinic with Rescue America, another splinter rescue group.

Gunn's killing shocked the nation as abortion again made front-page headlines, but the violence did not let up. In her first press conference on March 24, 1993, Attorney General Janet Reno called for "federal legislation to protect women" against clinic violence (Reno 1993). During the same month, the Freedom of Access to Clinic Entrances Act (FACE) was introduced in both houses of Congress. Thus, clinic violence was now on the public agenda, and a specific federal policy for dealing with the violence had been suggested.

As FACE was being studied and debated in Congress, another physician was shot. In August 1993, as Dr. George Tiller was driving away from a Wichita clinic that had been the target of protest and rescue activity, he was shot by Rochelle Shannon of Oregon, who had come to Wichita specifically for the purpose of killing him. Shannon, it was soon learned, had been in frequent contact with Gunn's assailant.

It looked to many as if a conspiracy was, indeed, under way; but the Court had only recently ruled that conspiracies could not be prosecuted under existing federal civil rights laws. This time, however, even the National Right-to-Life Committee denounced the shooting. But those in the radical wing of the right-to-life movement continued to justify the violence. For example, Paul Hill, an excommunicated minister and organizer of Defensive Action—a small group of men who advocate the murder of those who perform abortions (Blanchard 1994, p. 101)—appeared on *Donahue* to defend the violence.

While national attention was focused on the escalating violence, Janet Reno testified before Congress on behalf of the administration, urging congressional passage of the Freedom of Access to Clinic Entrances Act; indeed, she described it as "essential legislation." Different versions of FACE were then passed in both houses of Congress in November 1993. FACE, as proposed, made it a federal crime either to block access to reproductive health clinics or to harass and use violence against women seeking reproductive health care and those providing it. The proposed legislation also gave federal courts jurisdiction to order injunctive relief and damages, while specifically allowing for First Amendment protections for peaceful demonstrations. However, the House and Senate were not able to reconcile the differences in their bills before the Christmas recess.

Meanwhile, in response to *Bray*, while waiting for the U.S. Congress to act, several states enacted anti-clinic violence statutes on their own. Several "No Picketing Zone" laws were passed, and Colorado and Washington States specifically passed their own version of FACE. Other states used existing anti-stalking laws to stop physician/provider harassment. The radical right's reaction was immediate. As one pro-lifer proclaimed, "Stalking laws, trespassing laws—they're immoral laws if they protect immoral action, and we won't follow them" (Puente 1993).

Anti-stalking laws, however, did not deter Paul Hill of Defensive Action from shooting and killing a physician and his escort as they were leaving a Pensacola clinic where the physician performed abortions. This incident was the last straw. FACE was passed by the House on May 5, 1994, in a vote of 241 to 174, and then by the Senate on May 13 in a vote of 69 to 30.

The Right-to-Life Movement Responds

As FACE awaited the president's signature, the right-to-life movement launched a new offensive—this time, an orchestrated campaign of "telephone terrorism" designed to shut down the executive offices. Specifically, Christian Coalition members were urged to call the White House again and again, so as to wreak havoc on its communications system. The American Life League and Operation Rescue also promised to challenge the constitutionality of FACE in court as soon as possible.

***NOW v. Scheidler* Decided.** Even before the telephone terrorism had begun, while Congress was considering FACE and the states were enacting their own versions of it, the Court heard oral arguments in *Scheidler*. The Clinton administration also weighed in on the issue by filing an amicus curiae brief on the side of pro-choice activists—an executive action unprecedented in the history of the abortion issue. Interestingly, the ACLU filed a brief supporting neither side, because the case presented competing issues of First Amendment free speech and assembly guarantees versus a woman's right to secure an abortion.

In contrast to the ACLU, the Supreme Court did not appear to view the case as a free speech issue. Instead, the Court ruled *unanimously*, in January 1994, that economic motive was not critical to RICO actions in cases involving a conspiracy that negatively affected a business. According to Ellie Smeal, of the Fund for the Feminist Majority, this ruling gave the pro-choice movement a "powerful tool" in its arsenal to combat the escalation of violence (Hall 1994).

The combined impact of *Scheidler* and FACE was felt immediately among the ranks of the right-to-life movement. Now that protesters risked heavy fines and jail time for their protest activity, recruitment was more difficult than ever. "They are scared people," said Scheidler of his followers. "People have already quit [protesting] just by the fact we are charged with RICO" (Hall 1994). Nevertheless, violence against providers continued. In December 1994, two receptionists were killed and several people injured when a lone gunman went on a shooting rampage at two clinics in Brookline, Massachusetts.

The Freedom of Choice Act. FACE was not the only pro-choice legislation debated by Congress, although, ultimately, it was the only such legislation passed. As early as 1990, sensing the direction in which the Supreme Court was going in terms of accepting restrictions on abortion rights, the ACLU and other pro-choice groups began to seek co-sponsors for the Freedom of Choice Act (FOCA), which would prohibit state restrictions on abortion. Sponsored by Representative Don Edwards (D.–Calif.) and Senator Alan Cranston (D.–Calif.), it was initially drafted to codify *Roe* by protecting the right of a woman to an abortion before viability and by prohibiting restrictions such as parental notification and consent as well as the requirement that all abortions be performed in hospitals. Because President Bush had promised to veto the act, House and Senate leaders did not push for a vote on the floor.

After Clinton's election and the election of more than twenty new pro-choice women to the Democratic-controlled Congress, pro-choice activists failed to seize upon the opportunity to pass pro-choice legislation without fear of a presidential veto. In July 1993, FOCA became bogged down in congressional bickering when new provisions such as those barring minors' access to abortion and restricting public funding of abortions for indigent women were added to the original bill. Senator Carol Moseley-Braun (D.–Ill.) withdrew support from the proposed act, as did the ACLU and NOW, arguing that the added provisions discriminated against poor women and minors. As Moseley-Braun explained, "I cannot support a bill that trades off the rights of some women for the promise of rights for others" (Povich 1993, p. 14). In contrast, NARAL and Planned Parenthood believed that compromise was reasonable since so many of their members, and so many people in general, were on middle ground regarding abortion; that is, they opposed an outright ban but were willing to support some restrictions, especially the parental consent requirement, as inevitable if any law was to pass. Thus, NARAL and Planned Parenthood on one side of the debate, and NRLC on the other, were willing to accept less than full abortion rights/restrictions as a way of getting some of their policy preferences enacted into law.

Aiding the pro-life cause was contentment on the left. Pro-choice activists saw the election of a pro-choice president, record numbers of women legislators, and Clinton's appointment of Ruth Bader Ginsburg to the Supreme Court as signs that abortion rights were no longer being jeopardized to the extent they had been during the Reagan years. Recall from Chapter 6 that Clinton had settled on Ginsburg only "after becoming convinced that she was clearly pro-choice" (Devins 1995a, p. xxiv). Reinforcing that view was the Supreme Court's decision in *Scheidler*. In a unanimous opinion, the Court found that RICO could be applied to illegal, anti-choice violence and harassment, even though the perpetrators were not motivated by economic gain. This decision signaled to many that the Court was no longer going to stand by and allow violence, threats, and intimidation at clinics. With political prognosticators predicting that the threat to abortion rights was gone, many legislators were more than willing not to have to go on record by voting on FOCA and risking loss of votes over an issue that the Court and the president appeared committed to supporting. How wrong they were. By the end of election night 1994, it was clear that any further hopes for congressional action were dashed as one pro-life Republican after another defeated pro-choice incumbents.

The November 1994 Congressional Elections

On September 27, 1994, during the height of the 1994 congressional election campaign season, then–House Minority Whip Newt Gingrich (R.–Ga.) assembled in Washington, D.C., all of the Republican congressional candidates from around the nation to sign the party's Contract with America. The Contract, which constituted a framework for policymaking, pledged those who signed it to bring a series of legislative proposals to the floor of the House of Representatives for a vote. Among the key provisions in the Contract were a pledge to vote for term limits for members of Congress, a pledge to make all existing employment laws applicable to Congress, a pledge to pass the line-item veto, and a "personal responsibility" section that pledged Republicans to try to limit the use of federal funds for abortion services or abortion counseling. This last provision was a reaction to President Clinton's lifting of the gag rule (see Figure 7.1).

Never before had a political party sought election in a nonpresidential election in such a united fashion or with such a clear statement of purpose. The Contract with America clearly resonated with many American voters. Pollsters and political pundits alike were stunned by the magnitude of the Democratic Party's defeat. Twenty-nine Democratic pro-choice incumbents lost in their reelection bids, and thirty-four open seats were filled by pro-life Republicans (*Charleston Gazette* 1994). Not reelected was the longtime, pro-choice Speaker of the House, Thomas Foley (D.–Wash.), the first Speaker since 1862 to be able to claim that dubious distinction. The new, liberal, pro-choice women of the 103rd Congress were also hit disproportionately, as the House lost most of its first-term women. "The 104th Congress could well be the most anti-women, anti-choice Congress in our history," remarked Kate Michelman of NARAL on the day after the election (Michelman 1994).

Michelman's assessment was not far off target. In 1994, a record number of congressional votes—thirty-seven in all—were taken on choice issues (NARAL 1996), and fourteen passed. Among the fourteen actions taken by the Republican 104th Congress concerning abortion restrictions or choice through April 1996 are those that criminalize abortion speech on the Internet; ban abortions overseas for military women; ban abortions for women in federal prisons; deny abortion coverage for women in D.C., despite locally raised revenue; provide bonus grants to states that reduce the number of abortions; and severely limit Title X funds, thus reversing the current requirement that ob-gyn residency training programs in abortion procedures be provided to meet accreditation standards (NOW 1996, p. 4).

Perhaps most controversial was the 104th Congress's passage of the Partial Birth Abortion Ban Act, which marked the first time that Congress had banned a safe medical procedure. Partial birth abortions is a term coined by right-to-life forces to describe a relatively rare abortion method used in late-term abortions that involves a physician's use of a catheter to deflate a fetus's head in order to facilitate its extraction from a woman's womb. In February 1996, President Clinton sent a letter to lawmakers saying that he would veto the bill unless it contained an exception to allow the procedure if it was necessary to protect a pregnant woman's health (Politics USA 1996). As sent to the president, however, the bill contained language allowing only an exception to save the life of the mother. Catholic bishops kept up a

FIGURE 7.1

Clinton Memo Concerning the Gag Rule

Federal Register
Vol. 58, No. 23
Friday, February 5, 1993

Presidential Documents

Title 3—

The President

Memorandum of January 22, 1993

The Title X "Gag Rule"

Memorandum for the Secretary of Health and Human Services

Title X of the Public Health Services Act provides Federal funding for family planning clinics to provide services for low-income patients. The Act specifies that Title X funds may not be used for the performance of abortions, but places no restrictions on the ability of clinics that receive Title X funds to provide abortion counseling and referrals or to perform abortions using non-Title X funds. During the first 18 years of the program, medical professionals at Title X clinics provided complete, uncensored information, including nondirective abortion counseling. In February 1988, the Department of Health and Human Services adopted regulations, which have become known as the "Gag Rule," prohibiting Title X recipients from providing their patients with information, counseling, or referrals concerning abortion. Subsequent attempts by the Bush Administration to modify the Gag Rule and ensuing litigation have created confusion and uncertainty about the current legal status of the regulations.

The Gag Rule endangers women's lives and health by preventing them from receiving complete and accurate medical information and interferes with the doctor-patient relationship by prohibiting information that medical professionals are otherwise ethically and legally required to provide to their patients. Furthermore, the Gag Rule contravenes the clear intent of a majority of the members of both the United States Senate and House of Representatives, which twice passed legislation to block the Gag Rule's enforcement but failed to override Presidential vetoes.

For these reasons, you have informed me that you will suspend the Gag Rule pending the promulgation of new regulations in accordance with the "notice and comment" procedures of the Administrative Procedure Act. I hereby direct you to take that action as soon as possible. I further direct that, within 30 days, you publish in the Federal Register new proposed regulations for public comment.

You are hereby authorized and directed to publish this memorandum in the Federal Register.

William J. Clinton

THE WHITE HOUSE,
Washington, January 22, 1993.

[FR Doc. 93-2973
Filed 2-3-93; 1:16 pm]
Billing code 3195-01-M

This memo, which suspended the so-called gag rule, was issued by President Clinton to the secretary of Health and Human Services in 1993.

candlelight vigil outside the White House, and National Right-to-Life Committee members were urged to contact Clinton to urge him to sign the bill, but the president vetoed it on April 8, 1996. Underscoring his belief that the law, as written, went too far in limiting reproductive options, Clinton gathered five women around him in the Oval Office. Each, in turn, spoke movingly about having undergone the controversial procedure to save their own lives or else to avoid long-lasting, adverse physical consequences. As a result of this veto, abortion again became a key issue in the 1996 presidential election.

Clinic Violence and Abortion Availability

In spite of pro-life victories in the 1994 congressional elections, violence continued unabated. As noted earlier, in December 1994 two receptionists were killed during a shooting spree at two Brookline abortion clinics and five others were injured. It was also in 1994 that Operation Rescue again became involved in internal debates over the use of force. It finally opted to reject the idea of what some more radical groups call "justifiable homicide." Operation Rescue refused to sign the justifiable-homicide petition originally drafted by Paul Hill, the convicted killer of a Pensacola physician and escort. Thus, in January 1995 disgruntled members of Operation Rescue formed the American Coalition of Life Activists (*Abortion Report* 1995). Soon, this organization produced what it termed a "Deadly Dozen" list that contained the names of thirteen of the most well-known physicians who still performed abortions. Despite the fact that federal marshals were immediately dispatched by the Justice Department to the homes and offices of those on the list (Frantz 1995), by January 1996 five on the list had become the objects of shooting and other forms of violence and intimidation (McGeown 1966).

At least partly on account of clinic violence and mixed public attitudes, abortions were in fact unavailable to women in about 85 percent of all U.S. counties in 1994. Recall that in 1976, just three years after *Roe*, more than one-fourth of the residency programs in gynecology required that physicians learn to perform abortions; an additional two-thirds offered it as an option. But by 1992, the number of programs requiring training in the procedure had declined to only 12 percent—and in almost one-third of the programs, it was not even taught (Estrich 1995). Recent congressional actions specifically allowing medical schools the option not to teach the procedure are likely to decrease the number of trained physicians even further. Adding to this problem is the fact that, in the aftermath of *Webster* and *Casey*, states throughout the country have enacted, and continue to enact, a variety of restrictions that limit or impede women's access to safe *surgical* abortions.

Indeed, as we saw in Table 7.1, nearly all of the states have enacted one or more abortion-specific restrictions. Some states have no restrictions; but others have a variety, including bans on the performing of abortions in public hospitals or by physicians on the public payroll, twenty-four-hour waiting periods that often require women to travel long distances and find lodging overnight before obtaining an abortion, parental consent requirements, and detailed informed consent procedures designed to deter women from exercising what is still a constitutional, albeit limited, right. It is worth noting that the widespread availability of nonsurgical, pharmaceutical abortions would allow most women to bypass these restrictions, thus going a long way toward resolving many aspects of the abortion dilemma itself.

Pharmaceuticals: A Lasting Solution?

While Congress, the president, the states, and the courts continue to grapple with the making of abortion policy, the development of two new, nonsurgical methods of abortion are likely to dramatically change the nature of the abortion debate. In 1995, a study conducted at the Mt. Sinai Hospital in New York City was reported in the *New England Journal of Medicine.* Physicians/researchers there reported that two drugs, methotrexate and misoprostol—already approved by the FDA for other purposes—were a "safe and effective" alternative to surgical abortions. (Note that drugs approved by the FDA can be used for any reason by a licensed physician.)

A single dose of methotrexate, followed five to seven days later by a vaginal suppository containing misoprostol, produced spontaneous abortions with no serious side effects within twelve to twenty-four hours in 96 percent of the 178 women studied (Schieszer 1995). (Methotrexate is generally used to treat certain cancers; misoprostol is an ulcer medication.) In short, an abortion could be obtained by means of three visits to a physician at a cost of $300 to $400 instead of up to $600 (depending on the city). So remarkable were these findings that the National Abortion Federation held workshops in San Francisco in early April 1996 to train doctors how to perform nonsurgical abortions. And Planned Parenthood clinics in Massachusetts announced that, by June 1996, they would begin using this combination of legal drugs to produce spontaneous nonsurgical abortions (*Abortion Report* 1996).

After considerable delay, RU-486 is another pharmaceutical likely to soon come on the market in the United States. RU-486, which is used alone, also produces spontaneous abortions.

Manufactured in France and available by prescription in England, France, and Germany, RU-486 is taken in pill form at the point when a pregnancy is confirmed. Initial tests have shown that, when taken within the first seven weeks of pregnancy, RU-486 causes shedding of the fertilized embryo after implantation in the uterine wall 95 percent of the time. There are also indications that it can be used to treat endometriosis, a leading cause of infertility. Thus, somewhat ironically, the same drug that can be used to terminate a pregnancy could potentially be used to facilitate pregnancies. This possibility, however, has not stopped right-to-life activists and the Roman Catholic Church from denouncing the drug. The Catholic Church was especially active in successfully pressuring the Reagan and Bush administrations to outlaw the testing or use of RU-486 in the United States, despite its success in France and the fact that Sweden and Great Britain also licensed the drug.

In 1989, the FDA issued an "Import Alert" barring the importation of RU-486 into the United States even for personal use, on the grounds that it had not been approved by the agency (see Figures 7.2 and 7.3). When the U.S. government also prohibited trials of the drug in this country, Lawrence Lader, a longtime pro-choice activist, planned a test case to challenge the constitutionality of the ban: Just two days after *Planned Parenthood of Southeastern Pennsylvania v. Casey* (1992) was decided, Leona Benten, a pregnant, twenty-nine-year-old woman, was arrested at a New York airport for bringing RU-486 into the United States from France.

Leona Benton was selected to challenge the law because she fit the clinical profile for safe and appropriate use of the drug. In addition, customs officials had been notified in advance to ensure that she would be arrested. A U.S. District Court judge ordered that Benton's RU-486 pills be returned to her. His order was immediately appealed to the U.S. Circuit Court of Appeals. The three judges on the appeals panel—all of whom were pro-life Reagan appointees—stayed the district court order, and, later, by a vote of 7-to-2, the U.S. Supreme Court refused to review the policy.

Immediately after taking office in 1993, President Clinton ordered his administration to "promote the testing, licensing and manufacturing" of RU-486. Because he also lifted the Import Alert banning importation of RU-486, it now could be imported for personal use. The Clinton administration also allowed the nonprofit Population Council to sponsor trials of RU-486, which it encouraged throughout 1995. And on April 1, 1996, the FDA confirmed that the Population Council had filed an application to sell RU-486 in the United States based both on clinical trials in which the drug was tested on 2,100 American women and on the experiences of 150,000 European women. The Population Council also announced that

FIGURE 7.2

Import Alert, 1989

Regulatory Procedures Manual
Part 9, Imports
Chapter 9-79

IMPORT ALERT

ORO/DFI (HFC-131)
IMPORT OPERATIONS

No.: 66-47

Date: June 6, 1989

[illegible] DETENTION OF ABORTIFACIENT DRUGS

TYPE OF ALERT: Automatic Detention

PRODUCT : Abortifacient Drugs (drug that induces abortion)

PROBLEM : New Drug without NDA/Safety from unsupervised use (DRND/DRHL)

PRODUCT CODE : 66[ ][ ][ ][ ][ ]

PAC :

COUNTRY : All

MANUFACTURER/
SHIPPER : ALL UNAPPROVED

CHARGE : "The article is subject to refusal of admission pursuant to Section 801(a)(3) in that it appears to be a new drug without an effective new drug application (NDA) as required by Section 505(a)."

RECOMMENDING
OFFICE : HFC-131 Import Operations Branch

REASON FOR
ALERT : Questions have been raised about a new abortifacient product, RU486 or "Mifepristone", (Import Bulletin 66-B13 9/26/88) and whether the agency should use its discretion, pursuant to the Pilot Guidance for Release of Mail Importations (7/20/88), or otherwise, to allow its importation for personal use. FDA has concluded that unapproved products of this kind would be inappropriate for release under the personal importation policy. The intended use of such drugs could pose a risk to the safety of the user.

INSTRUCTIONS : Automatically detain all shipments of unapproved abortifacient drugs.

[illegible] : No purging is required of this alert.

The FDA's Import Alert prohibited the importation of the abortifacient drug known as RU-486, charging that "it appears to be a new drug without an effective new drug application" and, as unapproved, "could pose a risk to the safety of the user."

FIGURE 7.3

Clinton Memo Concerning RU-486

29 Weekly Comp. Pres. Doc. 89
Jan. 22, 1993

Memorandum on Importation of RU-486

Memorandum for the Secretary of Health and Human Services
Subject: Importation of RU-486

In Import Alert 66-57, the Food and Drug Administration ("FDA" A) excluded the drug Mifepristine -- commonly known as RU-486 -- from the list of drugs that individuals can import into the United States for their "personal use," although the drugs have not yet been approved for distribution by the FDA. (See FDA Regulatory Procedures Manual, Chapter 9-71.) Import Alert 66-47 effectively bans the importation into this Nation of a drug that is used in other nations as a nonsurgical means of abortion.

I am informed that in excluding RU-486 from the personal use importation exemption, the FDA appears to have based its decision on factors other than an assessment of the possible health and safety risks of the drug. Accordingly, I hereby direct that you promptly instruct the FDA to determine whether there is sufficient evidence to warrant exclusion of RU-486 from the list of drugs that qualify for the personal use importation exemption. Furthermore, if the FDA concludes that RU-486 meets the criteria for the personal use importation exemption, I direct that you immediately take steps to rescind Import Alert 66-47.

In addition, I direct that you promptly assess initiatives by which the Department of Health and Human Services can promote the testing, licensing, and manufacturing in the United States of RU-486 or other antiprogestins.

You are hereby authorized and directed to publish this memorandum in the Federal Register.

William J. Clinton

President Clinton lifted the Import Alert's ban in 1993 with this memo directing the Department of Health and Human Services to begin testing of RU-486.

it had given the exclusive rights to manufacture RU-486 in the United States to a newly formed private company: Advances in Health Technology (Neergaard 1996). FDA Commissioner David Kessler told Congress in 1995 that it would take his agency about six months to determine whether RU-486 was safe. Of course, a change of administrations could forestall approval of RU-486 if it is not approved by January 1997, in the same manner that the Bush administration worked to keep it out of the United States.

Although FDA approval of new drugs often takes years, there are indications that a Democratic FDA would be predisposed toward licensing RU-486. Indeed, the head of the FDA, in 1993, took the unprecedented step of convincing the European maker of the drug to allow testing in the United States. Conversely, Pennsylvania governor Robert Casey has hinted that the Clinton administration's unbiased position toward RU-486 could ultimately serve as the basis for a lawsuit enjoining its sale. "The FDA should not be an advocate for a drug that hasn't been tested here," said Casey (Van Biema 1993, p. 53).

RU-486 and the combination medications that can also be used to terminate a pregnancy nonsurgically will clearly be the next frontier in the abortion wars—so long as both the Congress and the executive branch are not in Republican control. These pharmaceuticals move abortion out of clinics into physicians' offices, allowing abortion to become a truly private decision (though still not an easy one) for millions of women.

Abortions will still be too costly for many poor women, and access to them will be limited because of parental consent requirements or other policies designed to deter those seeking abortions. But the widespread availability of RU-486 and/or the use of methotrexate and misoprostol in combination could go a long way toward transforming the abortion debate, a possibility that is all too real for those who oppose the procedure under any circumstances. "You can't stop a woman from visiting a doctor," said one drug industry analyst. "It becomes a private transaction. And that's the end of the abortion battle" (Van Biema 1993). In short, abortions would become much more difficult to regulate as they become simpler, safer, cheaper, and available virtually *anywhere at any time.*

If RU-486 *were* approved during a Democratic administration, pro-life Republicans would probably have difficulty turning back the clock. Consider what happened in France: Once RU-486 became available there, the manufacturer attempted to withdraw it from the market because of Catholic Church and pro-life opposition. The outcry from French women, however, was so great that the drug remained on the market.

The Clinton administration's aggressive stance on RU-486, along with the FDA director's apparent support of it, has put right-to-life activists on alert. The American

Life League, for example, has devised a six-point plan to deal with RU-486 that includes staging protest rallies and inundating the FDA with anti–RU-486 calls and mail. And on the state level, pro-lifers have pledged to try to win the same kinds of regulations that they have secured concerning surgical abortions. In fact, to prevent women from taking "a quick pill" to end a "problem" pregnancy, pro-life activists have vowed to seek longer waiting periods than those already in place for surgical abortions.

The administration of a pill, or two drugs in combination, would allow more physicians to perform or facilitate abortions in their offices, because there would be no need for surgical intervention—thus making abortions available to many more women, and without intimidation to the women or their physicians. In addition, right-to-life activists would have a much more difficult time targeting individual physicians who facilitated abortions through dispensing medicine. Said Professor Laurence Tribe in reference to the violence committed against providers, "You won't know whom to kill. You won't know where to lie down" (Van Biema 1993). Thus, by limiting the potential for violence and increasing the privacy of the decision, while at the same time making it imperative that an abortion be secured early in the pregnancy (because both nonsurgical types of abortions must be performed early in the first trimester), these pharmaceuticals could well be the "route around the dilemma" (Tribe 1992, p. 214).

Right-to-life activists have vowed to make RU-486, and any other drugs used to induce abortion, a national issue. Joseph Scheidler, in particular, has cautioned, "[W]e will probably know which physicians were dispensing it. We'll sneak in women to ask for RU-486. . . . There will be doctors who will not deal with it. For those who do, we'll go to their homes, to their offices, to their hospitals" (Van Biema 1993, p. 54).

Conclusion

As we have seen, the use of combination drugs to produce spontaneous abortions or FDA approval of RU-486 would go a long way toward providing a peaceful solution to the dilemma that the abortion issue represents for many policymakers. During his 1992 presidential campaign, Bill Clinton repeatedly mentioned his belief that abortion "should be safe, legal and *rare*"—a position he reiterated as he vetoed the Partial Birth Abortion Ban Act. Most other constitutional rights—civil rights and equality, for example—are not discussed as being better under limited terms or conditions. Thus, although abortion has the same characteristics as many other policy issues, it continues to be different in ways that render coherent policymaking very difficult.

Especially because of the religious, moral, and feminist values that have long been associated with abortion, perspectives on the issue tend to be polarized. Exacerbating this problem is the fact that men and women who "come to be pro-life and pro-choice act as the end result of lives that center around different definitions of motherhood" (Luker 1984, p. 214) *and* of male and female roles in society. Finally, because the people on both sides live in such different worlds, yet within the same world, "the scope of their lives fortifies them in their belief that their own views on abortion are more correct, more moral, and more reasonable" (Luker 1984, p. 215). Thus, finding a neutral, or common, ground for those at the opposite ends of the spectrum may be impossible. Just as certainly as some will always believe that O. J. Simpson was guilty while others will forever celebrate his innocence, universal agreement on abortion is likely never to occur. Many of those on opposite ends of the abortion issue spectrum, for example, do not appear to agree even about what justifiable violence is, in the context of clinic violence, the latest phase of the abortion wars. On one side, pro-choice activists believe that clinic picketing and verbal harassment should and must be prohibited. On the other side, many pro-life activists believe that only overt criminal acts such as bombings, shootings, and arson should be prohibited. And those on the radical right—like earlier radical activists on the right or left such as the abolitionist John Brown or student radicals during the 1960s, believe that no act is wrong if it is committed to stop what they consider a greater evil.

In many ways history is repeating itself. It has not been at all unusual to see groups splinter and develop radical fringes that detract from the prestige and acceptability of the original organization. Clearly, the radical "rescue" wing of the right-to-life movement has hurt that movement, as evidenced by the efforts of the more conventional advocates to distance themselves from Paul Hill and, to a lesser extent, Scheidler and Terry. Moreover, in the aftermath of the Pensacola and Brookline murders and other acts of violence, some activists on *both* sides of the abortion issue organized a group called Common Ground Network for Life and Choice and publicly described themselves as "unanimous in [our] strong opposition to the use of physical violence by any person as a means of advocating or expressing beliefs concerning abortion" (Common Ground 1995, p. 3). Common Ground has also sought to find issue areas on which both sides can compromise, such as adoption.

At first glance, a group like Common Ground appears to be a much-overdue first step toward compromise. But it's also possible that compromise, at least in terms of the way our democratic system was intended to work by the Framers, already has been reached. As revealed in Table 1.1, a majority of the public do not believe that abortion should "always be legal." Instead, along a continuum of sorts, recent polls show that increasing numbers of the public believe that abortion should be legal to save the life of the mother, to protect the life of the mother, in cases of rape or incest, or with a husband's or parent's permission. In essence, that ambivalence toward abortion is reflected in the U.S. Supreme Court's recent decisions concerning abortion. In both *Webster* and *Casey,* the Court upheld state efforts to restrict abortion by the narrowest of margins. The Court adopted a compromise position by allowing the states to curtail some abortion rights without banning the procedure altogether—a position not that far from what public opinion polls indicate Americans want or accept. And, reflecting public opinion regarding legality, for those who needed or wanted an abortion (and could pay for one) it did in fact remain legal, a far cry from the circumstances in most states before *Roe.*

Our present structure of government may not be the best way to forge policy on a controversial issue. Still, although interest groups have tried to shape the discourse of abortion and the two major political parties have taken opposite positions on it, the courts, especially the U.S. Supreme Court, have, over time, come perhaps the closest to mirroring public sentiments on the abortion issue. Confusing at times, yes. Inconsistent? Sometimes. Yet that may be the best the present political system can do in the way of finding a neutral ground or point of compromise on an issue that involves as many religious and moral overtones as it does health-related and political ones.

Throughout this book, the way that governments and lawmakers—at the national, state, and even local levels—have reacted to the abortion issue as it has been defined and redefined within the policy cycle was analyzed to highlight some of the key facets of the American political system. At times, the system has appeared to work well; at others it has not. Given the complex nature of the abortion issue, and the tendency of Americans to frame issues in terms of rights while relying on undemocratic institutions, especially the courts, to allocate those rights, the national and state legislatures' inability to forge and maintain coherent and consistent policy in the face of some widely divergent, and possibly irreconcilable, views on abortion policy is not surprising. Yet one could take the view that at least one branch of government, the Supreme Court, has found a neutral ground by allowing for some restrictions on abortion while continuing to guarantee the right to an abortion to most women. Similarly, the Court, the Congress, and, of late, the executive branch have been unified in their opposition to clinic violence and harassment, again reflecting public opinion. Both the Court's decision in *Scheidler* and Congress's passage of FACE suggest that the political system has effectively responded in the wake of activity deemed abhorrent by most of the polity.

As of April 1996, the U.S. Supreme Court has agreed to hear yet another challenge involving the scope of clinic protest. In 1994 the Court upheld the requirement for a 36-foot buffer zone around clinics; in 1997 it will decide whether a 15-foot no-speech zone, prohibiting sidewalk counselors from continuing to talk to women as they enter clinics and who indicate that they wish to be left alone, is constitutional.

The abortion issue has indeed been defined and redefined as it has made its way onto the public agenda. Initially the abortion issue concerned the right to secure an abortion, then the right to have the government pay for one, then the right of states to implement certain restrictions, then the right of picketers essentially to close clinics through protest activity, and finally the right of the administration to ban the testing, import, or sale of a pharmaceutical. Throughout all of these stages, the scope of the conflict has widened and narrowed, the arenas of lobbying have shifted, and the policy implementation and evaluation processes have been realigned. In the final analysis, then, the abortion issue may not be all that different from other policy issues, including civil rights and the environment. All such policy issues have gone off on tangents, incurred violence, and, ultimately, moved toward neutral ground. It appears that the abortion issue is now reaching that stage of equilibrium.

Discussion Questions

Chapter 1

1. How does the abortion policy cycle mirror that of other policy issues?

2. Why does abortion seem to be an issue or practice regulated by the government?

3. What are the stages of the policymaking process? What issues aside from abortion can it be applied to?

4. How might you begin to evaluate how well or how badly abortion policy has been implemented?

5. What is it about abortion that makes some politicians shy away from going "on the record" about it? In that regard, is it different from other issues?

Chapter 2

1. What factors contributed to the passage of restrictive state abortion laws in the 1800s, especially after the Civil War? And what factors, if any, do you view as valid reasons for limiting access to legal abortions?

2. How did the Comstock Act link the ideas of birth control and abortion?

3. How did the "reform" versus "repeal" factions of the fledgling abortion rights movement resolve their disagreements?

4. What set of factors acted together to put the issue of abortion on the national public agenda?

5. What kind of dilemma did the abortion issue first pose for state lawmakers in the 1960s and early 1970s?

6. Does the Hippocratic oath present a dilemma for physicians?

7. How or why did abortion become a political issue as opposed to a medical issue?

8. The courts have been chosen as the prime target of women's rights advocates; what are the implications of this choice for democratic government?

Chapter 3

1. How did the federal nature of the U.S. political system affect the course and development of abortion and contraceptive laws?

2. What are test cases? How and why were they used by Planned Parenthood in the 1960s?

3. What was the privacy doctrine described by the Supreme Court justices in *Griswold v. Connecticut?* How did the Court apply it in *Roe v. Wade?*

4. What was the trimester approach to pregnancy developed by the majority in *Roe v. Wade?* How did it affect a woman's right to an abortion at each stage of pregnancy?

5. In the aftermath of *Roe*, numerous interest groups on both sides of the abortion issue were formed and/or activated. What kinds of strategies were pursued by these groups? How effective were they?

6. Is Solicitor General Lee's assessment of the role of the states in the federal system accurate for all issues, or just for abortion?

7. Is federalism a protection for civil liberties, as the Federalists argued, or an impediment, as the Anti-Federalists charged?

Chapter 4

1. In what way did *Roe v. Wade* function as a catalyst instead of providing the final answer on abortion policy?

2. How has the evolution of interest groups supported David Truman's theory of interest-group development?

3. Given the mandate in the First Amendment concerning the importance of the separation of church and state, is the Roman Catholic Church's role in the abortion debate appropriate? Why or why not?

4. Explain how various interest groups on both sides of the abortion issue came together to become a social movement.

5. What role has the Right-to-Life Party played in state and national elections? Is it likely ever to become a strong third party? Why or why not?

6. What difficulties might right-to-life supporters encounter at the state level if Congress actually passes a right-to-life amendment?

7. What factors led to pro-choice advocates' misjudgment of their opponents? And how does this outcome reflect the political capacity of interest groups in general?

Chapter 5

1. How did the rise in prominence of the Christian right affect the abortion issue?

2. By what means did President Reagan advance his pro-life beliefs in spite of the *Roe v. Wade* decision?

3. In what ways did Joseph Scheidler's tactics cause controversy within the anti-abortion movement?

4. What was the significance of *Akron v. Akron Center for Reproductive Health, Inc.?*

5. How was the abortion issue affected by changes in the composition of the Supreme Court?

6. Can a president be assured that each judicial appointee will decide in the way intended by the president when the judge or justice was appointed?

Chapter 6

1. What impact did the election of George Bush have on the abortion policy cycle?

2. What role did the media play in getting the objectives of Operation Rescue on the public agenda? In what ways did Operation Rescue and the Pro-Life Action League represent the objectives of the right-to-life movement?

3. What role did *Webster v. Reproductive Health Services* play in mobilizing both sides of the abortion debate?

4. What impact do amicus curiae briefs tend to have on the outcome of Supreme Court litigation? Is abortion like other issues in its ability to attract so many "friends of the court" briefs on both sides?

5. Why, in *Webster*, did the Supreme Court stop short of overruling *Roe?*

6. What kinds of restrictions might the Court invalidate as an undue burden?

7. Does the Supreme Court have the capacity to make effective public policy?

Chapter 7

1. What, if any, were the long-term consequences of abortion as a policy issue after the election of a pro-choice president? Should major policy decisions affecting the polity turn on the election of a single individual?

2. Can you see any patterns in state abortion restrictions? Is there anything about political culture or the role of women that would explain abortion rights differences across the states?

3. What factors led up to Congress's passage of FACE? What are the long-term implications of FACE? Would any groups other than "rescue" organizations be affected by this act?

4. How can you explain the stark differences between the Supreme Court's decision in *Bray* and its decision in *Scheidler?*

5. What impact did the 1994 congressional elections have on the abortion policy cycle?

6. Are RU-486 or other forms of drug therapy a final solution to the abortion dilemma? A partial solution?

7. Has the abortion dilemma been solved to the extent that it can be, within the limits of our democracy's capacity to mediate differences? Do you think it will ever be fully solved?

Glossary

Abortifacients. Medicines or drugs used to induce or cause an abortion.

Abortion. A miscarriage or premature expulsion of the fetus.

Agenda-Setting Stage. The second stage of the policymaking process; generally a time when groups are trying to get positive media attention to frame an issue in a favorable way.

Akron v. Akron Center for Reproductive Health, Inc. (1983). A case in which the Supreme Court, by a 6-to-3 vote, invalidated several parts of a city ordinance, including provisions requiring (a) second- and third-trimester abortions to be performed in hospitals; (b) a twenty-four-hour waiting period; (c) informed and written consent; (d) physician "counseling," which in turn required doctors to inform patients that the unborn child is a human life from the moment of conception; (e) parental notification; and (f) the "humane and sanitary" disposal of the aborted fetus. The Court concluded that these provisions interfered with a woman's right under *Roe.*

Amicus Curiae. "Friends of the court," such as interest groups or affected individuals who file briefs; they are not direct parties to the case but, rather, weigh in to voice their opinion about the legal issues involved.

Anti-Abortion Movement. A movement largely begun in the aftermath of *Roe v. Wade* (1973) to limit or end legalized abortion.

Belotti v. Baird (1979). A case in which the Supreme Court, by an 8-to-1 vote, struck down a Massachusetts law requiring parental consent of both parents for abortions for minor women.

Bill of Rights. The first ten amendments to the U.S. Constitution.

Birth Control Movement. A social movement begun in the early 1900s; its aim was to make access to contraceptives legal.

Bray v. Alexandria Women's Health Clinic (1993). A case in which the Supreme Court, by a 6-to-3 vote, ruled that the KKK Act could not be used to limit threatened clinic blockades.

Budgeting. The fifth stage of the policymaking process, in which it is determined how the policy will be paid for.

Christian Coalition (CC). A powerful grassroots conservative religious/political movement headed by televangelist Pat Robertson.

Christian Right (also called the religious right). A powerful political force that emerged during the mid-1970s; its leaders and followers believed that public morals affected their Christian faith.

Commerce Clause. A section of the U.S. Constitution contained in Article I, section 8, that grants Congress the authority to regulate interstate commerce. It was used as the legal basis for the Comstock Act.

Common Law. The basis of the U.S. legal system, which in turn is derived from unwritten English law.

Comstock Act. A federal law passed in 1873 that prohibited the use of the U.S. mails for distribution of any "obscene" materials. Information about birth control and abortion were included in the Congress's definition of obscene.

Connecticut v. Menillo (1975). A case in which, in a per curiam (unsigned) opinion, the Supreme Court ruled that a state law limiting performance of abortions to physicians was constitutional and did not contravene *Roe.*

Doe v. Bolton (1973). The companion case to *Roe v. Wade* in which the Court held that a physician's best medical judgment regarding the necessity of an abortion encompasses all factors, including a woman's mental health.

Equal Protection Clause. The section of the Fourteenth Amendment guaranteeing that all citizens receive equal protection under all state laws. It has been used to bar discrimination against African Americans, women, and other groups.

Evaluation. The final stage of the policymaking process, in which the effectiveness of a policy is measured.

Executive Order. A presidential directive to an agency that provides the basis for carrying out laws or for establishing new policies.

Federal Campaign Financing Act of 1974. The basic law that regulates the federal election process. It establishes strict reporting requirements and places limits on contributions.

***Federalist* No. 78.** The essay in which Alexander Hamilton wrote that the judiciary "would be the least dangerous branch" of government.

Federal System. The form of government in the United States in which national government and state government have defined roles, and in which the former receives its powers directly from the people.

Fetal Viability. The time at which a fetus is considered able to live outside its mother's womb.

Fetus. A flexible term referring to an unborn child.

Freedom of Choice Act (FOCA). Proposed congressional legislation that would make the Supreme Court's decision in *Roe* the law of the land through national legislation.

Fundamental Freedom. A freedom considered so vital that the Supreme Court subjects proposed governmental restrictions of it to heightened scrutiny. A state must show a compelling reason to infringe a fundamental freedom.

Fundamental Right. A right that can be abridged by government only when demonstrably necessary to achieve a "compelling" objective.

Gag Rule. A series of regulations stating that organizations receiving federal funds cannot counsel patients regarding abortion or provide referrals for abortions.

Gender Gap. The disparity between the partisan choices of women and men in the aggregate.

Griswold v. Connecticut (1965). A case in which, by a 7-to-2 vote, the Supreme Court ruled that there existed a constitutional right to privacy, derived from the Bill of Rights, which included the right of married couples to use birth control.

Harris v. McRae (1980). A case in which, by a 5-to-4 vote, the Supreme Court upheld the constitutionality of the Hyde Amendment by finding that states are not required to fund "medically necessary" abortions when federal funds are not available.

Hyde Amendment. An amendment to a congressional appropriations bill, originally passed in 1976, that limits the use of Medicaid funds for the payment of abortions for indigent women.

Human Life Amendment. A proposed constitutional amendment that bans abortion and would overturn *Roe v. Wade.*

Implementation. The sixth stage of the policymaking process, in which a policy is put into practice.

Injunction. A legal order restraining a person from committing an action or commanding a person to commit an action.

Institutional Agenda. A set of concrete, specific items scheduled for action and consideration by a decisionmaking body.

Judicial Bypass Provision. A provision in parental consent legislation that allows a minor to petition a court for permission for an abortion rather than obtaining consent from a parent.

Madsen v. Women's Health Center **(1994).** A case in which, by a 6-to-3 vote, the Supreme Court ruled that the use of a buffer zone to limit picketing does not violate a clinic protester's rights.

Maher v. Roe **(1977).** A case in which, by a 6-to-3 vote, the Supreme Court ruled that Connecticut's refusal to extend state Medicaid benefits to Medicaid-eligible women was constitutional.

Moral Majority. A pro-life fundamentalist and evangelical ministry founded by the Reverend Jerry Falwell to defend religious practices and the family through political action.

National Abortion Rights Action League (NARAL). The leading pro-choice organization, founded in New York as the New York Abortion Rights Action League. Subsequently known as the National Association to Repeal Abortion Laws, it became the National Abortion Rights Action League after *Roe;* and, in 1994, to reflect its expanded interests, it became the National Abortion and Reproductive Rights Action League.

National Conference of Catholic Bishops (NCCB). A group consisting of all the Catholic bishops in the United States.

National Right-to-Life Committee (NRLC). The largest anti-abortion group, founded in 1973 with the assistance of the NCCB.

NOW v. Scheidler et al. **(1994).** A case in which, by a 9-to-0 vote, the Supreme Court ruled that RICO statutes could be used to prohibit clinic violence and harassment.

Operation Rescue. An organization founded in the 1980s by Randall Terry, which, unlike many other, more conventional anti-abortion groups, uses civil protest in the form of blockading abortion clinics as its main tactic for preventing abortions.

Penumbras. The emanations from the First, Third, Fourth, Fifth, Ninth, and Fourteenth Amendments that, taken together, allow the Supreme Court to find a right to privacy guaranteed by the Constitution.

Planned Parenthood Association of Kansas City v. Ashcroft **(1983).** A case in which, by a 6-to-3 vote, the Supreme Court ruled that second-trimester hospitalization for abortions in Missouri was unconstitutional. However, five justices upheld the second physician requirement as well as the parental consent provision.

Planned Parenthood Federation of America. The organization created by the merger of the National Birth Control League and the Birth Control Federation of America.

Planned Parenthood of Central Missouri v. Danforth **(1976).** A case in which, by a 6-to-3 vote, the Supreme Court struck down Missouri's spousal consent law, citing an unconstitutional veto power by a third party. A 5-to-4 majority also struck down a parental consent requirement for unmarried, minor women on the same grounds.

Planned Parenthood of Southeastern Pennsylvania v. Casey (1992). A case in which, in a badly fractured ruling, a majority of the Supreme Court upheld requirements specifying a twenty-four-hour waiting period, parental consent, and detailed provider filing information; only a husband notification requirement was deemed an undue burden and therefore unconstitutional.

Plurality. A Supreme Court opinion that has the support of fewer than a majority of the Court but, because of divisions on the Court, becomes the controlling opinion of the Court.

Poelker v. Doe (1977). A case in which, in a per curiam (unsigned) opinion, the Supreme Court ruled that St. Louis may opt to pay for childbirth for indigent mothers without being forced to also pay for nontherapeutic abortions.

Police Power. The right of the states to legislate for the public health and welfare of their citizens.

Policy Adoption. The fourth stage in the policymaking process, in which policymakers are required to adopt a policy.

Policy Formulation. The third stage in the policymaking process, in which policies are defined.

Policymaking Process. A seven-stage process in which political actors and institutions interact to make policy.

Political Action Committees (PACs). Federally sanctioned, officially registered fundraising committees that represent interest groups in the political process and generally fund political campaigns.

Privacy. A fundamental constitutional right, emanating from several specific guarantees found in the Bill of Rights, that has been used as the constitutional basis for a woman's right to an abortion. (See also *Roe v. Wade* [1973].)

Problem Definition. Part of the first stage in the policymaking process, in which an existing problem is defined.

Problem Recognition. Part of the first stage in the policymaking process, in which a determination is made that a problem exists.

Pro-Life Action League. A group founded by Joseph Scheidler that advocates violence as a strategy to prevent the implementation of existing abortion laws.

Quickening. The time at which a woman first feels the movement of the fetus in utero.

Reproductive Freedom Project (RFP). A separate entity created by the American Civil Liberties Union, whose goal was to ensure full compliance with the decision in *Roe v. Wade.*

Right-to-Life Movement. Collectively, the groups and individuals opposed to legalized abortion, often regardless of the reason for which the procedure was being sought.

Right-to-Life Party. A political party founded to focus attention on abortion issues. It ran a presidential candidate nationwide for the first time in 1976.

Roe v. Wade (1973). A case in which, by a 7-to-2 vote, the Supreme Court invalidated all state abortion restrictions. The Court situated the right to an abortion in the right to privacy, which was derived from the penumbras of the First, Third, Fourth, Ninth, and Fourteenth Amendments to the U.S. Constitution.

RU-486. A drug, taken in pill form, that induces abortion in the early stages of pregnancy, thus making surgical abortion unnecessary.

Rust v. Sullivan (1991). A case in which, by a 5-to-4 vote, the Supreme Court upheld the federal gag rule, finding that it did not violate freedom of speech, the right to privacy, or Title X.

Solicitor General. A member of the Justice Department appointed by the president to represent the United States before the Supreme Court.

Standing. The legal basis to bring a case.

Suffrage Campaign. The campaign to win the right to vote for women; describes the period from 1890 to 1920, when the Nineteenth Amendment was ratified.

Tenth Amendment. The amendment to the U.S. Constitution that reserves to the states all powers not delegated to or prohibited by the national government.

Test Case. Litigation in which plaintiffs are chosen to challenge or test the constitutionality of a law or practice in order to advance an interest group's policy goals in court.

Thornburgh v. American College of Obstetricians and Gynecologists (1986). A case in which, by a 5-to-4 vote, the Supreme Court invalidated several abortion restrictions, including the requirement that a woman seeking an abortion must receive specific information from her physician and be told in detail about the stages of fetal development.

Undue Burden. Justice Sandra Day O'Connor's belief that state restrictions of abortion are permissible so long as they do not pose an undue burden on a woman's efforts to secure the procedure. Under this test, most state abortion restrictions have been upheld by the Supreme Court.

Voluntary Motherhood. A woman's right to limit her family by natural means.

Webster v. Reproductive Health Services (1989). Marked the first time that only four justices voted to uphold *Roe* as the Court let stand several abortion restrictions including ones prohibiting use of public funds or public employees and testing of fetal viability at twenty weeks.

Time Line: Key Dates Concerning Abortion and Birth Control

1821	Connecticut enacts first state statute forbidding abortion.
1940s	The Connecticut law undergoes its first legal tests.
1959	American Law Institute and American College of Obstetricians and Gynecologists urge that abortion be decriminalized.
1962	Sherri Finkbine has an abortion in Sweden.
1963–1964	Several states experience a German measles epidemic.
1964	The first pro-choice groups are founded by Lawrence Lader and Patricia McGinnis.
1965	*Griswold v. Connecticut.*
1967	NOW calls for repeal of all state abortion laws; AMA endorses abortion law reform.
	NCCB creates Family Life Bureau to stop abortion.
1967–1970	Twelve states pass abortion law reforms.
1968	Citizens Advisory Council on the Status of Women and ACLU call for abortion law repeal; NARAL founded.
1970	Four states, including New York, repeal abortion laws.
	Right-to-Life Party is founded.
1973	*Roe v. Wade* and *Doe v. Bolton.*
	National Right-to-Life Committee is founded.
	Human life amendments to overturn *Roe* are proposed in Congress.
1974	ACLU creates the Reproductive Freedom Project.
	Abortion becomes an issue in congressional elections for the first time.
1975	Catholic bishops announce their Pastoral Plan to combat abortion at the parish level.
1976	The Republican and Democratic parties adopt abortion planks in their platforms for the presidential election.
	The Hyde Amendment, which barred the use of federal funds for abortions, is enacted.
	Right-to-Life Party candidate Ellen McCormack enters the presidential race.
	Planned Parenthood of Central Missouri v. Danforth, the first major abortion case since *Roe v. Wade,* is decided by Supreme Court.
1977	Supreme Court holds that neither the Constitution nor the Social Security Act requires states or the federal government to fund nonmedical abortions. The Hyde Amendment is thus upheld in *Maher v. Roe, Beal v. Doe,* and *Poelker v. Doe.*
	ACLU launches Campaign for Choice.
1978	Several pro-choice representatives and senators are defeated in November elections.

1979 Parental consent provision is ruled unconstitutional in *Bellotti v. Baird*.
Moral Majority is founded; helps elect pro-life president Ronald Reagan.

1980 NARAL PAC is founded.
Republican and Democratic platforms adopt opposing positions on abortion in the presidential campaign.

1981 President Reagan appoints the first woman justice, Sandra Day O'Connor, to Supreme Court.
Adolescent Family Life Act (originally intended to prevent teen pregnancy) is passed.

1982 Army of God, an anti-abortion group, firebombs an abortion clinic in Illinois and kidnaps the doctor and his wife.

1983 In *Akron v. Akron Center for Reproductive Health, Inc.*, the undue burden standard is articulated for the first time, though not adopted by the Court.

1984 Archbishop John J. O'Connor of New York urges Catholics to vote against political candidates who approve of abortion.
The Republican Party platform endorses a human life amendment to the Constitution.

1985 Acting Solicitor General Charles Fried files a brief for the United States in *Thornburgh v. American College of Obstetricians and Gynecologists* asking the Supreme Court to overrule *Roe v. Wade.*

1986 NOW stages a pro-choice March for Women's Lives in Washington, D.C. An estimated 85,000–125,000 people attend.
Supreme Court ruling in *Thornburgh v. American College of Obstetricians and Gynecologists* reaffirms *Roe v. Wade* by a vote of 5 to 4.
NOW files a lawsuit against Joseph Scheidler and the Pro-Life Action League and other radical groups, seeking a court order that would stop harassment of abortion clinics.
President Reagan nominates William H. Rehnquist, a *Roe* dissenter, to be chief justice of the United States.
France announces successful tests of RU-486.

1987 The Department of Health and Human Services rules that family planning clinics that receive federal funds may not offer abortion counseling (a restriction set forth in the so-called gag rule).

1988 Operation Rescue demonstrates at the 1988 Democratic Convention.
Pro-choice "Who Decides?" campaign is launched.
George Bush is elected president on a right-to-life Republican Party platform.

1989 FDA bans the importation of RU-486.
In *Webster v. Reproductive Health Services,* the Supreme Court signals that the Court will defer to state legislation limiting abortions.
Freedom of Reproductive Choice Act is introduced in Congress.
Rally for Safe and Legal Abortions is held in D.C.
"Who Decides?" campaign continues.
Right-to-life movement launches boycott of Planned Parenthood contributors.
Christian Coalition is founded.

1990	Cardinal John O'Connor of New York warns Roman Catholics that they risk excommunication for supporting legal abortion; a public relations firm is hired by O'Connor to mount an anti-abortion campaign.
	Supreme Court upholds two state laws requiring notification of parents when minors seek abortions.
1991	"Summer of Mercy" is launched by Operation Rescue.
	Supreme Court upholds the gag rule in *Rust v. Sullivan.*
	Freedom of Choice Act is introduced in Congress.
1992	Operation Rescue blocks abortion clinics in Buffalo, New York.
	Congress passes a law nullifying the gag rule, but the law is vetoed by President Bush.
	In *Planned Parenthood of Southeastern Pennsylvania v. Casey,* Supreme Court upholds a Pennsylvania law limiting abortions, but refuses to overturn *Roe v. Wade.*
	Bill Clinton is elected along with a record number of pro-choice women representatives.
	DeMoss Foundation begins "Life, What a Beautiful Choice" campaign.
1993	Bill Clinton takes office as president of the United States; removes five federal restrictions on abortion by executive order.
	In *Bray v. Alexandria Women's Health Clinic,* Supreme Court refuses to allow use of the KKK Act to enjoin anti-abortion demonstrations that block abortion clinics.
	Physician/provider is shot and killed in Pensacola, Florida.
	Roussel-Uclef S.A. of France, maker of RU-486, agrees to license the drug for testing in the United States.
	More shootings occur at abortion clinics.
1994	FACE is passed by Congress.
	In *NOW v. Scheidler,* Supreme Court rules that the RICO law can be applied to illegal anti-choice violence and harassment.
	In *Madsen v. Women's Health Center,* Supreme Court upholds portions of an injunction creating a buffer zone around an abortion clinic.
	Violence against clinics and providers continues.
	Republicans win House and Senate majorities.
	American Coalition of Life Activists is founded.
1995	RU-486 clinical trials continue.
	"Dirty Dozen" doctors are targeted for violence.
	Methotrexate and misoprostol are found to safely induce abortions in combination with each other.
	The House and Senate vote to limit methods used in second-term abortions.
	Supreme Court upholds the constitutionality of FACE.
1996	Congress passes the Partial Birth Abortion Ban Act.
	President Clinton vetoes Partial Birth Abortion Ban Act.
	Population Council files application to sell RU-486.
	Planned Parenthood announces that it will begin methotrexate/misoprostol nonsurgical abortions in June 1996.
	Supreme Court agrees to hear clinic protest case.

Table of Cases

Akron v. Akron Center for Reproductive Health, Inc., 462 U.S. 446 (1983).
Beal v. Doe, 432 U.S. 438 (1977).
Belliotti v. Baird, 443 U.S. 622 (1979).
Benton v. Kessler, 112 S. Ct. 2929 (1992).
Berman v. Parker, 348 U.S. 26 (1954).
Bigelow v. Virginia, 421 U.S. 809 (1975).
Bowen v. Kendrick, 487 U.S. 589 (1988).
Bray v. Alexandria Women's Health Clinic, 115 S. Ct. 753 (1993).
Brown v. Board of Education of Topeka, 348 U.S. 886 (1954).
Connecticut v. Menillo, 423 U.S. 9 (1975).
Doe v. Bolton, 410 U.S. 179 (1973).
Engle v. Vitale, 370 U.S. 421 (1962).
Epperson v. Arkansas, 393 U.S. 106 (1968).
Griswold v. Connecticut, 381 U.S. 479 (1965).
Harris v. McRae, 448 U.S. 297 (1980).
Madsen v. Women's Health Center, 114 S. Ct. 2516 (1994).
Maher v. Roe, 432 U.S. 464 (1977).
National Organization for Women (NOW) v. Scheidler, 114 S. Ct. 798 (1994).
Ohio v. Akron Reproductive Health Center, 497 U.S. 502 (1990).
Planned Parenthood Association of Kansas City v. Ashcroft, 462 U.S. 476 (1983).
Planned Parenthood of Southeastern Pennsylvania v. Casey, 112 S. Ct. 2791 (1992).
Planned Parenthood of Central Missouri v. Danforth, 428 U.S. 52 (1976).
Poe v. Ullman, 367 U.S. 497 (1961).
Poelker v. Doe, 432 U.S. 519 (1977).
Roe v. Wade, 410 U.S. 113 (1973).
Rust v. Sullivan, 111 S.Ct. 1759 (1991).
State v. Murphy, 27 N.J.L. 112 (1858).
Swann v. Charlotte-Mecklenburg Board of Education, 402 U.S. 1 (1971).
Thornburgh v. American College of Gynecologists and Obstetricians, 476 U.S. 747 (1986).
Tileston v. Ullman, 318 U.S. 44 (1943).
United States v. One Package, 86 F.2d 737 (1936).
United States v. Vuitch, 305 F. Supp. 1032 (1969).
United States v. Vuitch, 402 U.S. 62 (1971).
Webster v. Reproductive Health Services, 492 U.S. 490 (1989).
Williams v. Zbaraz, 448 U.S. 358 (1980).

References

Abortion Report. 1996. "RU-486: FDA Confirms Population Council Submission." April 2.

———. 1995. "Missouri: ACLA Plans Protest in the Gateway City." July 24.

Abramowitz, Alan. 1993. "It's Abortion, Stupid: Policy Voting in the 1992 Presidential Election." Paper prepared for delivery at the annual meeting of the American Political Science Association.

American Civil Liberties Union. 1988–1995. *Reproductive Rights Update*. Published biweekly.

Anderson, James E. 1994. *Public Policymaking: An Introduction*, 2nd ed. Boston: Houghton Mifflin.

Arieff, Irwin. 1989. "Supreme Court Abortion Ruling Energizes Right-to-Life Forces." *Reuters*, July 4, P.M. cycle.

Back, Kurt W. 1989. *Family Planning and Population Control: The Challenges of a Successful Movement*. Boston: Twayne.

Baer, Judith A. 1991. *Women in American Law*. New York: Holmes and Meier.

Banner, Lois. 1984. *Women in Modern America: A Brief History*, 2nd ed. San Diego: Harcourt Brace Jovanovich.

Barringer, Felicity. 1993. "Abortion Clinics Preparing for More Violence." *New York Times*, March 12, p. A1.

Barry, Norman P. 1987. *The New Right*. London: Croom Helm.

Beck, Melinda, with Peter Katel. 1994. "Propaganda Makes Me Do It." *Newsweek*, February 28, p. 34.

Berke, R. 1991. "Groups That Back Right to Abortion Ask Court to Act." *New York Times*, November 8, p. A1.

Blair, Bea. 1973. "Abortion: Can We Lose Our Right to Choose?" *MS.*, October, pp. 72–95.

Blanchard, Dallas A. 1994. *The Anti-Abortion Movement and the Rise of the Religious Right: From Polite to Fiery Protest*. New York: Twayne.

Boeth, Richard, et al. 1978. "Abortion: Getting Violent." *Newsweek*, March 13, p. 33.

Bonafede, Dom. 1980. "Let's Look at the Record." *National Journal*, May 24, p. 865.

Bork, Robert H. 1990. *The Tempting of America: The Political Seduction of the Law*. New York: Free Press.

Brief of 281 American Historians. 1988. Submitted in *Webster v. Reproductive Health Services, Inc.*

Broder, David S. 1988. "Why Not Take a Risk? Debate, George, and Debate and Debate." *Washington Post*, August 16, p. A15.

Byrnes, Timothy A., and Mary C. Segers, Eds.1992. *The Catholic Church and the Politics of Abortion: A View from the States*. Boulder, Colo.: Westview Press.

Califano, Joseph A. 1981. *An Insider's Report from the White House and the Cabinet*. New York: Simon & Schuster.

Carabillo, Toni, Judith Meuli, and June Bundy Csida. 1993. *Feminist Chronicles, 1953–1993.* Los Angeles: Women's Graphics.

Center for Reproductive Law & Policy. 1993–1995. *Reproductive Freedom News.*

Charleston Gazette. 1994. "Election Heightens Pro-Abortion Rhetoric." December 10.

Church & State. 1991. "Bennett, Bork Launch Catholic Campaign to Promote Church Views." October, p. 16.

Ciolli, Rita. 1992. "Next: Fight Shifts to Legislatures." *Newsday,* June 30, p. 4.

Clift, Eleanor. 1991. "The GOP's Civil War Over Abortion." *Time,* August 5, p. 31.

Clinton, William. 1992. "Remarks on Supreme Court *Casey* Ruling," June 22, U.S. Newswire.

Cobb, Roger W., and Charles E. Elder. 1983. *Participation in American Politics: The Dynamics of Agenda Building,* 2nd ed. Baltimore: Johns Hopkins University Press.

Common Ground. 1995. *News from the Common Ground Network for Life and Choice.* Washington, D.C. Mimeo.

Conason, Joe. 1992. "The Religious Right's Quiet Revival: Pat Robertson's Christian Coalition." *The Nation,* April 27.

Conduit, Celeste Michelle. 1990. *Decoding Abortion Rhetoric: Communicating Social Change.* Urbana: University of Illinois Press.

Congressional Quarterly Weekly Report. 1987. "Senate Labor OKs Family Planning Legislation." November 14, p. 2821.

Cook, Elizabeth Adell, Ted G. Jelen, and Clyde Wilcox, Eds. 1992. *Between Two Absolutes: Public Opinion and the Politics of Abortion.* Boulder, Colo.: Westview Press.

———. 1994. "Issue Voting in Gubernatorial Election: Abortion and Post-*Weber* Politics." *Journal of Politics,* vol. 56, February, pp. 187–189.

Craig, Barbara Hinkson, and David H. O'Brien. 1993. *Abortion and American Politics.* Chatham, N.J.: Chatham House.

Crawford, Alan. 1980. *Thunder on the Right: The "New Right" and the Politics of Resentment.* New York: Pantheon Books.

Degler, Carl. 1980. *At Odds: Women and the Family in America from the Revolution to the Present.* New York: Oxford Books.

D'Emilio, John, and Estelle Freedman. 1988. *Intimate Matters: A History of Sexuality in America.* New York: Harper & Row.

Devins, Neal, Ed. 1995a. *Federal Abortion Politics: A Documentary History,* Vol. 1, *Congressional Action, Part 1.* New York: Garland Publishing.

———. 1995b. *Federal Abortion Politics: A Documentary History,* Vol. 1, *Congressional Action, Part 2.* New York: Garland Publishing.

———. 1995c. *Federal Abortion Politics: A Documentary History,* Vol. 2, *Executive Action, Part 1.* New York: Garland Publishing.

———. 1995d. *Federal Abortion Politics: A Documentary History,* Vol. 2, *Executive Action, Part 2.* New York: Garland Publishing.

Diamond, Sara. 1994. "The Religious Right Goes to Court." *The Humanist,* May, pp. 35–38.

Dixon-Mueller, Ruth. 1993. *Population Policy and Women's Rights: Transforming Reproductive Choice.* Westport, Conn.: Praeger Publishers.

The Economist. 1980. "Anti-Abortionists: The Right Takes Aim," October 4, NEXIS.

Eisenstein, Zillah. 1988. *The Female Body and the Law.* Berkeley: University of California Press.

English, Deirdre. 1981. "The War Against Abortion—Inside the Anti-Abortion Movement." *Mother Jones*, February/March, p. 17.

Estrich, Susan. 1995. "'Roe vs. Wade' Dead? Foster Debate Says So." *USA Today*, February 16, p. 11A.

Faludi, Susan. 1991. *Backlash: The Undeclared War Against American Women*. New York: Crown Publishers.

Faux, Marian. 1988. *Roe v. Wade*. New York: New American Library.

Ford, Gerald R. 1976. "President Ford on Abortion," Public Forum, Lower West Bend High School (Indiana), April 2. In *Weekly Compilation of Presidential Documents*, vol. 12, no. 15, p. 522.

Frantz, Douglas. 1995. "The Rhetoric of Terror." *Time*, March 27, p. 48.

Freeman, Jo. 1988. "Feminist Activities at the National Conventions." *News & Notes About Women Public Officials, vol. 6*, Winter, pp. 9–15.

Friendly, Fred W., and Martha J. H. Elliott. 1984. *The Constitution: That Delicate Balance*. New York: Random House.

Gallup, George, Jr., and Alec Gallup. 1988. "Attitudes on Abortion: Little Changes Since Supreme Court's 1973 Ruling." Poll for release on October 23, 1988.

Gallup Organization. n.d. *America's Opinion on: Abortion, 1962–1992*. Mimeo.

Garrow, David J. 1994. *Liberty & Sexuality: The Right to Privacy and the Making of Roe v. Wade*. New York: Macmillan.

Ginsburg, Ruth Bader. 1992. "Speaking in a Judicial Voice." *New York University Law Review*, vol. 67, December, pp. 1185–1209.

Glendon, Mary Ann. 1987. *Abortion and Western Law*. Cambridge, Mass.: Harvard University Press.

Goodman, Ellen. "Blackmun the Emancipator." *Boston Globe*, April 7, p. 15.

Gordon, Linda. 1977. *Women's Body, Woman's Rights: Birth Control in America*. New York: Penguin Books.

Greeley, Andrew. 1990. *The Catholic Myth: The Behavior and Beliefs of American Catholics*. New York: Scribner's.

Green, Robert. 1986. "Democratic Senators Oppose Rehnquist's Confirmation." *Reuters*, September 9.

Groer, Ann. 1994. "Justices Near Vote on Clinic Protests." *Orlando Sentinel*, April 29, p. A1.

Hall, Mimi. 1994. "RICO Ruling Sends 'Chill' Through Activists." *USA Today*, January 25, p. 4A.

Halva-Neubauer, Glen A. 1993. "The States After *Roe*—No 'Paper Tigers.'" In Malcolm L. Goggin, Ed., *Understanding the New Politics of Abortion*. Newbury Park, Calif.: Sage.

Herman, Robin. 1980. "Taking Up Political Arms Against the Right to Lifers." *New York Times*, November 9, p. 8.

Horne, William W. 1991. "Defending Disobedience." *The American Lawyer*, November, p. 58.

Hugick, Larry. 1991. "Pro-Life Wichita Demonstrations Fail to Change Opinion on Abortion." *Gallup Poll Monthly*, September.

Hyer, Marjorie. 1988. "Catholic Bishops Speak Out on the Democratic Platform." *Washington Post*, May 28, p. C16.

Jeffreys, Daniel. 1995. "Her case legalized abortion in the U.S. She is the very symbol of the pro-choice movement. But now 'Jane Roe' has switched sides. She tells Daniel Jeffreys why." *The Independent*, August 24, p. 4.

Kennedy, David. 1977. *Birth Control in America: The Career of Margaret Sanger*. New Haven, Conn.: Yale University Press.

Kenworthy, Tom. 1988. "House Rejects Easing Abortion Rules: Approval of Compromise Spending Bill Is Delayed." *Washington Post,* September 10, p. A6.

Lacayo, Richard. 1990. "The Justice in the Middle: For Both Sides of the Abortion Debate, O'Connor Is a Moving Target." *Time,* July 9, p. 27.

Lader, Lawrence. 1955. *Margaret Sanger and the Fight for Birth Control*. Boston: Beacon Press.

———. 1966. *Abortion*. Boston: Beacon Press.

———. 1973. *Abortion II: Making the Revolution*. Boston: Beacon Press.

———. 1991. *RU-486: The Pill That Could End the Abortion Wars and Why American Women Don't Have It*. Reading, Mass.: Addison-Wesley.

Lee, Rex E. 1974. *A Lawyer Looks at the ERA*. Provo, Utah: Brigham Young University Press.

Lewin, Tamar. 1988. "Legal Abortion Under Fierce Attack 15 Years After *Roe v. Wade* Ruling." *New York Times,* May 10, p. A20.

Liebman, Robert C., and Robert Wuthnow, Eds. 1983. *The New Christian Right: Mobilization and Legitimation*. New York: Aldine.

Luker, Kristin. 1984. *Abortion and the Politics of Motherhood*. Berkeley: University of California Press.

Lynn, Frank. 1980. "Anti-Abortion Groups Split on Reagan's Candidacy." *New York Times,* June 22, p. A28.

Malloy, Michael T. 1973. "Despite Court's Ruling Abortion Fight Goes On," *National Observer,* February 3.

Mansbridge, Jane J. 1986. *Why We Lost the ERA*. Chicago: University of Chicago Press.

Marcus, R. 1992. "The Court's Ruling Assures More Abortion Litigation." *Washington Post,* July 1, p. A1.

McGeown, Patricia. 1996. "Security of Staff, Patients a Priority of All Clinics." *The Times Union,* January 5, p. A12.

McGlen, Nancy, and Karen O'Connor. 1995. *Women, Politics, and American Society*. Englewood Cliffs, N.J.: Prentice-Hall.

———. 1983. *Women's Rights*. New York: Praeger.

McKeegan, Michelle. 1992. *Abortion Politics: Mutiny in the Ranks of the Right*. New York: Free Press.

Michelman, Kate. 1993. "Kate Michelman: Predicts Attacks on Abortion Rights." *Abortion Report,* December 12.

"Missouri: ACLA Plans Protest in the Gateway City." 1995. *Abortion Report,* July 24.

Moen, Matthew C. 1989. *The Christian Right and Congress*. Tuscaloosa: University of Alabama Press.

Mohr, James C. 1978. *Abortion in America: The Origins and Evolution of a National Policy*. New York: Oxford University Press.

Moriwaki, Lee. 1992. "Robertson Readies 'Voter Guide'—500,000 Copies Aimed at State." *Seattle Times,* October 25, p. B1.

NARAL (National Abortion Rights Action League). 1996. "Key Findings from NARAL's 1995 Congressional Scoreboard." Mimeo.

National Commission on Americans Without *Roe*. 1992. *Facing the Future Without Choice: A Report on Reproductive Liberty in America*. Washington, D.C.: National Abortion Rights Action League.

National Conference of Catholic Bishops. 1975. *Pastoral Plan for Pro-Life Activities.* Washington, D.C.

National Women's Conference. 1979. *What Women Want from the Official Report to the President.* New York: Simon and Schuster.

Neergaard, Lauran. 1996. "Group Seeks OK to Sell Abortion Pill in U.S." *Chicago Sun Times,* April 2.

Newport, Frank, and Leslie McAneny. 1992. "Whose Court Is It Anyhow? O'Connor, Kennedy, Souter Position Reflects Abortion Views of Most Americans." *Gallup Poll News Service,* July 5.

NOW (National Organization for Women). *NOW Bill of Rights.* Washington, D.C.

———. 1996. "Late Term Abortion (D&X)," Legislative Update, April 5.

O'Connor, Karen. 1980. *Women's Organizations' Use of the Courts.* Lexington, Mass.: Lexington Books.

O'Connor, Karen, and Lee Epstein. 1985. "Abortion Policy." In Tinsley E. Yarbrough, Ed., *The Reagan Administration and Human Rights.* Westport, Conn.: Greenwood Publishing Group.

Olasky, Marvin. 1992. *Abortion Rites: A Social History of Abortion in America.* Wheaton, Ill.: Crossway Books.

Osofsky, Howard J., and Joy D. Osofsky, Eds. 1973. *The Abortion Experience: Psychological and Medical Impact.* New York: Harper & Row.

Paige, Connie. 1983. *The Right to Lifers: Who They Are, How They Operate, and How They Get Their Money.* New York: Summit Books.

Petchesky, Rosalind. 1984. *Abortion and Women's Choice.* New York: Longman.

Peterson, Bill. 1982. "Kidnapping Focuses Tensions and Fears on Abortion Clinic." *Washington Post,* August 22, p. A2.

Politics USA. 1996. "House Sends Partial Birth Abortion Bill to Clinton." March 28, p. 1.

Povich, Elaine S. 1993. "Abortion Rights Bill Rejected by Moseley-Braun." *Chicago Tribune,* July 10, p. 14.

Puente, Maria. 1993. "Clinic Protestors Under Pressure from Stalking Laws." *USA Today,* May 10, p. 2A.

Reagan, Ronald. 1988. "State of the Union Address." *Congressional Quarterly Weekly Report,* January 30, pp. 220–227.

Reed, James. 1978. *From Private Vice to Public Virtue: The Birth Control Movement and American Society Since 1830.* Princeton, N.J.: Princeton University Press.

Reno, Janet. 1993. "Reno: Calls on Congress to Pass Clinic Access Bill." *Abortion Report,* March 24.

Ronn, Susan L. 1995. "Comment: FACE-ing RICO: A Remedy for Antiabortion Violence?" *Puget Sound Law Review,* Winter, pp. 357–386.

Rubin, Eva R. 1982. *Abortion, Politics, and the Courts.* Westport, Conn.: Greenwood Press.

Rubin, Eva R., Ed. 1994. *The Abortion Controversy: A Documentary History.* Westport, Conn.: Greenwood Press.

Schieszer, John. 1995. "Drugs Combine to Terminate Pregnancy." *St. Louis Dispatch,* December 18, p. 1E.

Simon, James F. 1995. *The Center Holds: The Power Struggle Inside the Rehnquist Court.* New York: Simon & Schuster.

Smolowe, Jill. 1993. "New, Improved, and Ready for Battle." *Newsweek,* June 14, pp. 48–51.

Spitzer, Robert J. 1987. *The Right to Life Movement and Third Party Politics*. Westport, Conn.: Greenwood Press.

Staggenborg, Suzanne. 1991. *The Pro-Choice Movement*. New York: Oxford University Press.

Terry, Randall. 1989. Monday Transcript No. 3506 from *The MacNeil/Lehrer NewsHour*, July 3.

Thomas, Evan, et. al. 1991. "Where Does He Stand?" *Newsweek*, July 15, p. 16.

Thomas, Judy. 1995. "*Roe vs. Wade* Lawyer Regrets Picking McCorvey as Plaintiff." *Kansas City Star*, October 26, p. A8.

Toner, Robin. 1993. "Settling In: Easing Abortion Policy." *New York Times*, January 1, p. 1.

Tribe, Lawrence H. 1992. *Abortion: The Clash of Absolutes*. New York: Norton, 1992.

Truman, David B. 1951. *The Governmental Process*. New York: Knopf.

United States Catholic Conference. 1974. *Documentation on the Right to Life and Abortion*. Washington, D.C.

Van Biema, David. 1993. "But Will It End the Abortion Debate?" *Time*, June 14, p. 52.

von Drehle, David. 1994. "Roe Opinion Reshaped Nation's Public and Private Life." *Washington Post*, April 7.

Weddington, Sarah. 1992. *A Question of Choice*. New York: Grosset/Putnam.

"Why the New Uproar over Abortions." 1976. *U.S. News & World Report*, March 1, p. 14.

Willke, John C. 1978. *Abortion Questions and Answers*. Cincinnati: Hayes Publishing.

Wills, Gary. 1989. "Evangels of Abortion." *New York Review of Books*, June 15, p. 19.

Zremski, Jerry. 1994. "Focus Changes as *Roe v. Wade* Turns 21." *Buffalo Evening News*, January 21, p. 3.

About the Book and Author

In a single year, Dr. David Gunn was killed, Jane Roe recanted, the Supreme Court began to backpedal from its landmark 1973 decision, Congress became fixated on a rare late-term abortion procedure, and numerous states imposed legislation limiting a woman's right to choose. It was a year of extremes for an issue that seems to know no middle ground, and it is the polarizing quality of abortion as a policymaking dilemma that *No Neutral Ground?* seeks to address.

One of the most heated and often violent issues of our time, abortion continues to challenge leaders, citizens, and policymakers alike. Is it a question of morality? Personal liberty? The right to privacy? Keeping the peace? What are the implications of the Supreme Court's rulings on abortion for future legislation? And what does it mean for every level of government when an issue defies consensus the way that abortion does?

In her unique treatment of this complex subject, Karen O'Connor builds on the history of abortion as a political issue—how it was first defined in the early 1800s and how it got on the political agenda—and takes us through the tug-of-war development of abortion politics to the present, using the policy process framework. Examining key court cases, institutions, dramatic events, and opinions from the public to the Supreme Court, O'Connor highlights the dilemma of how a polity attempts to make decisions about issues on which agreement or compromise is unlikely. She questions whether such divisive issues can ever be satisfactorily resolved, but gives us the tools to explore every avenue toward potential resolution.

Karen O'Connor is professor of government at American University. Prior to joining the faculty there in 1995, she was professor of political science and associate faculty in the Women's Studies Program at Emory University in Atlanta, Georgia, where she taught since 1977. She is also a member of the Georgia bar. Professor O'Connor has published several books including *Women, Politics and American Society* (with Nancy McGlen, 1995), *American Government: Roots and Reform* (with Larry J. Sabato, 1993, 1994, 1995, 1996), *Public Interest Law Groups* (with Lee Epstein, 1989), *Women's Rights: The Struggle for Equality in the 19th and 20th Centuries* (with Nancy E. McGlen, 1983), *Women's Organizations' Use of the Courts* (1980), and more than fifty articles in journals including the *Harvard Journal of Law and Policy*, *Judicature*, the *Western Journal of Political Science*, the *Journal of Politics*, and *Women & Politics*, among others.

Index